A
GENOCIDE
IN THE
MAKING?

A GENOCIDE IN THE MAKING?

ERDOĞAN REGIME'S CRACKDOWN ON THE GÜLEN MOVEMENT

BÜLENT KENEŞ

Blue Dome Press
New Jersey

Pictures of Ahmet Burhan Ataç, Haluk Savaş, and *Zaman* newspaper are courtesy of Selahattin Sevi. Other pictures are by AST (Advocates of Silenced Turkey).

Published by Blue Dome Press
335 Clifton Ave. Clifton, NJ, 07011, USA
www.bluedomepress.com

Paperback 978-1-68206-025-4   Ebook: 978-1-68206-531-0

Library of Congress Cataloging-in-Publication Data

Names: Keneş, Bülent, 1969- author.
Title: A genocide in the making? : Erdoğan regime's crackdown on the
   Gülen movement / Bülent Keneş.
Other titles: Erdoğan regime's crackdown on the Gülen movement
Description: New Jersey : Blue Dome Press, [2020] | Includes
   bibliographical references and index.
Identifiers: LCCN 2020030071 (print) | LCCN 2020030072 (ebook) | ISBN
   9781682065310 (eBook)
Subjects: LCSH: Turkey--Politics and government--21st century. | Gülen
   Hizmet Movement. | Erdoğan, Recep Tayyip. | Crimes against
   humanity--Turkey--21st century. | Genocide--Turkey--21st century. |
   Protest movements--Turkey--History--21st century. |
   Authoritarianism--Turkey. | Islam and politics--Turkey--21st century.
Classification: LCC DR603 .K453 2020 (print) | LCC DR603 (ebook) | DDC
   364.15/109561--dc23
LC record available at https://lccn.loc.gov/2020030071
LC ebook record available at https://lccn.loc.gov/2020030072

Printed in Canada

To
Furkan, Feridun, Ahmet, Esma, Gülsüm ...
and all victims of Erdoğan's despotic regime

Contents

ABBREVIATIONS

AA: Anadolu News Agency
ADL: Anti-Defamation League
AKP: Justice and Development Party
BBC: British Broadcasting Company
BHRC: Bar Human Rights Committee of England & Wales
CHD: Contemporary Lawyers Association
CHP: Republican People's Party
CoE: Council of Europe
CPT: European Committee for the Prevention of Torture and Inhuman ·
or Degrading Treatment or Punishment
DP: Democrat Party
DSI: State Waterworks Authority
ECHR: European Convention on Human Rights
ECtHR: European Court of Human Rights
ENCJ: European Network of Councils for the Judiciary
EP: European Parliament
EU: European Union
"FETO: Fethullahist Terror Organisation"
HOH: People's Private Forces
HSK: Board of Judges and Prosecutors
HSYK: High Council of Judges and Prosecutors
IBAHRI: International Bar Association's Human Rights Institute
IBDA/C: Islamic Great East Raiders/Front
ICC: International Criminal Court
ICCPR: International Covenant on Civil and Political Rights
IHD: Human Rights Association
IHH: Foundation for Human Rights and Freedoms and Humanitarian
Relief
IPI: International Press Institute
ISIL: Islamic State in Iraq and the Levant
JWF: Journalists and Writers Foundation
MGK: National Security Council
MHP: Nationalist Movement Party
MIT: National Intelligence Organisation

MSH: National Mobilization Movement
NATO: North Atlantic Treaty Organisation
NGO: Nongovernmental organisations
OHCHR: Office of the United Nations High Commissioner for Human Rights
OKK: Special Forces Command
OSCE: Organisation of Security and Co-operation in Europe
PKK: Kurdistan Workers' Party
R2P: Responsibility to Protect
SADAT: International Defense Consulting
SCF: Stockholm Center for Freedom
SCO: Shanghai Cooperation Organisation
TL: Turkish lira
TMSF: Savings Deposit Insurance Fund
TPC: Turkish Penal Code
TRT: Turkish Radio and Television
TSK: Turkish Armed Forces
TUSKON: Turkish Confederation of Businessmen and Industrialists
UN: United Nations
WJP: World Justice Project
YARSAV: Judges and Prosecutors Association

PREFACE

All Islamists are Muslim, but we cannot say that all Muslims are Islamists. This simple logic, which is applicable to the Islamic world, is true for Turkey as well. Modern Turkish history is full of interwoven and multi-layered contradictions and controversies. Until recently, the tension between the religious segments of society, which have taken on various appearances and discourses within themselves, and the rigid, French-style secularism imposed by the state that had long dominated Turkey have left an indelible imprint on Turkey's socio-political agenda. Outsiders were able to see this tension as the main and perhaps only tension in Turkey through the contradictions between these religious and secularist segments. With its deep-rooted history, this socio-political polarisation has prevented people from seeing the intra-group tensions, contradictions and controversies.

The struggle of political Islamism in Turkey, which built its political projects based on the exploitation of the feelings of religious people who have defined their socio-political identity mostly with religion against a staunchly secularist/laicist understanding that is flawed with serious democratic shortcomings, had turned over time into a hatred of all types of secularism and diverse lifestyles. To make myself clear, I would like to draw the reader's attention as early as in the preface to the usage of words like "Islamism – Islamist" in contrast to "Islamic – Muslim," which will appear throughout the book. While the former pair refers to an ideology represented by political figures across the Muslim world (like Erdoğan in Turkey), the latter underscores religious practices and culture that have flourished on the axis of Islam's socio-spiritual dynamics in the form of worship, charitable works, and community networks. By polarising the society over religious-secularist contradictions, Turkey's political Islamists, who planned to transform this tension into political capital, have increasingly headed toward a discriminatory and hateful discourse that overshadows the peaceful and inclusive messages of Islam. Society had felt to the bone how this led to a major political devastation in Turkey during the post-modern coup era after the notorious, military-dominated National Security Council (MGK) intervened the democratic process on February 28, 1997.

As a matter of fact, there had never been an autochthonous (native) political Islamism as we know it today in Turkey. Political Islamism, which deeply affects Turkey, is comprised of different versions of the political Islam that was imported from Pakistan, Egypt and North Africa, developed in reaction to colonialism and based on reactionary experiences in those lands. From this point of view, we can easily say that the Muslim Brotherhood (Ikhvan) in Egypt and Jamaat-i Islami in Pakistan were the fathers of the political Islamism on which Recep Tayyip Erdoğan's political origins are based. However, following the 1979 Iranian Revolution, the influence of Ayatollah Ruhullah Khomeini and his fellow mullahs became more dominant over Turkish political Islamists. The political and religious thoughts of Erdoğan's political mentor, Necmettin Erbakan, were based on inflammatory Islamist conceptions that were hardened and radicalised by anti-colonialist movements and the revolutionary mindset in Iran rather than the moderate and inclusive local religious concepts in Turkey.

Most of the books that significantly influenced the political and religious thoughts of Erbakan and his inner circle were generally Turkish translations of works published by such radicalised Islamist groups outside of Turkey. Although political Islamism became evident in Turkey especially after the 1960s, a more moderate, tolerant mainstream Muslim tradition – the Islamic tradition, I would call it – has always remained powerful. This Islamic tradition has steadfastly approached Islam as a pure religion descended from the Prophet Muhammad, not as a political ideology that would present the opportunities of political power as the Islamists see it. Islamists have not refrained from using this sacred religion as an "appetizer" for their political agenda and dangerous social polarization.

These traditional or more modern Islamic social movements, which have encompassed the entire society, have assumed the role of important sociological bearers of a peaceful culture of co-existence that has flourished throughout history by deriving its soul from Islam. These religious groups, including some hundreds-year-old religious orders, embarked on a quest to gradually rehabilitate the ultra-secular political regime through mutual interaction rather than clashing with it.

As well as many other socio-religious groups, the Gülen movement, which has been inspired by the thoughts and teachings of Turkish Muslim scholar Fethullah Gülen and has been on the stage of Turkish society since the early 1970s, has also preferred to pursue a reformatory Islamic process and an all-embracing democratic path against the provocations of political Islamism. Just like other deep-rooted civilian Islamic movements, the Gülen movement has never lent support to any political formations or parties established by the political Islamists who pursue a political agenda in the pursuit of power and seek revenge on the secularist regime.

The Gülen movement has always kept its distance from the political Islamist discourse and actions that differentiate, polarize and divide the society, and found itself much closer to the centre, centre-right or centre-left political parties, which have at least been trying to embrace the whole society. Therefore, the Gülen movement, with its penetration into society, its media and its civil society capabilities, has always supported the political formations that appeal to the entire society and has tried to democratise the state and the society and prioritise basic freedoms, fundamental human rights, transparency and accountability.

Against such a background, Erdoğan established the Justice and Development Party (AKP) with a group of associates in 2001 and publicly declared that he was maintaining a distance from the political Islamism formulated by his political Islamist mentor Necmettin Erbakan, saying, "I have taken off the shirt of Milli Görüş [National View]." The party programme and the election manifesto announced by the AKP before the elections of November 3, 2002 were consistent with democratic reformist commitments in support of Erdoğan's "I have changed" discourse. Indeed, the AKP and Erdoğan had undertaken to fulfil their commitments to rapidly democratise the state, unify the society and integrate Turkey with the world during their first years in power as stated in the party programme and election manifesto. Thus, they gained a reputation and credibility both in Turkey and around the world. The Gülen movement, with its rich and well-educated human capital, civil society entities and media organs fully supported Erdoğan's and his party's revolutionary democratisation policies and long-expected reforms during that period, which embraced the entire society in line with the goal of membership in the European Union.

Starting from 2007, however, the notorious deep-state formations began to resist these reforms. In the face of these anti-democratic interventions, all other democratic circles in Turkey and worldwide, including the Gülen movement, took sides with the AKP government. The struggle against deep-state entities and the democratic and social reforms realised by Erdoğan and the AKP created great excitement in the society and increased their support to 50 per cent. In the course of this struggle against the anti-democratic, deep-state structures, not only was the dominant military tutelage broken, but also a strong pro-Erdoğan media and civil society were created.

As the tide started to change in Erdoğan's favor, he won a landslide (almost 50%) election on June 12, 2011. Among his promises before the election was to draft a new civil and democratic constitution. Erdoğan realised a great opportunity lay before him in which the regime of military tutelage and the bureaucratic oligarchy were paralysed, and the judiciary in particular was democratised with a referendum on September 12, 2010. Instead of using this opportunity any further in line with the expectations of democratic circles to fulfil the commitments he made before the elections, Erdoğan utilised this opportunity to return to his ideological factory settings, in other words, to his controversial political Islamist origins.

The Arab revolts that erupted in early 2011 also led to the inclusion of imperial motivations to Erdoğan's pursuit of absolute power within. Thus, the opportunity of the political power he pursued within the framework of the objectives of political Islamism in the country and his passionate, imperial plans encouraged by the assumptions of the Arab revolts intersected, and Erdoğan turned to brand new targets. In this process Erdoğan not only attempted to radically change Turkey's regime in line with the targets of political Islamism; he also intervened directly or indirectly in the internal affairs of regional countries, including Egypt, to change their regime in the same direction.

He used proxy groups and organisations to influence political developments in those countries in order to carry out his interventions into the internal affairs of the countries he targeted. If there was no such organisation in a targeted country, he formed new ones. As in the case of Syria, since he could not afford the cost of these illegitimate and illegal activities, which were without doubt international crimes, with legitimate public funds he embarked on both national and international black money and bribery operations including laundering black money from the illegal oil trade conducted by Iran, which was under UN and US sanctions.

Erdoğan was not only caught up in this dirty business; he also expected all segments of society, including the Gülen movement, to support these illegitimate initiatives. Finally, part of Erdoğan's illegal international business was exposed by a corruption and bribery scandal that became public knowledge on December 17/25, 2013 and by the apprehension of Turkish National Intelligence Organisation (MIT) trucks carrying weapons and ammunition to radical Islamist terrorist organisations in Syria in early 2014.

Contrary to the expectations of support, the Gülen movement started to distance itself from Erdoğan and his AKP, which gave signs of returning to his political Islamist roots after the 2011 elections and of acting in line with the objectives of political Islamism both at home and abroad. This distance increased as the AKP and Erdoğan deviated from democracy and moved towards political Islamism.

Because of this divergence, Erdoğan launched a witch-hunt to annihilate the Gülen movement and started his genocidal program by halting the educational activities of the movement, which is widely known as a global educational force. Erdoğan has argued that the December 17/25, 2013 corruption operations were a "coup" to topple his government despite the abundance of evidence related to corruption and bribery. He claimed the graft and bribery operations were carried out by police, prosecutors and judges who were close to the Gülen movement, and he embarked on the demolition of state mechanisms and the judiciary.

At the same time, he launched an intense, systematic and widespread campaign of hatred to discredit in public opinion both Fethullah Gülen and the Gülen movement. Unfortunately, his efforts were facilitated by shutting down all media organs opposed to him, and Erdoğan became the only voice appealing to the community. In spite of all this, he could not fully convince the society and the world of the unfounded arguments he put forward against the Gülen movement. Therefore, by plotting a great conspiracy on July 15, 2016, he attempted to achieve his ultimate objectives by staging a false-flag military coup as if it were against himself.

He has realised his goal, so far, to a great extent in this way. Thus, hundreds of thousands of members of the Gülen movement have been victimised since 2013, when the December 17/25 corruption and bribery investigations incriminated Erdoğan and his inner circle. The level of victimisation, the "witch-hunt," as Erdoğan publicly put it, further escalated following the controversial coup attempt in 2016 that President Erdoğan defined as a "gift from God" while the attempt was still under way. More than 160,000 public servants have been branded as "terrorists" without any administrative or judicial investigation and purged from government jobs without benefits or compensation. In most cases, they were also deprived of the right to work for private enterprise, leaving their families at risk of hunger.

Turkey has suffered from tyranny, a loss of reputation and failure in every sense as Erdoğan, who considers himself to be the caliph of the Islamic world, continues his unlawful, immoral and arbitrary persecutions and widespread and systematic human rights violations targeting alleged members of the Gülen movement. Looking at the credentials of the targeted individuals they mostly represent the well-trained, well-educated and qualified human capital of the country.

When AKP came to power in early 2000s, Erdoğan had vowed that he had "taken off the shirt of the political Islamist Milli Görüş" and initiated a process of democratisation, which was supported by the Gülen movement. The prestige and credibility of Turkey, which had rapidly risen among the international community with this process, have unfortunately been devastated, along with all its democratic institutions and principles in the aftermath of the coup attempt.

In brief, the Gülen movement, as a moderate, liberal, Islamic civil society group, has tried to prevent the radical Islamist Erdoğan from taking Turkey to a political Islamist hell. However, despite all these efforts that led it to pay a very heavy price, the movement could not stop the country from becoming a complete hell due to the uncritical support given by the masses, who were influenced by the intensive propaganda campaign through a media totally under the direct control of Erdoğan.

As an outspoken critic of oppressive policies, the author of this book has been a target of the Erdoğan regime, too. President Erdoğan and his ruthless government have tried to take all measures including threats, detention, arrest and imprisonment to intimidate and silence me. Even long before the coup attempt in 2016, the Erdoğan regime opened more than 30 court cases against me based simply on what I wrote in newspapers and on social media and what I said on TV programs. The courts, which are also under Erdoğan's direct control, handed down a number of penalties to me including long prison sentences at the end of sham trials.

However, the heaviest blow came in the wake of the controversial coup attempt on July 15, 2016. My name appeared in the second rank of a list of 47 critical journalists on July 26, 2016 to be arrested on the baseless accusation of involvement in the abortive putsch. I had to hide for weeks at a variety of addresses and finally managed to cross the Maritsa River, which forms the border between Turkey and Greece. Thus, was I able to save myself from the inevitable persecution of the Erdoğan regime, which indicted me with a demand by the prosecutor of three aggravated life sentences plus 15 years in prison based on one of my articles, which consisted of just around 500 words.

Acknowledgements
After I fled to Stockholm, I realised that a number of my journalist colleagues also managed to escape the Erdoğan regime and had arrived in Sweden. We immediately met and decided to establish the Stockholm Center for Freedom (SCF) to raise our voices for the hundreds of thousands of people who have been victimised by the oppressive Erdoğan regime and to document the massive human rights violations in the post-coup-attempt period. Hence, a crucial part of the information and statistics I used in this book are based on the exhaustive work of my hard-working and devoted colleagues and myself during our reporting activities at SCF. So, I owe infinite thanks to my colleagues Ahmet Dönmez, Bülent Ceyhan, Abdullah Bozkurt, Bülent Korucu, Levent Kenez, Erkam Tufan Aytav, Süleyman Sargın and Menaf Alıcı for their direct and indirect contributions to the writing of this book. I especially thank them for serving as such a strong voice for the voiceless victims at such a difficult time despite the fact that they, too, have been victims of this oppressive process. I must also thank my dear copy editor, who proofread this book but requested to remain anonymous because of her understandable fear of the Erdoğan regime.

Before I sent the manuscript to the publishing house, this book was read by my dear friends Prof. Dr. İhsan Yılmaz, Prof. Dr. Mehmet Efe Çaman, two respected Swedish academicians who are specialized on human rights issues and my veteran colleague Ali Halit Aslan. Their valuable criticism and recommendations gave this book a better shape and a vivid soul. I also owe many thanks to Hakan Yeşilova and other respected editors of Blue Dome Press.

Special thanks to AST (Advocates of Silenced Turkey) for their support in the promotion of this book, for providing pictures, and especially for their advocacy on human rights violations in Turkey.

Since they have patiently shared all the burdens and suffering of this difficult process with me, as experienced by millions of innocent people who are victims of the Erdoğan regime in Turkey, and as they have lent all possible support during my writing of this book, my beloved wife Ipek, my son Umut Sina and my daughter Elif Leyla deserve my profound gratitude.

My greatest hope and expectation for this humble book is that it plays a crucial role in the creation of a worldwide awareness that will prevent an easily predictable human catastrophe in the form of a new genocide, the many symptoms of which have already appeared in Turkey under the brutal rule of the Erdoğan regime.

Dr. Bülent Keneş
Stockholm, June 2020

INTRODUCTION

Against the background of the poor track record of the international community in underestimating genocidal acts before their occurrence, it is necessary to examine the Turkish government's mounting crimes against the participants of a civic group, namely the Gülen movement, also known as the Hizmet (service) movement, with the deliberate intention of destroying this social group, in whole or in part.

This comprehensive book reasonably concludes that the acts committed by the Turkish government in an unprecedented persecution targeting one specific social group may be classified at the very least as crimes against humanity and could very well be the harbinger of what comes next in terms of a full-scale genocide to exterminate hundreds of thousands, if not millions, of innocent people.

Unfortunately, the establishment of basic humanitarian values, the development of a pluralistic culture, the promotion of democratic principles such as the rule of law and fundamental human rights included in international conventions and the nurturing of a climate of tolerance have not followed a linear pattern in world history. The cruelty of humanity has not moderated even in our times when the world has almost become a global village, with enormous advancements in communications and transportation technologies. This trend finds its manifestation in the eruption of more than 250 wars and conflicts in the last 90 years and the death of more than 90 million civilians, most notably women and children.

Large-scale killings, ethnic cleansing, massacres and policies of genocide that can still be observed in the modern day have led to profound human rights violations and mass grievances. Although some intellectual endeavors were initiated after World War I to prevent mass killings, it took until the end of the 1940s to conceptualise the crime of genocide and attach legal consequences to it. The crime of genocide was codified by UN General Assembly Resolution No 96 (1) on December 11, 1946 and was approved as an international legal norm on December 9, 1948.

The Convention on the Prevention and Punishment of the Crime of Genocide was approved by the UN General Assembly on that date, and the convention was put into force following approval by 20 states on January 12, 1951. However, it was not until the 1990s that the initial legal and actual consequences of this initiative took effect. The term "crime of genocide" was first used in Bosnia, then in Rwanda and Darfur, to put the responsible parties on trial, and it is still developing as an international legal norm.

Experts believe that preventive mechanisms can be established by detecting early acts that may lead to genocide. One of these experts is Gregory H. Stanton, head of Genocide Watch, who drafted a report titled "The 8 Stages of Genocide" in 1996. He argued that genocides are committed as a consequence of "predictable" and "preventable" processes and claimed that the situations and actions that occur pre-genocide, at the time of the genocide and post-genocide are predictable and preventable. He later on increased the number of stages to 10 to boost awareness for early detection.

Hundreds of thousands of members of the Gülen movement have been victimised since 2013, when major corruption and bribery investigations that were made public December 17/25, 2013 incriminated autocratic Turkish Prime Minister (now President) Recep Tayyip Erdoğan and his inner circle.[1] The level of victimisation, the "witch-hunt," as Erdoğan publicly put it, further escalated following a controversial coup attempt on July 15, 2016 that President Erdoğan defined as a "gift from God" while the attempt was still under way. More than 160,000 public servants have been branded as "terrorists" without any administrative or judicial investigation and purged from government jobs without benefits or compensation. In most cases, they were also deprived of the right to work for private enterprise, leaving their families at risk of starvation.

Over 600,000 people have been investigated on allegations of terrorism, and some 500,000 have been detained on false charges that cannot be regarded as lawful under the rule of law. At least 77,000 people were formally arrested, around 200 media outlets were shut down and 240 journalists were jailed as well as countless left unemployed or forced to seek asylum overseas in the wake of the coup bid.

Fifteen private universities and more than 1,000 private schools have been shuttered and their assets confiscated, some of which have been plundered by pro-Erdoğan circles. As a consequence of this process, which affected more than 22,000 academics, analytical and critical thinking in colleges and universities has been dealt a huge blow. Official figures indicate that more than 1,000 major companies have been seized along with TL 56 billion in assets. One hundred sixty-nine flag officers including four-star generals and thousands of lower-ranking officers have been arrested on charges of being 'putschists' or 'Gülenists,' resulting in the severe undermining of the Turkish military's combat capabilities. Essentials of democracy, like impartiality of the judiciary along with due process, the right to a fair trial and the right to a defense have been destroyed. More than 1,320 lawyers have been detained, 593 were sent to jail and 216 were sentenced to a total of 1,361 years in prison.

Systematic torture and ill treatment, which were by and large eliminated in Turkey in the early 2000s, have been revived and become systematic and widespread. Thousands of people have been tortured in detention centers and jails and in some cases in unofficial holding facilities. The number of people who died under suspicious circumstances in detention and who committed suicide exceeds 126. Twenty-six Gülen movement members have been abducted in broad daylight.

After the July 15, 2016 failed coup, the persecution reached a level that is impossible to express in numbers. With the open or covert support of opposition parties for the Erdoğan regime's discourse against the Gülen movement, the growing witch-hunt targeting members of the movement, the systematic and widespread hate speech and increasing persecution and injustice all appear to have been laying the groundwork for a possible genocide.

The Erdoğan regime, which admitted to having been making preparations to crack down on the movement since 2010, has made significant headway in wiping out the movement. The widespread torture, systematic persecution and rounding up of hundreds and in some instances thousands of the group's members on a weekly basis have given rise to allegations that an early stage of the crime of genocide is being carried out against real and alleged followers of the Gülen movement.

Many believe these figures must be taken seriously, and it is incumbent on all national and international stakeholders to take urgent action to halt and reverse these alarming developments in Turkey before they become an actual genocide. Therefore, this book was written to sound the alarm for the international community and international organisations and inform them of the steps taken against the Gülen movement, with full recognition of internationally accepted norms, definitions and criteria in relation to the crime of genocide.

As is known, although it has its own limitations, the best and the most functional definition of genocide is found in Article 2 of the Convention on the Prevention and Punishment of the Crime of Genocide. This definition and description were quoted in the Rome Statute, the founding document of the International Criminal Court (ICC), as well. Moreover, components of the crime of genocide have been determined through generally accepted criteria. As Stanton correctly observed, it is possible to predict and prevent genocide by assessing the situation in a society by means of this definition, description and these criteria.

Realisation of just one of the five criteria in Article 2 of the Convention on the Prevention and Punishment of the Crime of Genocide is legally deemed sufficient to define the incidents as genocide. Therefore, a decision can be made as to whether a process is underway towards genocide by analysing the criminal acts "with intent to destroy, in whole or in part, a national, ethnical, racial or religious group."

According to the definition in Article 2 of the convention, genocide means "any of the following acts committed with intent to destroy, in whole or in part, a national, ethnical, racial or religious group, as such:

(a) Killing members of the group;
(b) Causing serious bodily or mental harm to members of the group;
(c) Deliberately inflicting on the group conditions of life calculated to bring about its physical destruction in whole or in part;
(d) Imposing measures intended to prevent births within the group;
(e) Forcibly transferring children of the group to another group."

With serious concerns that members of the Gülen movement in

Turkey are at risk of genocide, we will analyse the campaign against the Gülen movement from the perspective of acts defined in Article 2 of the convention. In doing so, we aim to raise awareness and contribute to the prevention of such a tragedy.

On the other hand, M. Hassan Kakar, who is also known for his genocide studies, suggests that for genocide to occur, there must be certain preconditions. Foremost among them are (a) a national culture that does not place a high value on human life; b) a totalitarian society, with its assumed superior ideology; and (c) members of the dominant society must perceive their potential victims as less than human, or non-human. He further argues even these conditions are not enough for the perpetrators to commit genocide. To do that -- that is, to commit genocide -- the perpetrators need (d) a strong, centralised authority and bureaucratic organisation as well as (e) pathological individuals and criminals.[2]

Like Stanton, Kakar argues that a campaign of vilification and dehumanisation of the victims must be launched by the perpetrators, who are usually new states or new regimes attempting to impose conformity to a new ideology and its model of society, as is the case in Turkey. There is no doubt that a comprehensive study to analyse whether preconditions for a genocide targeting different social groups including members of the Gülen movement have been met in Turkey needs to be initiated. In this book, the situation in Turkey will also be analysed in light of these preconditions.

This book aims to show that the Erdoğan regime goes beyond merely engaging in hate speech and making threats and remarks about annihilating the Gülen movement. To this end, this book will examine how many preconditions of a potential genocide are present in Turkey and how many stages of a potential genocide as formulated by Stanton have been realised by Erdoğan's regime against followers of the Gülen movement. However, it should be borne in mind that this book was written in an environment in which access to information has been restricted, the free media have been silenced and most independent journalists have either been imprisoned or fled into exile, and also that it has become almost impossible to conduct an independent academic study in the country.

Despite the ongoing mass persecution in Turkey, which includes various aspects of ideological, pragmatic, domestic, economic and cultural genocide, the issue has not been highlighted in the international community. Therefore, this book intends to explain the current state of the Erdoğan regime's reprehensible campaign against the Gülen movement in order to make the international community aware of the real nature of the persecution in the hope that all national and international mechanisms which have the potential to prevent the possible lethal consequences can be mobilized.

CHAPTER I

WHAT IS GENOCIDE?

1.1. Definition of genocide

Genocide means the intentional destruction of, in whole or in part, a group that differs from others based on its nationality, ethnicity, race, political view or religion, in line with a plan and the advantage of the destroyers. The term "genocide" did not exist before 1944. It is a very specific term, referring to systematic violent crimes committed against groups with the intent to terminate their existence. Genocide was defined for the first time by British Prime Minister Winston Churchill as "a crime without a name."[1] In 1944 Polish lawyer Raphael Lemkin[2] coined the term "genocide."[3]

Lemkin defined genocide as: "Generally speaking, genocide does not necessarily mean the immediate destruction of a nation, except when accomplished by mass killings of all members of a nation. It is intended rather to signify a coordinated plan of different actions aiming at the destruction of essential foundations of the life of national groups, with the aim of annihilating the groups themselves. The objectives of such a plan would be the disintegration of the political and social institutions, of culture, language, national feelings, religion, and the economic existence of national groups, and the destruction of the personal security, liberty, health, dignity, and even the lives of the individuals belonging to such groups."

At the 5th Conference for the Unification of Penal Law in Madrid in 1933, Lemkin put forward a proposal to consider the destruction of racial, religious and social groups as a crime in international law. His proposal for enacting two new offences, the act of barbarity and the act of vandalism, was not accepted. The main reason for the rejection of Lemkin's proposal was the views of the states on their national sovereignty. At that time, the prosecution and trial of a crime committed within the national boundaries of a country by an international court was generally considered to be a foreign intervention. As a result, acts of genocide were considered to be "a crime without a name" until the end of World War II.

In any case, Lemkin was the first person to use the term genocide in his book *Axis Rule in Occupied Europe: Laws of Occupation, Analysis of Government, Proposals for Redress*. In the book he described genocide as: "a coordinated plan of different actions aiming at the destruction of essential foundations of the life of national groups, with the aim of annihilating the groups themselves. … Genocide is directed against the national group as an entity, and the actions involved are directed against individuals, not in their individual capacity, but as members of the national group."[4]

With this definition, Lemkin was saying that genocide is a very broad term and that it can take place in various contexts, including political, cultural, social, economic, biological, physical, ethnic and religious. It was the Holocaust, Hitler's policy of destroying the Jews in line with his plan, which led the way for the definition of the crime of genocide. As an eyewitness, Lemkin was inspired by what he had experienced in defining genocide.[5] At the Nuremberg International Military Tribunal, established in 1945, the accusation leveled against high-ranking Nazis was the commission of a crime against humanity. However, the term genocide was used in the indictment as a definitive concept but not as a legal term.[6]

In the General Assembly's decision of December 11, 1946, no. 96 (1), which was unanimously adopted, genocide was accepted by the UN: "Genocide is a denial of the right of existence of entire human groups, as homicide is the denial of the right to live of individual human beings; such denial of the right of existence shocks the conscience of mankind, results in great losses to humanity in the form of cultural and other contributions represented by these human groups, and is contrary to moral law and to the spirit and aims of the United Nations. Many instances of such crimes of genocide have occurred when racial, religious, political and other groups have been destroyed, entirely or in part. The punishment of the crime of genocide is a matter of international concern."[7]

The importance of this resolution was the criminalisation of genocide in international law. In line with this resolution, the international prosecution and trial of acts of genocide committed within a country are not considered a matter of national concern and as a result are not a violation of national sovereignty.

The clearest definition of genocide appears in Article 2 of the Convention on the Prevention and Punishment of the Crime of Genocide, which was adopted by the UN General Assembly in December 1946. Article 2 of the convention reads as follows:

"In the present Convention, genocide means any of the following acts committed with intent to destroy, in whole or in part, a national, ethnical, racial or religious group, as such:

(a) Killing members of the group;

(b) Causing serious bodily or mental harm to members of the group;

(c) Deliberately inflicting on the group conditions of life calculated to bring about its physical destruction in whole or in part;

(d) Imposing measures intended to prevent births within the group;

(e) Forcibly transferring children of the group to another group."

Within the scope of this legal definition, genocide means annihilating a certain group of people who have specific features and are recognised by law, as part of a plan and with exclusive intent. In that sense, genocide points to a different situation than massacre or mass killing, all of which define various types of killing.[8]

That said, the qualification of the crime of genocide in the five acts listed in Article 2 of the convention has been criticised, and it is still contentious. Experts argue that these five acts pertain to the Holocaust. In particular sub-articles (d) and (e) are not flexible enough to cover other genocides since they refer to sterilisation in death camps and the forcible dispersal of the group. Therefore, this description is considered inadequate.[9] On the other hand, it is emphasised that it is wrong to understand from the 'group' definition in the convention that only national, ethnical, racial or religious groups that have fixed and perpetual characteristics can be victims of genocide and that political, cultural and even economic groups can be as well. For this reason, the exclusion from genocide of events such as the annihilation of more than 1 million communists by Indonesian dictator Suharto in the 1960s and the massacre of more than

1 million anti-communists by Cambodian dictator Pol Pot gives way to criticism.[10]

According to Horowitz, anybody can be a perpetrator of genocide. Nevertheless, genocides have been carried out in most cases by states. Radical political elites use the state bureaucracy to carry out genocide for their own interests. The goals of banishment or annihilation that have been put into practice within the scope of a plan or strategy have been the product of an official policy.[11] Therefore, before everything else, genocide is a state crime. This thesis is supported by the fact that genocides have usually been perpetrated by dictatorial regimes. The research shows that 170 million people were massacred by states in the 20th century alone.[12]

The identity of the perpetrators of genocide, be they soldiers or civilians, or even a member of the victim group, is irrelevant. Moreover, the legal entity of a state is not tried in court even if genocide is carried out as a systematic state policy. In the instance of genocide, officials who took decisions and carried them out and people who participated in the genocide as principal offenders are the ones who stand trial. Genocide is the worst crime to be committed in legal and human history. Even though crimes against humanity and war crimes are considered serious crimes as well, these crimes are not as serious as genocide in terms of human rights violations.[13]

1.2. The types of genocide

In light of the genocide literature, we can classify genocides as ideological, pragmatic, domestic, international, economic and cultural.

Ideological genocide: The ultimate objective in ideological genocides is banishment or annihilation of the targeted group. The ideology adopted by the offender points to a certain group as the target. A state policy is designed and carried out according to this ideology. The most prominent example of ideological genocide is the Holocaust since the annihilation of the Jews had a central place in Nazi ideology. Likewise, people who were sent by Stalin to certain death in Siberia and communists who were massacred by Suharto's special commandos in Indonesia were the victims of ideological genocide. The situation in Rwanda was no different.[14]

Pragmatic genocide: These kinds of genocides are generally carried out as the cleanup of a certain group that is perceived to be an obstacle. Since the victimized group is seen as an obstacle in the way of a certain goal, it is exposed to massacre and exile. Throughout history, pragmatic genocides have been carried out more often than ideological genocides. The slaughtering of the population in eastern Iranian cities by the armies of Genghis Khan because they were considered an obstacle to Mongol incursions[15] and the genocide of American Indians because they were considered an obstacle in the way of the white advance to the West[16] are examples of pragmatic genocide.

Domestic and international genocides: Domestic genocides are generally carried out by dictatorial regimes. These kinds of genocides are perpetrated by one of the ethnic groups that has captured state power and are used against other ethnic, racial or national groups with the intention of genocide in multiethnic countries. Social crises in multiethnic and multicultural societies can lead to political tensions. Therefore, such societies are more vulnerable to genocide. This is because the co-existence of different religious, ethnic and political groups is dependent on very fragile conditions.

The degeneration of democracy, freedom, equality and rule of law, etc., increases the risk of genocide.[17] In this respect, Bosnia and Herzegovina was a typical example of how a multiethnic and multi-religious region could be drawn into genocide.

International genocides are geographically and technically different than domestic genocides. There are two kinds of international genocides: massacres carried out on soil that has been invaded, and massacres carried out remotely.

Economic genocide: Economic genocide is the slaughtering or banishment of the local or autochthonous people of a certain region to exploit the region's natural resources. This concept is also used to define a massacre carried out to seize the properties of relatively wealthy minority groups or the policies of collective usurpation.

Cultural genocide: This is a type of non-violent genocide to assimilate or annihilate different cultures or nations. It is a method used to melt or assimilate a minority or weak group within a majority group without violence and normally manifests as a compulsory assimilation. Forcing the target group to adopt the oppressor group's religious identity, the banning of the native language, separating children and babies from their families and raising them in line with the majority's cultural and national characteristics in boarding schools, etc., are examples of cultural genocide.[18] As a result of this method employed in Australia until the 1960s, aboriginal generations were raised as strangers or even hostile to their own cultures.[19]

1.3. Development of law for the prevention and punishment of genocide

The Convention on the Prevention and Punishment of the Crime of Genocide was adopted by the UN General Assembly on December 9, 1948 as General Assembly Resolution 260. The convention entered into force on January 12, 1951. The first article of the convention reads: "The Contracting Parties confirm that genocide, whether committed in time of peace or in time of war, is a crime under international law which they undertake to prevent and to punish."[20] This article first and foremost advises the contracting parties of the convention to prevent genocide and to punish its perpetrators. One of the most important features of the convention is the codification of genocide as a crime in international law. In this way, prosecuting genocide has become possible regardless of the limits of national regulations, the principles of national sovereignty or domestic affairs. The convention aims to bring perpetrators to justice irrespective of their official titles or social or political status.[21]

The Article 2 in this Convention stipulates that political groups are vulnerable to genocide and that killing civilians, even in part, participating in a political group is genocide: "In the present Convention, genocide means any of the following acts committed with intent to destroy, in full or in part, a national, ethnical, racial or religious group...." In this regard crimes against humanity are considered equal to genocide. By excluding the condition of "being committed during war time," this article marks a significant difference between genocide and a crime against humanity. The convention states that genocide is a crime that can be committed during peacetime as well. This implies that for a crime to be categorized as genocide it does not have to be committed by a foreign power on another country's soil it invaded; such crimes taking place within the country itself are also considered genocide. Therefore, regardless of where and when it took place, the killing of a considerable number of people is accepted as genocide.

According to Article 3 the following acts shall be punishable: (a) Genocide; (b) Conspiracy to commit genocide; (c) Direct and public incitement to commit genocide; (d) Attempt to commit genocide; and (e) Complicity in genocide. Article 4 states that "[p]ersons committing genocide or any of the other acts enumerated in Art. 3 shall be punished, whether they are constitutionally responsible rulers, public officials or private individuals." Defining genocide as "an odious scourge," the remainder of the articles in this fundamental convention, consisting of 19 in total, concern judicial procedure and process as well as technical issues such as the entry into force of the convention.[22]

Genocide is also clearly defined as a crime in Article 6 of the Rome Statute, the founding statute of the International Criminal Court (ICC), which entered into force in 2002. The definition of genocide in the Rome Statute is based on the definition contained in the UN Genocide Convention. According to the Rome Statute the crime of genocide is characterised by the specific intent to destroy in whole or in part a national, ethnic, racial or religious group by killing its members or by other means. The five above-mentioned criminal acts against these four groups are accepted as genocide.[23]

As the commission of this crime can put the right to life, physical unity and honour of the persons and other rights and freedoms under assault, codification of the crime of genocide serves the purpose of protecting the physical and psychological integrity of the targets. Another aim of the development of international criminal law is the protection of the international order. Being the most egregious of crimes, genocide not only targets the legal order of nation-states; it also causes the deterioration of the international order and security either directly or indirectly. It is obvious that the codification of the crime of genocide plays a crucial role in safeguarding international security and the legal order.

1.4. The crime of genocide in Turkish law

By the adoption of Law No. 5630, dated March 25, 1950, the Republic of Turkey became a party to the Convention on the Prevention and the Punishment of the Crime of Genocide without any reservations. Law

No. 5630 was published in the Official Gazette No. 7469, dated March 29, 1950.[24] Article 76 of the Turkish Penal Code (TPC) was directly drafted from Article 2 of this convention.[25] Article 76 of the TPC states that acts of genocide must be committed with special intent. Within this context, there must be a deliberation before committing the crime of genocide, and the acts must be perpetrated with the intent to destroy a national, ethnical, racial or religious group as a whole or in part. According to the last paragraph of the article, the crime of genocide is not subject to a statute of limitations.[26]

In a departure from the Genocide Convention, Article 76 of the TPC includes an objective criterion, saying that the crime can only be committed as a result of deliberation. The lawmakers emphasized in particular the intentional and systematic nature of the crime of genocide.[27] However, the incorporation of such a criterion in the definition of the crime narrowed its scope. In fact, deliberation has become an element of the crime. As a result, the crime of genocide cannot be committed if it is not carried deliberately.[28]

National and international legal documents first and foremost aim at protecting the physical and psychological unity of individuals who are part of a certain group. Furthermore, the right to exist as a group has also been protected.[29] In addition, preservation of the international order is another legal aspect that has been brought under protection.[30] As the crime of genocide threatens not only individual rights but also the safety of the international community, no exceptions have been made to this crime, either at the national or the international level.[31]

1.4.1. Who is the perpetrator of the crime of genocide?

Genocide can be perpetrated by anyone.[32] The perpetrator need not have an official title or be related to any state or a similar organisation. Not only can heads of state or ministers who plan or order a genocide be held criminally responsible; even privates in the military and civilian accomplices can be perpetrators. Since the existence of an organisational structure, i.e., a chain of command, and arms make committing genocide easier, paramilitary groups, terrorist organisations and military powers are more likely to be perpetrators of this heinous crime.[33] Article 4 of the Genocide Convention does not offer an exhaustive list of possible perpetrators of genocide. Moreover, it does not mention any certain characteristics of the perpetrators.[34]

Legal justifications such as self-defence, the implementation of laws, consent of the victim and the assertion of rights as well as being at war, defending one's homeland or following orders cannot justify the perpetration of genocide.[35] In short, there is no legal justification that can absolve the perpetrator of criminal liability. Moreover, complicity in committing genocide is possible in many ways. People aiding and abetting in the commission of the crime of genocide will be tried in line with the relevant articles of the TPC. Article 3 of the convention states that conspiracy, complicity and direct and public incitement to commit genocide are punishable. Definitions in the convention and the TPC overlap in this regard.[36]

Considering it one of the most serious crimes against humanity and undertaking the obligation to try the perpetrators of genocide, Turkey accepted the principle of universality in prosecuting the acts of this crime and trying the perpetrators. In accordance with the Convention on the Non-Applicability of Statutory Limitations to War Crimes and Crimes Against Humanity, signed by Turkey on November 26, 1968 and entering into force on November 11, 1970, prosecution of the crime of genocide and the trial of its perpetrators are not subject to a statute of limitations.

Article 3 of the Genocide Convention enumerates the punishable acts as: Genocide, conspiracy to commit genocide, direct and public incitement to commit genocide, attempt to commit genocide and complicity in genocide. According to this article not only is the commission of genocide a punishable act, but conspiracy, incitement, attempt and complicity are as well. Evaluating Articles 2 and 3 of the convention together, it is understood that some of the punishable acts are not required to have a concrete result.

1.4.2. Who is the victim of genocide?

First of all, the victim of genocide must be a member of a national, ethnic, racial or religious group. These groups are exhaustively listed in the Genocide Convention and the TPC. Nevertheless, no criterion was mentioned for defining these groups. Groups have been defined in national and international case law.[37]

Victims of genocide must be targeted in their capacity of being members of certain groups. The acts, first and foremost, should be directed at a certain group.[38] The acts of the crime target people because they are considered to be and labelled as part of the targeted group. Therefore, being a member of the group matters with regard to the perpetrator. However, the perpetrator's perception of the status of the victims is also important for the perpetrator's criminal liability.

Victims of genocide are put under pressure and persecuted for their identity and their membership in a group. There is no special reason for them to be targeted personally; it is considered sufficient for them to be part of a certain group. For groups that have been marginalised by exclusion from the society to which they belong and by humiliation, being a victim of genocide is more likely.[39] Despite being the most integrated of all groups in their community and the most secular in all of Europe, the Jews of Germany were massacred by the Nazis because they were labelled and redefined as a group by the Nazis.[40] The same is true for the Muslim Bosnians who were massacred by the Serbian authorities. The more defenceless the targeted group, the more likely is the possibility of genocide. The common feature of groups that are collectively oppressed and annihilated is the inability to defend themselves. The protected groups in Turkey listed in the TPC can be defined as follows:

National group: Common history, customs, culture and language are among values that define a national group. Typical examples of national groups are national minorities.

Ethnic group: The main characteristic of an ethnic group is the possession of common traditions and customs. A commonality of race is not a condition for forming an ethnic group. Points in common for the members of an ethnic group are speaking the same language, sharing the same traditions and customs and having a common lifestyle.[41]

Racial group: A race is a grouping based on shared physical traits, ancestry or genetics.[42]

Religious group: Members of a religious group have the same beliefs, follow the same spiritual guide, share the same spiritual values and perform the same rituals. These groups are under the protection of the TPC regardless of size.

The victims of genocide will be defined in accordance with the acts of the crime as enumerated in Article 76 of the TPC. The victim of genocide is one who has been killed on the basis of his/her group association. Similarly, in the case of causing physical or psychological harm, the victims are those who are harmed on the basis of their group association. The victims are the members of the group if the group is forced to live in dire conditions that will result in its total or partial destruction. The same rule applies to members of groups who are subject to measures preventing births within the group. For instance, sterilised members or children who are forcibly transferred from their families are the victims. Determination of the group with which the victims are associated plays a vital role with regard to qualifying the crime committed as genocide.[43]

In cases of acts of genocide, general deliberation is not sufficient to prosecute a perpetrator. The perpetrator must know the result of his/her act. Article 6 of the Rome Statute also states that the acts of genocide to destroy a national, ethnical, racial or religious group, in whole or in part, must be committed with obvious intention. Article 76 of the TPC also seeks intention during the commission of the crime. Intention to destroy is what separates genocide from other crimes, especially crimes against humanity. Destruction of the group can be in whole or in part. Within this framework, destruction of the representatives or the leaders of the group is considered sufficient for the commission of the crime.[44]

Namely, the acts of genocide can only be committed deliberately. Special intent is a sine qua non for the crime of genocide, and it is the difference between genocide and similar international crimes.[45] However, intention and deliberation must be separated. Killing someone on the basis of his membership in a certain group does not have to be deliberated before the commission of the crime. Devising a plan and subjecting even only one person to genocide in line with that plan is sufficient for committing genocide.

Chapter II

Susceptibility to Genocide: Aggravating Factors in Turkey

2.1. A political culture afflicted with genocidal tendencies

A number of prominent experts known for their genocide studies emphasize that there must be some prerequisites for the commission of genocide against a community or a social group and point to the necessity of the presence of a national culture that does not value human life. Massacres that took place in Turkey's recent history render it impossible to say that conditions in the country make it an unlikely place for a possible genocide.

Erdoğan, who attracted supporters and accumulated power by using the rhetoric of "Keep humans alive to keep the state alive" during a period in which the driving force for democratic reforms was a bid for European Union membership, has started to talk more about death than life and to glorify 'martyrdom' in recent years. And it has not been perceived as a simple coincidence. Erdoğan's "Those who are against one state and one flag can go wherever they want" rhetoric and former Defense Minister Vecdi Gönül's statement, "If Greeks and Armenians continued to live in Turkey today, we would not have our current nation-state," hint at many things about the prevalent mentality in Turkey.[1]

Turkey's modern history, especially since the beginning of the 20th century, was marked by mass killings and violence that arose from a political culture that does not value human life, and which has been rekindled by Erdoğan's provocations, agitations and massive propaganda in recent years. Recalling these crimes against humanity will help us to understand the seriousness of the danger awaiting members of the Gülen movement, which has been targeted and demonised by the Erdoğan regime with incessant and systematic propaganda for years.

2.1.1. Armenians

The Ottoman state, under the revolutionist and nationalist government of Committee of Union and Progress, caused the death of between 800,000 and 1.5 million Armenians in 1915, during World War I, through systematic ethnic cleansing, deportation and massacres.[2] Today, significant number of countries and researchers recognize these massacres as genocide while other countries like the United States continue to call it the Great Catasrophe (Medz Yeghern). Regardless of the differences in description this crime against Armenians is widely believed to have started when the CUP government ordered the deportation of 250 Armenian intellectuals and political activists, from Istanbul to Ankara, on April 24, 2015, most of whom eventually got killed. According to various sources, what has come to be accepted by many as a genocide was realized in two phases. In the first phase, the healthy Armenian male population was recruited and used as forced labor. In the second phase, Armenian masses including women, children and the elderly were exiled to a desert in Syria under "death march" conditions. Armenians who were exiled from their homeland by the Ottoman soldiers experienced severe food and water shortages during their march. They were also subjected to robbery, rape and massacre along the way.[3]

Lemkin also used the term genocide to describe the systematic and deliberate massacre of Armenians.[4] The Republic of Turkey appropriated the heritage of the CUP policy of denial and has always opposed demands for recognition of the Armenian massacres as genocide.[5] However, 29 countries to date have officially recognized that as genocide, and this definition is also widely accepted by genocide researchers.[6]

2.1.2. Assyrians (Sayfo)

The Assyrians are one of the oldest ethnic groups in the world. As an ethnic and religious minority in the Middle East, the Assyrians have long suffered from oppression and persecution. During World War I,[7] somewhere between 250,000 to 300,000 Assyrians – according to some sources – i.e., about half the population in Turkey, were killed or died from starvation or disease in a series of campaigns orchestrated by the Ottoman CUP government. Despite considerable attention at the time, it has faded from memory and is passed over in surveys of the history of genocide.

Turkey, which is known for denying the atrocities against Armenians as genocide, also continues to reject similar claims from the Assyrians. However, the International Association of Genocide Scholars has deemed what happened to them to have been genocide.[8] Moreover, the Swedish parliament also recognized the "Assyrian Massacre" as genocide in 2010.[9] Unlike the Armenians, the Assyrians have had difficulty in making these atrocities known throughout the world. The fact that today there are very few survivors of the massacres is considered to be one of the reasons. Sometimes the Assyrian massacres are also included in the massacres against Armenians.

2.1.3. Dersim

Just as Gregory H. Stanton pointed out, the first signs of genocide in Dersim appeared in the early years of the Turkish Republic. "Dersim is at a boiling point for the Republican government. It is absolutely necessary for peace and order in the country to have a definitive operation for this in order to prevent horrible possibilities," said Administrative Inspector Hamdi Bey in a report submitted to the Turkish government in February 1926. First General Inspector İbrahim Tali (Öngören) explained the method in 1931: "Preventing attacks by people and their trade with other cities by besieging Dersim to cut their relations with the world, forcing them by starvation to evacuate the region, detaining those who do not bow before the government and scattering them to the western parts of the country."[10]

Turkish Interior Minister Şükrü Kaya presented legislation, commonly known as the Tunceli Law, that once more labelled the region as 'a zone of illness that required surgery'. The law passed without opposition in parliament or in the press. On June 18, 1937, Prime Minister İsmet İnönü announced his 'Reform Program' for Dersim. According to the program, besides the other measures, "the properties of tyrants will be confiscated. ... Those who turned Dersim into a haven for bandits will be moved to the western provinces and settled there, and they will be trained as honourable citizens. Dersim will be completely evacuated, and nobody can reside or settle there without the permission of the Turkish cabinet. ..." Among the measures were the establishment of boarding schools for boys and girls in Turkish-dominated provinces and the transfer of 5-year-old boys and girls from Dersim to these schools in order to assimilate them through education.[11]

Between 1937 and 1938, a massive massacre was carried out after tension escalated between the Turkish government and the Alevi clans in Dersim. In order to ensure the absolute hegemony of the state in Dersim, the Turkish army organized a military campaign and bombarded houses, forests and caves, even using poison gas, to kill people indiscriminately in an attempt to exterminate an entire community and its culture.[12] According to some sources, 13,160 people living in the region were massacred and around 12,000 people were forced to migrate.[13]

In his book titled "*Dersim 1938 ve Zorlu İskan*" (Dersim 1938 and the Forced Resettlement) [14] Hüseyin Aygün noted that although the rebellion had started as a result of a provocation, family members and even those who did not participate in the uprising were subjected to massacre. Reports sent from the region to Ankara stated that people, including women and children, were massacred through the use of poisonous gas and firebombs.[15]

2.1.4. Property tax

An extraordinary property tax imposed by Law No. 4305 on November 11, 1942, as World War II was underway, led to great tragedies. The official justification for the property tax law was "to tax the high profitability created by the extraordinary conditions of war," claiming that it did not target any religious or ethnic group. However, at a Republican People's Party ([CHP]; Turkey was under single-party rule during this period) parliamentary group meeting, the reasons emphasised by then-Prime Minister Şükrü Saraçoğlu were different: "... We have an opportunity to achieve our economic independence. By eliminating the foreigners who dominate our markets, we will put the Turkish market into the hands of Turks."[16]

Throughout the summer of 1942, just as the Gülen movement is targeted today with fabricated news, Turkish newspapers published reports about theft, black marketeering and profiteering. Almost every day and in every national newspaper, cartoons characterizing the "Jewish black marketeer" were published.[17] On September 12, 1942, the Ministry of Finance demanded a tabulation of persons who were found to have reaped exceptional earnings due to the war conditions. In these lists Muslims were identified with an M, non-Muslims with a G, converts (*dönmeler*) with a D and foreigners with an E.[18] In fact, these lists were a study for the profiling of minorities in the last three groups (G, D, E) and revealing their assets.[19]

On November 11, 1942, the property tax law was legislated in the Turkish parliament without any debate. The law envisaged the establishment of wealth detection commissions that would determine who would pay how much tax in each province and district. The commissions' decisions would be final and conclusive; the tax payment period would be 15 days and the properties of those who did not pay the accrued tax within 15 days would be confiscated through foreclosure. Those taxpayers who did not pay the amount owing within one month would be forced to work for free in public and municipal service according to their abilities.[20]

When the tax lists were published on November 18, 1942, 70 percent of the total property tax was owed by taxpayers in Istanbul.[21] Eighty-seven percent of these taxes were owed by non-Muslims and 7 percent by Turks. The remaining 6 percent was owed by various minority groups such as the White Russians.[22] The tax rates applied to non-Muslims were hundreds of times higher than those applied to Muslims when considering the financial strength of both groups. The tax rate of the Armenians was the highest among the non-Muslims.[23] Nine out of 11 taxpayers whose assessed taxes were above 1 million Turkish lira belonged to the non-Muslim group, and two belonged to the convert group.[24] Between December 1942 and January 1943, thousands of properties belonging to non-Muslims in Istanbul changed hands. Sixty-seven percent of the properties sold were bought by Muslim Turks and 30 percent by official institutions and organisations.[25]

A total of 1,400 non-Muslim citizens were sent to labour camps because they failed to pay the property tax; 1,229 of them were from Istanbul and the rest hailed from Izmir and Bursa provinces.[26] Twenty-one (25 according to another source) of those sent to Aşkale district of Erzurum province, where the labour camp was located, died due to the adverse conditions. Some lost their mental or physical health or lost relatives due to grief.[27] The Aşkale exiles were able to return home only on December 17, 1943, on the eve of İsmet İnönü's arrival in Cairo to meet with US President Franklin Roosevelt and British Prime Minister Winston Churchill. The property tax was abolished on March 15, 1944 due to pressure exerted by the US when the Turkish government finally understood that the Nazis would be defeated.[28]

There was a total of 114,368 people on the property tax lists. The state collected 314.9 million Turkish liras, almost 80 percent of the state budget in 1942, which was 394 million Turkish lira. The property tax ignored the basic rights of Greek, Jewish and Armenian citizens in Turkey, neutralized their commercial and industrial activities, was used for the transfer of their commercial investments, wealth and capital to Turks and was a complete destruction of minorities.[29] In the 1935 census, non-Muslim minorities accounted for 1.98 percent of the population of Turkey, but due to a migration that began after the enactment of the property tax, it fell to 1.56 percent in the 1945 census and to 1.08 percent in the 1955 census.[30]

2.1.5. Istanbul Pogrom

The Istanbul Pogrom was an organised mob attack against the Greek minority living in Istanbul, on September 6-7, 1955. It was carried out by members of the Counter-Guerilla, the Turkish branch of Operation Gladio, and the National Security Service, the predecessor of the National Intelligence Organisation (MIT), along with the Turkish Armed Forces' Tactical Mobilisation Group (STK), out of which the Counter-Guerilla initially operated. The events were triggered by the Turkish media's deliberately fake news about the bombing of the house in which the founder of the Turkish Republic, Mustafa Kemal Atatürk, was born in Thessaloniki.[31] A Turkish consular officer who was apprehended confessed that they had fabricated the bomb attack to provoke the events. Yet, the Turkish media, ignoring this confession, maintained that the bomb was thrown by Greeks.[32]

The Istanbul Pogrom was a typical example of the organised and clandestine activity of the Turkish government, which was experiencing difficulty governing the country in the face of opposition criticism, in order to intimidate the opposition. Starting in 1955, the Democrat Party (DP) government encountered a worsening economic situation and lost the confidence of the people, whose standard of living decreased because of high inflation. Attempts to silence the opposition distanced the media, intellectuals and students from the DP.[33] So indeed, two weeks before the events of September 6-7, martial law was declared in Istanbul, Ankara and Izmir. New restrictions in the Law on Press and Demonstrations that were aimed at oppressing the opposition were justified by the September 6-7 events.[34]

In an interview Sabri Yirmibeşoğlu, who was working in the Tactical Mobilisation Group at the time of the September 6-7 events and served as secretary-general of the National Security Council from 1988 to 1990, said: "September 6-7 was the work of Special Operations. It was a magnificent undertaking. And it achieved its goal."[35] All newspapers, in particular the *Hürriyet* daily in Istanbul and *Gece Postası* in Izmir, published news unfavorable to the Ecumenical Patriarchate and Patriarch Athenagoras I[36] on an almost daily basis in order to lay the groundwork for the mass psychology necessary for such psychological warfare.

With an initiative by the Cyprus Is Turkish Association (KTC) and the blessing of other youth, professional and DP organisations and some governmental and nongovernmental authorities, local crowds and large groups brought from outside the city looted and ravaged neighbourhoods where non-Muslims lived on the evening of September 6.[37] Upon instructions, the security forces remained unengaged throughout the attacks on the houses, workplaces and churches of the Greek minority in Istanbul. However, the inner-city transportation of the 20 to 30-person groups, who had information on the location of Greek citizens, was enabled through vehicles such as private automobiles, taxis and trucks along with buses and ferries.

According to official records, more than 5,300 premises, including churches and a synagogue, were ruined by the morning of September 7; however, according to unofficial records the number was closer to 7,000. Millions of dollars in property were trashed and looted. All 73 churches in Istanbul were set on fire. It turned out that the majority of the attackers and looters were brought in from other cities. The death toll was announced to have been 11 in the Turkish media and 15 in the Greek media. Whereas 30 people were injured according to official records, unofficial sources placed it at 300.[38]

According to Dilek Güven, who wrote a Ph.D. thesis on the events of September 6-7, the reason for low death toll was the 'no death' order given to the mobs. Güven claims that the real number of women who were raped, 60 in official records, was actually closer to 400. Sixty women were treated for rape at the Balıklı Greek Hospital alone. Throughout the events, 4,214 houses, 1,004 workplaces, 73 churches, one synagogue, two monasteries and 26 schools were attacked.[39] According to the US Consulate in Istanbul, 59 percent of the workplaces attacked belonged to Greeks, 17 percent to Armenians, 12 percent to Jews and 10 percent to Muslims, while 80 percent of the houses attacked belonged to Greeks, 9 percent to Armenians, 5 percent to Muslims and 3 percent to Jews.[40]

As had been earlier decided, martial law was declared. A total of 5,104 suspects were detained in connection to the events. Although the first investigations and trials were focused on the KTC and youth organisations, the leftist opposition was later designated as a target. A case was opened against already blacklisted leftist intellectuals such as Aziz Nesin, Nihat Sargın, Kemal Tahir, Asım Bezirci, Hasan İzzettin Dinamo, Hulusi Dosdoğru and four dead communists.[41] The head of the KTC, Hikmet Bil, and some of its members were put in jail; however, they were freed after threatening to blackmail authorities, saying 'Release us, or we will reveal the true story!' It was said in court that "the Turkish nation boiled over and carried out the events." Nobody was punished, and the events were swept under the rug.

Immediately after the healing of the wounds inflicted by the September 6-7 events, as a response to the proliferation of clashes between Greece and Turkey in Cyprus in 1963, Turkey abrogated the Residence, Trade and Sea Transportation Agreement on March 16, 1964. This agreement, which was signed in 1930, granted citizens of the two countries the right to engage in trade, to reside and to own property in both countries. Just like the Erdoğan regime's suspension of title deed transactions for people blacklisted as members of the Gülen movement immediately after the failed coup of July 15, 2016, the title deed transactions of Greek citizens were halted on March 17, 1964. As a precaution, land registry offices suspended all sales and inheritance transactions, thus violating their property rights. The Greeks were arbitrarily deported and only allowed to take a suitcase, which could not exceed 20 kilograms in weight, and 200 Turkish lira, equal to nearly $20 at the time.

Following the Istanbul Pogrom 12,000 Greek citizens had left Turkey by the end of September 1955. Families were torn apart. Together with the departure of people worried about situation in Turkey, the number of exiles reached 45,000. The Greek population, which was 2 million in 1914, fell to 2,000.[42]

2.1.6. Maraş

A massacre of Alevis was carried out in Kahramanmaraş province on December 19-26, 1978. One hundred fifty people were killed, and 200 houses belonging to Alevis were burned down. Nearly 100 workplaces were looted. According to the records of the prosecutor's office, of the 1,350 people involved in the incidents, 752 were arrested in the first stage of the investigation. Their trials took 23 years to conclude; 22 people were sentenced to death, seven were given life sentences and 321 were handed down prison sentences ranging between one and 24 years. On the other hand, according to the records, 68 people who played a leading role in the massacre were never prosecuted.[43]

The bloody events were triggered on December 19. A bomb was tossed into a theatre that was showing the movie "When Will the Sun Rise?" starring Turkish actor Cüneyt Arkın. The bomb was allegedly thrown by nationalist Ökkeş Şendiller or, according to another claim, by leftist Salman Ilıksu. On December 20, a café in Yeni Mahalle owned by an Alevi was bombed. A day later, two leftist teachers, Hacı Çolak and Mustafa Yüzbaşıoğlu, were killed. The funerals of the teachers transformed the events into a massacre. Upon hearing rumours such as "Alevis will attack the Sunnis tomorrow," a nationalist group gathered around the Ulu Cami mosque and then attacked Alevis after climbing over a police barricade. Following the death of three Sunnis in the evening, one of the most tragic events in Turkish history was triggered.

Several days before the incidents, the houses and workplaces of Alevi residents were marked by people who claimed they were conducting a census. When the events started to unfold, the leaders of the attackers gave orders to "Burn or tear down the marked houses, do not touch the others."[44] To prevent a clash between the police and the townspeople, all police officers were declared off-duty on December 24. Emotions were at a boiling point, and the situation got out of control. A state of chaos prevailed throughout the city. Finally, to put an end to the days-

long clashes between the sides, military forces were sent to Kahramanmaraş from Kayseri and Gaziantep provinces. In the wake of the incidents, Prime Minister Bülent Ecevit said the events were organised by
the Counter-Guerilla, which wanted to force him to declare martial law
against his will.

His words turned out to be prophetic. Under the pretext of the
events, martial law was declared in 13 cities on December 26, 1978. The
number of cities under martial law was subsequently increased.[45] Defence lawyers in the massacre case Ceyhun Can, Halil Sıtkı Güllüoğlu
and Ahmet Albay were killed on September 10, 1979, February 3, 1980
and May 3, 1980, respectively.[46] Thirty-five years later former Interior
Minister Hasan Fehmi Güneş, who went to the city 15 days after the incidents with a group of senators, characterised the events in an interview
as a "fascist plan." Saying that the massacre was planned in plain sight,
Güneş claimed that the National Intelligence Organisation (MIT) did
not provide any intelligence about the situation to the government, and
what was worse, contributed to the slaughter in Maraş.[47]

2.1.7. Çorum

In May-July 1980, 57 people -- mostly Alevis -- died and hundreds were
injured in bloody events with a politico-religious background in Çorum
province. Although the events were sparked by a nationalist attack on
the Milönü neighbourhood,[48] populated mainly by Alevis, several interesting developments had transpired immediately before the bloodshed.
Hasan Uyar, the chief of police in Çorum, was replaced by Nail Bozkurt,
who previously held the position in Tunceli. Fethi Katar from the MHP
was appointed provincial director of national education, and Rafet Ucel
was named governor of Çorum. Some 40 police officers were assigned to
other cities, and the positions of numerous school administrators, teachers and officials were changed.[49]

The killing of Gün Sazak, a prominent politician in the nationalist
MHP, on May 27, 1980 in Ankara heightened the tension in Çorum.[50]
On Wednesday, May 28, groups of youths started to march down the
busiest avenue of the city. The march quickly turned in to an attack.
Stores belonging to leftists on the avenue were looted. The governor of
Çorum declared a curfew and ordered the removal of barricades erected

by Alevis for self-defense, but these people denied removing barricades. At the same time in another district, a car (licence plate number 19 AN 709) with police officers in it sprayed the Milönü neighbourhood with bullets after getting through a weak barricade.

The tension increased with a report broadcast by state television station TRT claiming that "the events started after an explosive substance was thrown at the Alaaddin Mosque and a gun was fired from outside." This information, however, was not disseminated by military authorities, and the governor did not confirm or deny the report. Moreover, the Çorum reporter for TRT said he did not provide the information. The police officer who spread this fake news was never found. Like the prayers broadcast from mosque speakers on July 15, 2016, calls to jihad were made from the mosque speakers in Çorum. In such an environment groups with long barreled shotguns attacked Alevi neighbourhoods and a massacre took place.

2.1.8. Sivas – Madımak

On July 2, 1993 the Madımak Hotel was burned by radical Islamists in Sivas province during the traditional Pir Sultan Abdal Festival. Thirty-five people—authors, poets and intellectuals, mostly Alevis—including two hotel workers burned to death or died from smoke inhalation. Two people among the protestors outside the hotel also perished. The incident had started with a rock-throwing fight between rival groups. The police prevented the altercation from growing;[51] nevertheless, thousands of people gathered and stoned the governor's office in Hükümet Square. After that the group descended on the Madımak Hotel, burned the cars in front of it and set the hotel on fire after throwing rocks at it.

Thirty-five people in the hotel, including authors and poets Asım Bezirci, Nesimi Çimen,[52] Muhlis Akarsu, Metin Altıok and Hasret Gültekin, burned to death or were suffocated by the smoke. Fifty-one people, including famous author Aziz Nesin, were seriously injured but survived. Security forces gained control only after a curfew was declared that night. According to one claim, the Sivas massacre was planned by the Special Forces, just like the September 6-7, 1955 and Maraş massacres.[53]

2.1.9. Ongoing Kurdish crackdown

Turkey has a Kurdish problem whose roots lie in the pre-Republican era.[54] Due to shortcomings in democracy and the rule of law in the country, the Kurds' basic demands for social, cultural and political rights have not been met.[55] This situation has been exploited by some extremist and terrorist organisations. Giving way to bilateral distrust, the crisis has damaged relations between the Turkish and Kurdish peoples, who have managed to live together for almost a thousand years.

The Kurdish problem has led to hatred among society and thus increased the possibility of actual massacres committed by state forces and extremist groups. Since 1984 the outlawed Kurdistan Workers' Party (PKK) has exploited this fertile ground and has managed to attract the masses to its side.[56] The PKK experienced a calm period at the beginning of the 2000s after causing the death of more than 40,000 people. Yet, following the June 2015 elections, for the sake of forming a nationalist-Islamist alliance, President Erdoğan ended the peace process that he himself initiated in 2012 and as a result, the clashes between the PKK and Turkish security forces started up again.[57]

Kurdish cities and villages, for perhaps the first time in their history, were besieged by police and military forces. Under the pretext of the fight against terrorism in residential areas, hundreds of thousands of Kurdish citizens were displaced from their homes and forced to migrate. Hundreds of Kurds were slaughtered during this period of time. Historic cities, buildings and houses were demolished.[58] In a report dated February 2017 the UN had recorded the deaths and demolitions[59] as 2,000 people, including 800 security forces, lost their lives and that serious violations of human rights were committed. The 25-pages report also includes findings of massive destruction, killings and other human rights violations in the course of security force operations between July 2015 and December 2016.[60]

Emphasising the UN observers' inability to enter Turkey's Kurdish-populated southeastern cities despite a year-long effort, the report includes the testimony of residents and satellite images and states that in more than 30 cities in the region, residential areas were destroyed and 500,000 people were left homeless. According to the report, at the beginning of 2016 in the Cizre district of Şırnak province, 189 men, women and children were confined to their basements without food, water, medical assistance or electricity. They were subsequently killed in a fire sparked by artillery fire from Turkish security forces. The UN report indicates that not a single suspect was arrested or investigated and states that "Moreover, instead of opening an investigation into the circumstances surrounding the reported excessive use of force, recourse to heavy weapons and the resulting deaths, the local authorities accused the people killed of participating in terrorist organizations and took repressive measures affecting members of their families."[61]

Meanwhile, the Nusaybin district of Mardin province and the Sur district of Diyarbakır province suffered a cultural genocide. Seventy percent of the buildings in these districts were destroyed in a systematic bombardment.[62] After this destruction, the government pursued a policy of confiscation. By means of a cabinet decision certain neighbourhoods of Sur were expropriated.[63]

At the same time, with no respect for due process, 10,000 teachers were purged on allegations of ties to the PKK. Democratically elected Kurdish politicians and mayors together with scores of Kurdish journalists were arrested. Kurdish-language media outlets, media associations and NGOs were closed down.[64] In addition to the repression of the Gülen movement, oppressive practices against the Kurds were accelerated. Erdoğan succeeded in garnering unlimited support from his partisans for his massacres and oppression of the Kurds.

2.2. The Erdoğan regime and the reinvigoration of socio-political supremacism

Experts such as M. Hassan Kakar view "a totalitarian society with an ideology supposed to be superior" as a precondition of a process leading to genocide. A similar version of Hitler's supremacy complex that he infused in German society as well as the unfounded self-confidence that goes in parallel with the widespread perception of threat is systematically being pumped into the pro-Erdoğan masses by the Erdoğan regime.

Whilst the massive propaganda claiming that they can compete with all the nations of the world, which they see almost entirely as enemies, continues on the one hand, the ideology of Islamofascism, which has been derived from a kind of political Islamism blended with extreme nationalism and conspiracy theories, offers Erdoğan a wide range of possibilities upon which to act. The Erdoğan regime is paving the way to a possible genocide through dichotomies such as 'infidels' versus Muslims, Kurds versus Turks and 'FETO' [an acronym for the Fethullahist Terror Organisation, frequently used by Erdoğan and the pro-Erdoğan media in defamation of the Gülen movement] versus the nation.[65]

Erdoğan and the people around him who came from the political Islamist Milli Görüş (National View) tradition[66] had declared that they had "stripped off their Milli Görüş shirt" and for a while pretended that they had rejected their problematic political Islamist background. Actually, between 2002 and 2011, they pursued policies aimed at achieving democratisation, liberalisation and EU norms and standards on a fluctuating course.[67]

In this period, investigations were launched to neutralise the military tutelage that hampered democratisation, and these efforts at democratisation boosted public support for Erdoğan. However, when he garnered the votes of almost half the electorate in the parliamentary elections of June 12, 2011, Erdoğan, who had previously described democracy as "a tram that you get off when you come to the destination,"[68] believed there were no obstacles left before him and thus returned to his former ideological position and political factory settings. Instead of using public support for further democratisation in the direction of his pre-election promises, he preferred to use this support for his political Islamist agenda and for setting up a one-man rule.[69]

After the Gülen movement distanced itself from Erdoğan's new goals, Erdoğan first tried to ally with the Kurdish political movement in order to substitute the public support assured by the movement.[70] However, following the corruption and bribery scandal of December 17/25, 2013, he desperately needed to search for new partners who had more influence in the judiciary, the military and the state bureaucracy. Over the course of time, Erdoğan abandoned the idea of reinforcing political Islamism through the support of the Kurdish political movement, thus ending the 'Settlement Process,'[71] and rekindling the conflict. He tried to find the support he needed from the traditional nationalists, neo-nationalists and Eurasianists[72] with their presence in the bureaucracy, army, judiciary, civil society and the media in order to destroy both the Kurdish political movement and the Gülen movement.[73]

He derived a favourable result from these efforts and on the path initially set by pure political Islamist goals he established a pragmatic alliance and an ideological synthesis as well with nationalist/neo-nationalist/Eurasianist circles, which also have racist and fascist leanings. At this point, the Erdoğan regime was sitting on a troika of political Islamist, ultranationalist and Eurasianist discourses.[74] Those three extreme ideological discourses that were united on the basis of being anti-West, anti-Christian, anti-Jewish, anti-Kurd and anti-Gülen movement constitute the main elements of Erdoğan's new regime. Alliances and the process of ideological harmonisation have so far been able to be carried out smoothly, although there may be occasional disagreements between these three pillars, each of which subscribes to the supremacy of Muslims, the superiority of the Turkish race, which is viewed as having been chosen, and the uniqueness of the Kemalist revolution, all accompanied by a longing for the past.

The combination of those three ideological discourses provided a highly pragmatic and flexible space in which the Erdoğan regime could manoeuvre and gained Erdoğan the ability and opportunity to instrumentilise pan-Turkist ultranationalism, Eurasianist neo-nationalism and political Islamism for his political interests. From the composition of these three toxic ideological elements a lethal, oppressive regime has emerged for those who are not part of this equation.

Erdoğan, who has succeeded in recruiting rival conservative politicians with even the smallest of competitive potential such as Numan Kurtulmuş, Süleyman Soylu and Yalçın Topçu by providing material and political benefits, has managed to make the Nationalist Movement Party (MHP) with its 15 percent popular support a part of this ideological alliance.[75] Thus, he was able to build a populist, pragmatic and fascist regime, potentially addressing 50 to 60 percent of Turkey's population. Erdoğan, who succeeded in consolidating the support of the people in this way, also managed to develop a mafia-style give-and-take based on mutually concrete interests with the ultranationalist and Eurasianist/neo-nationalist establishments within the state.[76]

Like all totalitarian and authoritarian regimes, Erdoğan's regime also embarked on an intense propaganda campaign to create the perception that the Turkish nation is superior to other cultures, civilisations, states and societies. In fact, the origins of the perception of the superiority of the Turkish nation as expressed by traditional nationalists and Eurasianists/neo-nationalists date back to the beginning of the previous century.[77] For instance, a speech delivered by İsmet İnönü, who would later become a Mussolini-like national chief (Milli Şef), at the Turkish Hearths (Türk Ocakları) in 1925 was quite racist: "We are clearly nationalists ... and nationalism is our sole unity. In the majority of Turks, there is no influence of other elements. Our duty is to change non-Turkish people into Turks in the Turkish homeland. We will cut off those who oppose Turks and Turkishness. For those who are going to serve the country, above all, we want them to be Turks."[78] In a speech made in 1940 at the faculty of political sciences at Ankara University, İnönü also said, "You have these qualities, they are in your blood because our nation is the greatest and the most honourable nation."[79]

Today, this political movement, with its wide range of fascist tones from naked racism to pan-Turkism and nationalism, conveys the perception of racial superiority that is unfortunately not much different from that of the past. The following sentences from a lengthy text written by a typical nationalist are quite interesting: "... The mistake of those circles that want to equate Turks with the other cultures they live together with stems from missing this fact ... Turkish nationalism accepts Muslim micro-nationals such as Kurds, Circassians, Albanians, Georgians and Arabs as part of this nation, and lets them take part in the organisations of Turkish nationalism as a favour showing their determination to live together in the political organisations of Turkish nationalism. Turkish nationalism has developed with genetic codes, not short-range doctrinal discourses. It is slanderous to accept Kurdish identity and to claim that this identity is on an equal footing with Turkishness. Even if the concept of the Kurdish nation is real, it can never be in the same league as Turkishness."[80]

Murat Belge, well known for his expertise in nationalism, racism and militarism, is also among those who frequently express the risk that nationalist and racist cultures create: "You can often see slogans on Turkish nationalist/racist websites such as 'Not the nation's fraternity but the Turks' superiority!' So, it is very difficult for nationalism to eliminate a claim such as superiority."[81]

While a nationalist/racist understanding based on viewing the national existence and identity as superior to all other races and cultures constitutes in itself a threat and danger to differing thoughts and elements in the society, a much riskier and more dangerous situation has emerged in Turkey. That is because all the variants of this concept, merged with political Islamist radicalism, have become elements of a totalitarian regime that appeals to between 50 and 60 percent of the society.

This kind of dominant nationalism and racism on the one hand and radical Islamism leaning towards Salafism on the other produced this dire picture well portrayed by veteran Turkish journalist Hasan Cemal: "... Democracy is gradually being disparaged. It is reduced only to elections and votes. Human rights and freedoms are ignored. These values are the means of domination of Western imperialism in their eyes. ... So is the rule of law. Judicial independence and separation of powers, which make a democracy a real democracy, are seen as obstacles. ... Secularism, as one of the pillars of the republic and democracy, is one of the primary values towards which the enemies of the West are hostile. For this reason, they want to destroy secularism, especially by the Islamisation of education and increasing the number of religious schools [imam-hatip schools]. They aim at eliminating 'critical thought,' which is one of the cornerstones of democracy, law and freedom, and replacing it with the madrasa culture. Turkey is rapidly moving in this backwards direction. The hostility of the Erdoğan government to the West is day by day distancing Turkey from democracy, the rule of law and the system of liberties."[82]

Tayfun Atay, a sociologist of religion, also expresses the difference between Erdoğan and the AKP's point of departure and place of arrival: "... Turkey, after the '9/11' event that occurred in 2001 and sparked Islamophobia all over the world, was an almost unmatched country demonstrating that Islam and democracy, Islam and liberalism and Islam and secularism are compatible. This was the main reason why the AKP, which came to power as an example of 'liberal [moderate] Islam' in 2002, was a hope in the eyes of the world. The AKP is a political movement that squandered this hope. In particular since 2012, they have built Islamofascism on the one hand and fuelled Islamophobia on the other, with their policies towards the 'forced Islamisation' of the society so as to bring about a disastrous cultural polarisation within the country. Inside and out, to everything and everyone, they began to view things from the perspective of religion and destroyed 'secularism' which made them unique in the name of Islam in both the Muslim and non-Muslim worlds. They turned away from the experience of 'secular Islam' and embraced 'Salafi Islam.' While they might have been a bridge between the divided worlds of Islamofascism and Islamophobia, and acquired great political legitimacy in the eyes of everyone in the world, they burnt this bridge down. ... While they could have brought together civilisations, they preferred to be the instigator of the clash of civilisations. They were a hope for Turkey and for the world as well. They turned out to be a hopeless case."[83]

Throughout the political spectrum, from liberalism to socialist leftism, many authors and scholars now agree on this conceptualization of Islamofascism. Like Perihan Mağden, who describes the current regime as "an alliance of Kemalist neo-nationalists and Islamofascist Erdoğanists,"[84] political scientist Fatih Yaşlı, the author of a book titled "*Türkçü Faşizmden 'Türk-İslam Ülküsü'ne* (From Turkish Fascism to the Turkish-Islamist Ideal)"[85] is among those who mention an acceleration in the construction of a new regime in Turkey after the July 15, 2016 coup attempt.[86]

We can easily predict what kind of consequences racism and nationalism might have by looking at some past examples in Turkey, or bloody experiences in countries like Germany, Italy and Spain. In terms of radical Islamist fascism, we can understand the situation by considering what happened over time in countries such as Iran, Sudan and Saudi Arabia,[87] and what the Taliban regime recently did in Afghanistan[88] and ISIL in Iraq and Syria[89] in a very short period of time. Erdoğan's regime is much more dangerous than these regimes to differing mentalities, beliefs and lifestyles because his regime is based on a poisonous mix of all these oppressive regimes' dangerous ideologies. This assessment can easily be understood by examining the oppression and lawlessness engaged in by the Erdoğan regime in recent years, and a projection can also be made through them.

It seems that Erdoğan and his supporters internalised the understanding that they are the masters, the dominant and superior power, while other segments of society are obliged to obey them, and if they do not, then they deserve to be destroyed. In this regard, Erdoğanist theologians including Hayrettin Karaman, a professor of theology and Erdoğan's issuer of *fatwas*,[90] have been manipulating Islamic principles and rules to justify Erdoğan's crimes. The Directorate of Religious Affairs[91] has censored the Qur'an's verses and hadiths that curse theft, corruption and bribery[92] in Friday sermons (*khutbah*). A remarkable example of this censor was when they hastily changed a sermon on the subject of 'bribery' that was to be delivered on Friday, December 20, 2013, (just after the exposition of the Erdoğan's corruption and bribery scandal on 17 December 2013).

After the scandal erupted on December 17, 2013, Professor Karaman, in order to whitewash Erdoğan's illegalities and corruption, wrote that "corruption is not thievery,"[93] distorting clear Islamic principles, and said no one should "cut off their nose to spite their face."[94] Only two days after the December 17, 2013 graft scandal became public knowledge, Karaman used the words of a *fatwa* to legitimize the Erdoğan regime's efforts to annihilate the Gülen movement in retaliation for allegedly exposing Erdoğan's bribery and corruption. As to the meaning of religious authorisation and *fatwa*s for radical Islamists, the Salman Rushdi[95] and Taslima Nasrin[96] cases are still fresh in people's minds.

In an article titled "Türkiye'nin dostları ve düşmanları (Friends and enemies of Turkey)", published in the *Yeni Şafak* newspaper on December 19, 2013, Karaman indicated that opposition Grand Unity Party (BBP) leader Muhsin Yazıcıoğlu was in fact killed in the guise of a helicopter crash for the sake of Erdoğan's accumulation of power: "In order to prevent damage to the public [and to the Ummah], the risk of damage to a person, region or group is acceptable and can be tolerated. I am directing this to those politicians who have good and common sense, and as an example, I am commemorating the late martyr Muhsin Yazıcıoğlu with a prayer."[97] The idea put forward in these *fatwa*-like words is the exact opposite of the values of a liberal democracy that guarantee minority rights against the interests of the majority.

If these views were those of an ordinary theologian, perhaps they could be ignored with a brief criticism. However, what is at issue here is the radical *fatwa*s of Karaman, whose writings are accepted as Islamic guidance and immediately applied by Erdoğan's regime. At a time when radicalism associated with religion and sectarianism is causing bloodshed in the Middle East, there could not be any better justification for the injustices and inhuman actions that the Erdoğan regime is taking without any religious, ethical, moral or legal responsibility than this parlay. Erdoğan has exploited this opportunity to the utmost: He seized thousands of companies and private properties, shut down thousands of educational institutions and hundreds of media outlets,[98] purged at least 160,000 public servants, investigated over 600,000 people, detained some 500,000[99] and imprisoned at least 77,000 members of the Gülen movement.[100] He still continues to detain and jail them today.

Turkey is now going through a period of socio-political depression in which all power and authority are concentrated in the hands of one person, and the majority of society is positioning itself according to the one man in power. At such times, the danger posed by a leadership that guides the society according to its desires while seeking to destroy those it fails to guide, is obvious. This danger becomes even more concrete in the hands of a leader like Erdoğan, who has succeeded in establishing an one-man rule by easily manipulating his supporters' feelings through poetry, religious discourse, TV serials and the perception of victimisation.[101] Erdoğan has targetted social groups to varying degrees both in the past and in the present, as called for by the 'destructive narcissistic leadership' model. Erdoğan has turned republican circles, Alevis and Kurdish groups into low intensity targets and the Gülen movement into a high intensity target by demonising them.[102]

According to social psychologist Vamık Volkan, societies that find themselves in regression following a social disaster pave the way for the emergence of the narcissistic instincts of the leaders and the strengthening of their position in the eyes of the public. Moreover, narcissistic leaders satisfy their feelings of invincibility and grandeur by creating the false perception that they are the saviours of the people.[103] In these cases, leaders exploit social events and images. This is called 'selected trauma' or 'selected victory'. Selected trauma and victory are historical events, myths and rhetoric built upon these events which unify the people.[104] The controversial military coup attempt on July 15, 2016 has obviously functioned as a selected trauma/victory in the hands of Erdoğan.

Another characteristic of societies that have experienced a severe trauma and gone through a long period of regression is a cultural change that Volkan calls 'purification.' But purification can manifest itself as malicious purification, which leads societies to ethnic cleansing and genocide as we saw in the disintegration of Yugoslavia. In the form of destructive narcissism, just like in the case of Erdoğan, the leader wants to keep the society under control and lead them through this antagonism by pointing out enemy groups. It has often been seen that this kind of campaign, as Erdoğan did by demonising the Gülen movement, which started December 17/25, 2013 and intensified after July 15, 2016, has resulted in a humanitarian catastrophe. The best-known example is undoubtedly Adolf Hitler, who portrayed Jews as enemies and dragged his country and the world into an unmitigated disaster.[105]

Today, Erdoğan is extremely successful in repeating what Hitler did ahead of World War II, namely pumping extreme self-confidence into the society that he took over with a warped psychology in the wake of Germany's World War I defeat. Thanks to the coup attempt on July 15, 2016, Erdoğan managed to project overconfidence and a mood to the masses,[106] who were able to stop the tanks with T-shirts,[107] who challenged F-16 fighter jets with their bare hands,[108] who are made up of devout people, always kept away from the centers of power, in an atmosphere of desperate, humiliated and repressed feelings against the West that has existed for nearly two centuries.

Erdoğan has also succeeded in translating the regime, precisely calculated and created by him, into a mythological power in which the virtual and the real, the past and the present, are interwoven. Erdoğan, who has used all types of propaganda -- one of the main pillars of all dictatorships -- without any ethical concerns, has succeeded in diversifying these propaganda opportunities through music, movies and TV series. An article in the New York Times also pointed to Erdoğan's success in enchanting the masses by such methods.[109]

Just as Hitler identified with Frederick II, Erdoğan, widely said to be caught up in the "hubris syndrome,"[110] identifies mainly with Abdulhamit II, with the glorious names of the past and with unique heroism. According to the New York Times: "These themes are staples of President Erdoğan's populist appeal. For years he has portrayed the huge building projects reshaping the Turkish landscape as part of a struggle against jealous foreign powers out to frustrate Turkey's rise. A cult of personality has developed in which Mr. Erdoğan is seen as the sole embodiment of the 'national will.' He tells the faithful at public rallies that Turkey is fulfilling a sacred destiny under his presidency, returning to its historical role as a regional leader and global power."[111]

Because of such a self-perception and his belief in his ability to lead 50 percent (of the electorate) to any goal he desires,[112] Erdoğan may think of democratic support as a militia that can be driven on to the battlefield if required. Therefore, he was able respond to a friend who warned him that the polarising politics he embraces could lead to a civil war, "I don't care if a civil war takes place, we will crush them."[113]

When he was prime minister, the CHP, an opposition party, had announced that a public demonstration would be held in Istanbul's Kadiköy district to demand the protection of Gezi Park. Upon this, Erdoğan threatened with the masses, who he could radicalize or militarise whenever he wanted. "If the aim is to hold a public demonstration, I can gather 200,000 people where they gather only 20,000. On behalf of my party I can bring together 1 million where they can attract only 200,000. Don't make me do this."[114] Just two days after that, at a press conference, he threatened environmental activists with unleashing the masses on them and said: "At the moment we are keeping at least 50 percent of the country in their homes. We tell them, 'Be patient, don't buy into these games.'"[115]

In short, Erdoğan has built a fascist regime with which he has been able to manipulate 50 to 60 percent of the society by constructing it on three main ideological pillars: Islamists, ultranationalists and Eurasianists/neo-nationalists. Therefore, he has managed to create a 'superior' totalitarian mentality according to which people think they will rule the world and all other civilisations through a longing for the glorious days of the past and identifying themselves with the victories of that era. Since the Gülen movement did not want to be part or partner in this despicable propaganda and poisonous self-perception, like other educated groups in Turkey, and since the movement has been portrayed as being in concert with "foreign enemies," it has become the primary target for destruction by the Erdoğan regime. Unlike other dissident groups, the Gülen movement's potential to influence Erdoğan's voter base through its sociological and religious proximity has played a critical role in Erdoğan's preference for the Gülen movement as a primary target.

2.3. Erdoğan-centred autocracy and the institutional groundwork for genocide

As previously mentioned, genocide specialist Kakar underlines that even the existence of a national culture that does not value human life, the existence of a totalitarian understanding that claims to possess a superior ideology and the conduct of defamation and dehumanisation campaigns

that target the victims are not sufficient for the commission of genocide. Kakar emphasises that for genocide to take place against a targeted
group, the perpetrators should have a strong central authority and bureaucratic organisation. In this regard the Erdoğan regime, aiming to
annihilate the Gülen movement, does not face any problems since it has
the central authority and bureaucratic organisation that are totally free
from the law and mechanisms to enforce checks and balances.

In order to acquire the capability to commit genocide, the power
should be unrestrained and concentrated in the hands of one man or a
small group, just like the Ottoman Empire under the rule of the Committee of Union and Progress (İttihat ve Terakki Partisi) and Germany
under the rule of Hitler. This can only be possible if the constitutional
democracy is gradually removed and democratic dynamics, like checks
and balances and the rule of law that guarantee the prevention of political power from falling into the hands of one person, are deliberately corroded. Far from these ideal conditions, the Erdoğan regime has
effectively paralysed the mechanisms of checks and balances, not only
those enshrined in the Turkish constitution but also those included in
the international agreements to which Turkey is a party.

2.3.1. Seizure of the judiciary

In this regard, the judiciary, as one of the main pillars of democracies,
is the most crucial safeguard against legislative or executive excesses of
power. Therefore, ensuring its independence, objectivity, impartiality
and self-governance are critical. The experience of contemporary democracies manifests adherence to this fundamental standard. The first
priority of international agreements related to governance and created
by international organisations, particularly the United Nations and the
Council of Europe (CoE), to which Turkey is party and agreed to be
bound by, is the independence of judiciary.

However, the deterioration of the independence of the Turkish
judiciary has been extensively recorded and documented by the Venice Commission, EU progress reports and European Court of Human
Rights' (ECtHR) jurisprudence. Some human rights organizations have
also published extensive reports focusing exclusively on the subject.[116]
Turkey's judiciary is being widely criticized for acting on orders from

Erdoğan and not basing their rulings on the law. Judges in Turkey who make decisions that anger Erdoğan are either replaced or jailed. Therefore, Turkey has fallen to 109th place out of 126 countries in the World Justice Project's (WJP) Rule of Law Index 2019, a comprehensive measure of the rule of law.[117]

The tenure of judges, guaranteed by Article 139 of the Turkish constitution, has been completely terminated. The dismissal and arrest of judges and prosecutors en masse since July 15, 2016 and the pressure created through this unlawful aggression violate the right to a fair trial. In all, 4,238 judges and prosecutors, two-thirds of them in the hours following the coup attempt, were fired.[118] Their salaries and bank accounts were seized. Those judges and prosecutors who did not render dictated verdicts or defiantly ruled against Erdoğan's wishes were quickly punished.

Erdoğan had gradually taken over control of the High Council of Judges and Prosecutors (HSYK) after the December 17/25, 2013 corruption and bribery scandal. Constitutional amendments passed by a referendum on April 16, 2017 further granted Erdoğan the right to appoint all members of the HSYK (now HSK). As a result, the election of the majority of HSYK members by their peers has been eliminated. Erdoğan, taking advantage of his newly enhanced authority, appointed half the HSK members. The remainder were elected by the majority in parliament, which is the ruling AKP. The only criterion that Erdoğan and the ruling party, which he also chairs, applied in selecting the HSK members was loyalty.[119]

Starting in early 2014, the HSYK was harshly criticised by an international judicial society, despite its formation through relatively participatory elections. However, the HSYK's falling under the full control of the executive branch in 2016 was registered internationally by suspending the HSYK's observer status in the European Network of Councils for the Judiciary (ENCJ).[120] It was also stated in a recent report published by the International Commission of Jurists-Human Rights Joint Platform (ICJ-IHOP) that without an independent institution of self-governance and, therefore, without strong structural independence, it is difficult to see how judges and prosecutors in Turkey can carry out their duties independently in politically sensitive cases.[121]

When examining the process in which the judiciary has become the stick of the executive, one needs to draw particular attention to the

Penal Courts of Peace, which Erdoğan defined as "project courts." Fully authorised to deal with initial proceedings, including detentions and arrests, the Penal Courts of Peace were established to suppress opponents, particularly members of the Gülen movement and Kurdish politicians, from exercising their fundamental rights. According to the Code on Criminal Procedure (CMK), these courts have the power to issue search, arrest and detention warrants. They are also entitled to review decisions of non-prosecution made by public prosecutors. The power of the Penal Courts of Peace was, however, extended to include the removal of content and the closing down of Internet websites;[122] elimination of the right of a lawyer to engage in advocacy according to Decree Law no. 667 issued by the Erdoğan regime under the state of emergency;[123] and decisions on the merits on traffic offences.

Avenues for appealing the decisions of the peace court judges within their criminal jurisdiction are very limited. Apart from the highly exceptional circumstance in which a case can be referred to the Constitutional Court, the only appeal is to another Penal Court of Peace judge in the same district. Effectively, therefore, there is a closed system of appeal within the criminal procedural jurisdiction presided over by judges in Penal Courts of Peace, with minimal recourse to the broader court system. This situation is particularly worrisome given allegations of the lack of independence of the judges of these courts.[124] In addition, along with judicial process, judges are carefully handpicked by the government for all courts, from courts of first instance, which are authorised to hear cases targeting opponents although the AKP paints them as terrorist cases, to the Supreme Court of Appeals.[125]

Since their creation in 2014, the Penal Courts of Peace have been the focus of much criticism with regard to violations of human rights as they are at the forefront of the authorisation or judicial review of decisions restricting the right to liberty and other human rights. The report by the ICJ-IHOP also concludes that the system of the Penal Court of Peace judges in Turkey does not meet international standards for independent and impartial review of detention and suggests a set of detailed constitutional and legislative reforms to put the system back in line with Turkey's human rights obligations.[126]

Concerns about the independence and impartiality of the Penal Courts of Peace were brought to the Constitutional Court in 2015. The

Constitutional Court declined to annul the relevant provisions on the grounds that peace judges are appointed by the HSYK in the same manner as the judges of general jurisdictions and that they enjoy the same constitutional guarantees of independence.[127] In contrast to the Constitutional Court's decisions, the Council of Europe's Venice Commission concluded that the "system of horizontal appeals against decisions by the criminal peace judges does not offer sufficient prospects of an impartial, meaningful examination of the appeals."[128]

Indeed, according to ICJ reports, while around a third of the judiciary was arbitrarily and summarily dismissed immediately or soon in the aftermath of the attempted coup of July 15, 2016, all but one out of the 719 peace judges across the country remained in their jobs.[129] As the Venice Commission pointed out, the apparently political "screening" process in the selection of these judges casts doubts on the objectivity of the method of selection and consequently calls into question their impartiality.

Moreover, it is obvious that these peace judges are entrusted with the authorisation of requests for removal of content online made by the prime minister or other government ministers. Almost 212 such decisions have been issued since July 2015, and almost all of them were requested by the Prime Ministry. They were all executed by the presidency of the Telecommunications Directorate (TIB) and the Information Technologies and Communications Authority (BTK) and approved by a Penal Court of Peace in Ankara. One hundred thirty-seven of these decisions were issued by a single court in the Gölbaşı district of Ankara, blocking access to 575 websites, 482 news articles, 1,759 Twitter accounts, 736 tweets, 505 YouTube videos, 116 Facebook pages and 195 other pieces of content totalling 4,368 separate Internet addresses. All the appeals made against the decisions to block were rejected by other Penal Court of Peace judges.130 In other words, with regard to about 4,368 separate Internet addresses peace judges accepted all requests from the Prime Ministry and rejected all appeals made by potential victims. PEN International underlined in a recent report that "almost all appeals made against orders of pre-trial detention issued by Criminal Judgeships of Peace are rejected by another Criminal Judgeship of Peace."131

The Office of the UN High Commissioner for Human Rights also found that "the jurisdiction and practice of the [Penal Courts of Peace] gives rise to numerous concerns. These courts have been using the emergency decrees to issue detention orders, including decisions to detain journalists and human rights defenders, to impose media bans, to appoint trustees for the takeover of media companies, or to block internet."[132] The UN special rapporteur on freedom of opinion and expression in his report on Turkey found that "the system of horizontal appeal falls short of international standards and deprives individuals of due process and fair trial guarantees."[133]

While the courts are designed in line with the wishes of the executive, the right to a defense as an indispensable principle of law is about to be wiped out in Turkey. Especially in recent years, the tools of defense have gradually been eliminated on the pretext of fighting against terrorism. The Erdoğan regime's suppression of the right to a defense went further by recognising advocacy as a criminal act immediately after July 15, 2016. According to data compiled by independent monitoring site The Arrested Lawyers' Initiative, 555 lawyers have been arrested since July 15, 2016 and 1,546 were under prosecution as of January 24, 2019. Moreover, 216 lawyers have been sentenced to a total of 1,361 years in prison. Some of the arrested lawyers were reportedly subjected to torture and ill treatment. Fourteen of the detained or arrested lawyers are presidents or former presidents of provincial bar associations.[134]

The charges the lawyers faced were membership in a certain association and complicity with the suspects they were defending. The arrested lawyers are also facing suppression and forced to testify against their clients. Dozens of lawyers are known to have fled abroad to avoid the fate suffered by their colleagues. The loss of the right to a defense to that extent not only violates the right to a fair trial but also makes the Erdoğan regime's massive violations unquestionable.

According to a 34-page report on violations of the rights and protections of the legal profession in Turkey, which was submitted by the Bar Human Rights Committee of England & Wales (BHRC), the International Bar Association's Human Rights Institute (IBAHRI) and the Law Society of England and Wales to the United Nations special rapporteur on the independence of judges and lawyers in September 2018, "Primarily, new laws place in a statutory framework the pre-existing threats to the independence of the legal profession, including arbitrary arrest and detention, dismissals, and breaches of the right to a fair trial and due process. ... Legal professionals are being targeted with allegations of supporting a terrorist organization. The evidence points to these allegations as being a strategy to stop the legitimate exercise of their professional duties, including human rights-related work."[135]

Moreover, some bar associations give the government unconditional support in the witch-hunt against alleged members of the Gülen movement. For instance, the Istanbul Bar Association announced immediately after July 15, 2016 that it would not provide lawyers to people accused of membership in the Gülen movement. Also, some bar-appointed lawyers are allegedly misleading their clients into cooperating with the police and prosecutors and agreeing to plea bargains instead of defending themselves.

On the other hand, the Turkish Constitutional Court, the main function of which is the oversight of the constitutionality of legislative acts and the acceptance of individual human rights violation applications in line with the European Convention on Human Rights (ECHR), has been paralysed by the Erdoğan regime. Erdoğan in the past, when he was not in full control of the court, had tried to suppress it by denouncing the court's rulings and exerting pressure on the court through the media. In this regard Erdoğan once stated that "this may be the court's ruling, but I don't have to accept it. I don't pay any heed to it, and I don't respect it."[136] He eventually gained full control of the court after the July 15, 2016 coup attempt.[137]

Meanwhile, the top court, contrary to the Venice Commission's assessment,[138] declared that it was not authorised to oversee decree-laws in a petition submitted by the main opposition CHP to abrogate them. The Constitutional Court also rejected a petition filed by the CHP to abrogate 13 decree-laws issued under the state of emergency.[139] In addition, overseeing the compliance of legislative actions with the constitution and international conventions is not the sole duty of the court. It is also the antecedent authority to the ECtHR in terms of individual applications on human rights violations. By not exercising its authority on individual applications, in accordance with Erdoğan's wishes, the Constitutional Court has buttressed the formation of a dictatorship.[140] As in the cases of journalists Mehmet Altan and Şahin Alpay, the lower courts, which are under the direct influence of the government, have frequently defied the Constitutional Court's rulings on rights violations even if the high court has agreed to review some cases.[141]

If one leg of the ever-increasing human rights violations in Turkey has become the criminal justice system since the failed coup of July 15, 2016, the other leg is the system of administrative justice. Without administrative investigations, let alone court verdicts, over 160,000 people were dismissed from public service. These dismissals were carried out by decree-laws, adopted under the state of emergency declared in the wake of the abortive putsch. According to contemporary law and the Turkish constitution, "all actions and proceedings of the administration are subjected to judicial review." This review is carried out by the administrative justice system, the high court of which is the Council of State. The Constitutional Court, by rejecting the CHP's abrogation petition, granted the decree-laws the shield of immunity before other courts. It has expanded the gap of judicial oversight vis-à-vis injustices caused by the decree-laws.

The AKP government did not take any chances in terms of preventing oversight of actions and administrative proceedings and enforced additional measures. Some of the judges who were dismissed and/or arrested were administrative judges. With Law no. 6723, titled "The Law on Introducing Changes to the Law on the Council of State and Other Laws," all members of the Council of State, with the exception of the heads of chambers, were dismissed.[142] Out of 100 new members, while the Erdoğan-controlled HSYK appointed 75 of them, Erdoğan himself directly appointed the rest. Those critical dismissals and appointments took place only 10 days after the coup attempt.[143] It goes without saying that the main criterion for the appointments was alignment with the AKP. It is unreasonable to expect a high court, totally redesigned by disregarding the tenure of judges and the principle of natural justice, to oversee the actions of Erdoğan and the AKP government. It is not hard to predict the performance of the high court judges bearing in mind that 113 of their colleagues were arrested only a few days after the coup attempt.

The members of the Supreme Court of Appeals (Court of Cassation), one of the most important judicial mechanisms in Turkey, are supposed to have served with distinction for at least 15 years in courts of first instance. However, this rule has not been respected since the AKP's new regulations aiming to seize the judiciary have been in effect. The introduction of the law that brought changes to the formation and composition of the Supreme Court of Appeals and Council of State in the immediate aftermath of the coup attempt in 2016 has caused grave concern due to its effect on the independence of the judiciary. Frequent modifications to the internal structure of judicial organs, along with the network of courts and the criminal justice system, have caused legal confusion and vagueness.

Two hundred sixty-seven members of the Supreme Court of Appeals and 75 members of the Council of State were elected by HSYK just in four hours under the pretence of formal elections in the wake of the coup attempt. The EU Progress Report harshly criticised the dismissals and new appointments, stating: "There has been backsliding in the past year, in particular with regard to the independence of the judiciary which represents a significant challenge to the overall functioning of the judiciary. The extensive changes to the structures and composition of high courts are of serious concern as they threaten the independence of the judiciary and are not in line with European standards. Judges and prosecutors continued to be removed from their profession and in some cases were arrested, on allegations of conspiring with the Gülen movement. The situation worsened further after the July coup attempt, following which one fifth of the judges and prosecutors were dismissed and saw their assets frozen."[144]

As Turkish authorities announced at various times, the Turkish government has suspended or dismissed more than 160,000 judges, teachers, police officers and other civil servants since July 15, 2016. On December 13, 2017 the Justice Ministry announced that 169,013 people had been the subject of legal proceedings on coup charges since the failed coup. Interior Minister Süleyman Soylu announced on April 18, 2018 that the Turkish government had jailed 77,081 people between July 15, 2016 and April 11, 2018 over alleged links to the Gülen movement.[145] The Supreme Court of Appeals, as the final arbiter, in its current condition is not encouraging for the administration of justice.

2.3.2. Building a one-man rule

With the coup attempt in 2016, Erdoğan got the opportunity to build the government system he had been dreaming of. Through a constitutional referendum on April 16, 2017, an unprecedented and unique system of governance, dubbed the "Turkish-style presidency," was created. Prominent constitutional law scholars harshly criticised the government model set up by the constitutional amendments,[146] a mélange that includes the traces of many systems and a mixed system in which all roads lead to Erdoğan. It is called a presidency, but there is more of a fusion of powers than in a parliamentary system, to say nothing of a strict separation of powers.

President Erdoğan is the sole hegemon of not only the executive body but also the legislative body. As the leader of the ruling party, he is the only decision maker. Moreover, contrary to a traditional presidential system, there is a unicameral parliament in Turkey and in accordance with the Political Parties Law, Erdoğan drafts the list of candidates who will stand for election as members of parliament from his party. In addition, the legislature exercises almost no oversight over the appointment of cabinet ministers and their actions. The parliament has been turned into a 'consultative body' as evidenced during the post-coup period. An amendment to the parliament's rules of procedure drafted collaboratively by the AKP and its nationalist ally the MHP transformed the parliament into an assembly line for the serial production of legislation.[147] The opposition has been deprived of its tools to oppose any acts of the majority. As has already been stated in the "Seizure of the judiciary" section, Erdoğan seized full control of the judiciary either by a fait accompli or by transforming the legal infrastructure.

Moreover, on the road to establishing a dictatorship, Erdoğan closed down hundreds of unions, associations and civil society organizations. Pressure on human rights organisations and activists was intensified, as it was on all surviving civil society organisations. The representatives of both local and international human rights organisations have been forced to side with Erdoğan or face prosecution. For instance, Mazlum-Der, which once pursued an independent line on humanitarian issues including the Kurdish question and was known for its Islamist identity, was completely taken over by the Erdoğan regime. A trustee was appointed by the court and the association was brought under AKP control in an extraordinary plenary session that could not be attended by the then-administration of the association.[148]

Human rights activist Osman Kavala[149] and Taner Kılıç,[150] chairman of the board of Amnesty International Turkey, were arrested. Ten representatives of human rights organisations who held a meeting on the island of Büyükada, off the coast of Istanbul, were detained, six of whom were immediately arrested, followed by the rest.[151] Lawyers and human rights activists who want to visit Turkey are not allowed to enter the country, as experienced by Italian lawyer Barbara Spinelli, who was deprived of her liberty for 17 hours at Sabiha Gökçen Airport in Istanbul and then deported. Those who are already in the country are also deported.[152] These examples illustrate Erdoğan's quest for an 'iron curtain' country where he can freely carry out his unlawful and arbitrary plans as well as his inhuman activities.

2.3.3. Single-minded security bureaucracy, militias, jihadists and mafias

Another step that Erdoğan had already taken was to fill the security apparatus with people who had expressed unquestioned loyalty to him. As can be seen from the consequences, one of the objectives of the controversial 2016 coup attempt had been to open up this opportunity. Director General of Public Security Selami Altınok on December 12, 2017, said that 22,987 police officers in Turkey had been dismissed over alleged links to the Gülen movement.[153] Moreover, 169 generals and 6,810 colonels or below as well as 8,815 police officers were arrested because of their alleged links to the movement.[154]

Turkish Defense Minister Hulusi Akar, the country's former chief of general staff, said in October 2018 that a total of 15,153 members of the Turkish Armed Forces (TSK) had been expelled from the military since the failed coup attempt. The figure mentioned by Akar does not include cadets expelled from military academies or personnel at the Gendarmerie General Command. The Turkish government has dismissed over 40,000 military personnel including gendarmes and military cadets over alleged links to the Gülen movement, the TR724 online news outlet reported on Aug. 4. 2018.[155]

Long before the July 15, 2016 coup attempt, Erdoğan had already carried out massive purges in the police, which he accused of responsibility for the December 17/25, 2013 corruption probes, and he had even shut down police academies.[156] And in the aftermath of the July 15 coup attempt military academies were also closed, depriving the cadets of their right to receive an education at these academies.[157] AKP-linked history professor Erhan Afyoncu was appointed rector of the newly founded National Defence University, which replaced the military academies.[158] These developments, too, are seen as pieces of the plan in Erdoğan's mind.

Put aside the fact that Erdoğan's regime has released tens of thousands of rapists, murderers, pedophiles and sociopaths in order to make room in prisons for the targeted members of the Gülen movement,[159] the regime does not even feel the need to hide its intention to pave the way for the radical Islamist jihadists who it has supported on the ground in the civil war in Syria[160] and for various mafia groups and organised crime bosses such as Sedat Peker.

Erdoğan openly or secretly supports branches of radical Islamist terrorist organisations in Turkey such as Hizbullah[161] and al-Qaeda, while he integrated the IBDA-C radical Islamist terrorist organization into the dirty work of the regime, delegating clandestine missions to these kinds of terror and crime organisations. As if that were not enough, the Erdoğan regime established paramilitary organisations such as SA-DAT[162] and militia groups like Osmanlı Ocakları (Ottoman Hearths)[163] as well as the People's Private Forces (HOH), which now operates under the name of the National Mobilisation Movement (MSH) after changing its initial name.[164]

Erdoğan and his allies have been investing in paramilitary armed groups as well radical religious networks to threaten, harass and intimidate their opponents as part of the unprecedented persecution targeting vulnerable groups in Turkey. The man who runs Erdoğan's private army, SADAT, which has been training radical Islamist rebels who are fighting in Libya and Syria, is Adnan Tanrıverdi, an Islamist and retired lieutenant general who was given the official position of chief military advisor to the president in August 2016, a month after the failed coup.[165] He not only helps Erdoğan recruit more Islamists into NATO's second largest army but also trains radical militants from Turkey as well as rebels from foreign countries to fight in Erdoğan's proxy wars in Libya, Syria and other countries.

The militants in SADAT's paramilitary units are believed to have been drawn from the Islamic State in Iraq and the Levant (ISIL), al-Qaeda and other radical groups. Abdurrahman Dilipak, a top anti-Western

Islamist ideologue and a close ally of Erdoğan, is listed as an advisor to SADAT. SADAT's activities were brought to parliament's agenda with several questions submitted by opposition parties, but the government declined to respond to any of them.[166] SADAT forces were mobilised in the coup attempt of July 15, 2016 and were alleged to be responsible for some of the civilian deaths on the night of the coup.

The second force Erdoğan tapped in his war campaign is the radical Islamist Hizbullah, which is mainly rooted in the country's conservative Kurdish population. Hizbullah, which has openly declared its support for Erdoğan in every election in recent years,[167] was rewarded by Erdoğan when its convicted militants were released from prison in large numbers. Erdoğan has also lent support to Hizbullah for its accumulation of more power so he can secure the allegiance of this extremist group, which draws its strength from the Kurdish population, to deliver what he wants, from obtaining an all-powerful imperial presidency to garnering more votes for his AKP and mobilising the masses in support of his leadership at critical times.

Turkish Hizbullah, notorious for extrajudicial killings in the Southeast Anatolia in the late 1990s, was decimated in the early 2000s through a series of police operations. Its leader Hüseyin Velioğlu was killed in a raid on a safe house in Istanbul, many militants were arrested and convicted and the organisation was thrown into disarray. Erdoğan resuscitated Hizbullah by making an alliance with the group, secured the release of their operatives with favourable rulings in the high courts[168] and put the Kurdish political movement led by the Peoples' Democratic Party (HDP) in a vise while paving the way for the mushrooming of Hizbullah's political party, the Free Cause Party (Huda-Par).

The third group allied with Erdoğan is the fundamentalist militant Great Eastern Islamic Raiders-Front (IBDA/C or IBDA-C), known for its anti-Gülen movement stance. Erdoğan helped secure the release of the convicted leader of IBDA-C, Salih Mirzabeyoğlu (real name Salih İzzet Erdiş), popularly known to his followers as 'commander,' on July 23, 2014. Mirzabeyoglu was personally met at the gate of the Bolu maximum security prison by İhsan Ağcan, the deputy mayor of the city from the governing AKP, accompanied by dozens of people chanting "God is the greatest!" and with fireworks in the background.[169] In his first public comments to reporters immediately after he was released from prison,

Mirzabeyoğlu expressed surprise over his release and thanked Erdoğan for his interest in the case. He was later privately received by Erdoğan in a government office. [170]

This violent and armed group—which has claimed responsibility for a range of terrorist acts in Turkey including what authorities said was a joint plot with al-Qaeda in carrying out the 2003 Istanbul bombings of two synagogues, an HSBC bank and the British Consulate General as well as the 2008 attack on the US Consulate General in Istanbul and the killings of dozens of people in the 1990s—was given a fresh boost by the government-orchestrated release of its leader, who was serving a life sentence. The group is also among those that were mobilised on behalf of Erdoğan on July 15, 2016. Several indictments of al-Qaeda and ISIL groups in Turkey have shown that IBDA-C was involved in sending jihadists to Syria to fight the Bashar al-Assad regime. [171] The group's militants were out in the streets during the coup attempt and were reportedly involved in killings that occurred that night. [172]

Erdoğan has also struck a deal with mafia groups in Turkey in order to intimidate and harass his opponents and critics. Sedat Peker, a convicted felon who served jail time on various charges, receives VIP treatment at government functions and has been seen chatting with Erdoğan. On July 16, 2017, Peker threatened members of the Gülen movement with murder. [173] Peker's threat came a day after Erdoğan targeted people linked to the movement. "We're not just some nomadic tribe, we are a nation. They, however, are a disease, a disease. That's the difference," said Erdoğan, adding, "First we will cut off the traitors' heads." [174] Gang leader Peker had also threatened academics who signed a petition calling for peace in the Southeast Anatolia in early 2016. "We will spill your blood in streams and we will shower in your blood," [175] Peker said in a message titled "So-Called Intellectuals, the Bells Will Toll for You First," posted to his personal website on Jan. 13, 2017.

Erdoğan also helped set up a new group, the Ottoman Hearths (Osmanlı Ocakları), as a paramilitary nationalist youth network. The group was first mobilised during attacks on buildings belonging to pro-Kurdish and secular opposition parties on September 6-8, 2015. The Republican People's Party (CHP) headquarters in Ankara's Sincan district was among the buildings vandalized by angry mobs. CHP Secretary-General Gürsel Tekin said the assailants who vandalized the building presented themselves as members of the Ottoman Hearths.[176] CHP leader Kemal Kılıçdaroğlu was targeted in an intimidating protest during a June 8, 2016 funeral as a wreath bearing his name was torn apart before a man threw a bullet at him. Eren Erdem, a CHP deputy, said the person who lobbed the bullet at Kılıçdaroğlu was affiliated with Ottoman Hearths.[177] He added that the move was a mafia tactic aimed at intimidating the main opposition party.

Erdoğan's propagandists and media have also lent support to mafia-style structures and called for the murder of members of the Gülen movement. For example, Fatih Tezcan, a pro-government public speaker and columnist, said in a video posted on social media that he was sure the Turkish state had embedded a secret agent in the Gülen movement and that now was time for him to "terminate" Turkish Islamic scholar Fethullah Gülen.[178] In June 2017 he said people should gather in front of Silivri Prison, the inmates of which are primarily people jailed over links to the Gülen movement, and set it on fire, similar to the Madımak Hotel in Sivas when an angry mob in 1993 torched the hotel, killing 37 people, mostly members of the Alevi sect.[179]

CHAPTER III

DISTINCTIVE FEATURES OF
THE GÜLEN MOVEMENT AS A SOCIO-RELIGIOUS GROUP

The Gülen movement is known for its social, cultural and educational activities in Turkey and in nearly 170 countries[1] around the world and was widely appreciated in Turkey.[2] Following the December 17/25, 2013 graft probes that exposed the corruption of then-Prime Minister Erdoğan and his cronies,[3] the movement was turned into a scapegoat by the Turkish government. Labelled as members of the Gülen movement, the judges, prosecutors and police officers conducting the graft investigations were fired from public service and imprisoned.[4]

The purge of the Gülen movement has turned into a full-fledged witch-hunt by the Erdoğan regime.[5] Moreover, in the aftermath of the controversial coup attempt on July 15, 2016[6] a campaign has been launched to destroy the group. Under state of emergency decrees, more than 160,000 public servants who had nothing to do with the coup attempt, including military officers, policemen, teachers, diplomats, governors, district governors, doctors and academics, were fired from public service without any justification or due process. As the purge began on the very morning after the coup attempt, it was obvious that state authorities had been illegally profiling citizens for a long time. Private sector companies, including some 200 media companies, became victims of the purge, too. About 1,030 prominent firms and thousands of small-scale businesses were directly confiscated[7] or their ownership was transferred to the state by the appointment of trustees.[8] More than 2,000 educational institutions, including 15 private universities, were shut down.[9]

As a result of a gradually implemented plan, the Gülen movement has officially been declared a 'terrorist organisation' by the Erdoğan regime.[10] Some of the evidence used for incriminating the movement in terrorism includes having a bank account at legally operating private lender Bank Asya; sending children to or working at Gülen movement-affiliated schools or private test preparation schools; holding membership in certain unions; having books at home authored by Fethullah Gülen or books re-leased by Gülen movement-affiliated publishing houses; canceling a subscription to the pro-government private TV platform Digiturk; attending the International Language and Culture Festivals organized for years by the Gülen movement; and downloading the ByLock mobile phone messaging application, all clearly acts that can be considered part of daily life.[11] Within this framework, prosecutions have been launched into tens of thousands of alleged members of the Gülen movement. Moreover, the houses and workplaces of these people were raided under the cover of darkness by counterterrorism police. Although not a single weapon was found during these raids, 169,000 people have been detained on charges of terrorist organisation membership, and around 80,000 of them have been arrested.[12]

Why does a regime believe that a civic movement which conducts education, culture and dialogue activities based on universal principles of peace deserves such persecution and cruelty? Why is Erdoğan trying to destroy the movement and millions of members who have nothing to do with violence or terror? The answers to these questions can be found in the ideological background and affiliations of the Erdoğan regime, which is becoming more Islamofacist by the day, as well as the type of social organisation the Gülen movement constitutes.

Fethullah Gülen[13] was born in the village of Korucuk in Erzurum province, situated in the north-east of Turkey, a region known in the late 1930s when he was born – and in fact still so – for its highly conservative socio-cultural values,[14] from a young age he devoted himself to reflecting the problems and outdated cultural norms from the perspective of modern cultural values.[15] As a preacher and prominent opinion leader he traveled to cities and towns across Turkey to encourage people to invest in education. His ideas inspired many people and encouraged and mobilised benevolent individuals to turn his thoughts into practice.[16] His efforts were quite effective but also attracted negative reactions from conservative and religious circles,[17] because conservative circles traditionally sent their children to religious imam-hatip schools or Qur'an courses where the religious education was more concentrated. However, Gülen, believing that a religious education alone was wrong, encouraged people to send their children to schools where the positive sciences and social sciences were also taught. In his sermons he stressed that building a school is more important and a more urgent need than building a mosque.[18] This position was Gülen's first visible drift from more conservative and radical Islamist circles.

The movement launched by Gülen developed his faith-based philosophy of 'serving humanity' in the early 1970s. It was an authentic movement that developed its own tradition in religious and socio-cultural terms. The cultural codes of the Gülen movement are unique in the sense that they are in conformity with both traditional values and universally accepted, fundamental humanitarian values.[19] In particular the activities of the Journalists and Writers Foundation (JWF) contributed much to the visibility of the movement. The movement distanced itself from traditional Islamist rhetoric by asserting a position of 'no turning back from democracy.'[20] This approach was harshly criticised by political Islamist circles that saw democracy and secularism as a "non-religious" and even a "regime of infidels."[21] This was another important point that distanced the Gülen movement from the political Islamists.

According to their own discourse, tolerance and dialogue are the two most fundamental dynamics of the Gülen movement. These two concepts, re-invigorated by the relatively small-scale activities of the movement in the early 1990s, have been transformed into a quest for establishing a worldwide culture of reconciliation, as all peace builders, humanitarian organisations and international humanitarian laws have been trying to do, with the Gülen movement also aiming at laying the groundwork for peaceful co-existence. Actually, the movement fostered dialogue in response to the centuries-old adversaries of the people. To this end, Gülen initiated inter-religious dialogue activities and met with Patriarch Bartholomew I, the ecumenical head of the Greek Orthodox Church, on April 1, 1996. On September 10, 1997, he met Abraham Foxman, president of the Anti-Defamation League (ADL), and in 1997, he met John O'Connor, cardinal of the Catholic diocese of New York. On November 21, 1997, Georesmar Oviteh, representative of the Holy See in Istanbul, and representatives of the Syriac Christian community visited Gülen. He met with Pope John Paul II at the Vatican on February 9, 1998.[22] These meetings and dialogue activities were and are still the subject of intense criticism by the political Islamists and became another issue separating the Gülen movement from them.

The Gülen movement's conciliatory attitude toward the headscarf controversy and their constructive ideas on secularism[23] during the Feb.

28 post-modern coup period in the late 1990s were among the issues distancing Gülen further from the Islamists after hearing their harsh criticism. When he said, "A Muslim cannot be a terrorist, a terrorist cannot be a Muslim,"[24] in the aftermath of the September 11, 2001 terrorist attacks in the United States, his statements attracted the attention of the world media, in particular the US press. In fact, it was not Gülen's first stance against terrorism and radicalism. Gülen has always resolutely contradicted the 'fatwas' of Yusuf al-Qaradawi, a radical Egyptian Islamist who issued fatwas allowing suicide bombings for terrorist groups including the Islamic State in Iraq and the Levant (ISIL).[25]

The followers of the Gülen movement have proven throughout the years, with their discourse, projects and practices, that they are far from the thoughts and ideologies many see as 'extremist.' Today, the schools run by the Gülen movement are located in a vast geography stretching from Central Asia to Europe and from Africa to the Far East. These schools have been successful with their well-prepared curricula in providing high-quality education and working in harmony with the local socio-political cultures in various countries.

What lies behind the hatred of the autocratic Erdoğan regime for the Gülen movement? Why did Erdoğan and his authoritarian regime launch an intensive campaign to demonise the movement, engage in hate speech targeting it and conduct a witch-hunt and crackdown on its members? To understand this, it is necessary to look at the relations between the ruling AKP/Erdoğan and the Gülen movement in chronological order in addition to the aforementioned distinctive characteristics of Gülen and his movement.

The AKP was founded by Erdoğan and his colleagues on August 14, 2001. Democratic and liberal circles in the society welcomed and supported its program and rhetoric upholding democracy, the rule of law and individual rights and liberties, embracing all segments of society, as well as its stance against military tutelage and bureaucratic oligarchy.[26] The AKP, despite political Islamist background of its founders, had promised to pursue a mainstream policy embracing all and kept its promise in its early years in power. The Gülen movement, which has remained equidistant from all political Islamist parties during its entire history,[27] viewed the AKP as similar to the Motherland Party of Turgut Özal because of its liberal and democratic party program.

As did all liberal, democratic segments of Turkish society, international organisations and supra-national organizations such as the European Union (EU), the Gülen movement supported most of the policies of the AKP government during its first two terms in office because of the AKP's democratization reforms as part of the EU accession process; its steps for the integration of Turkey with more of the democratic world and its constructive approach to major foreign policy issues, notably the Cyprus question and efforts at normalisation with Armenia; its policy of zero problem with neighbours; its upholding of the rule of law; and its enhancement of rights and liberties in place of military and bureaucratic tutelage.[28]

Nevertheless, contrary to general perceptions, the Gülen movement's support for the AKP had never been unconditional. The movement openly expressed criticism and disagreement whenever the AKP was inclined to derail from the basic principles of democracy, the rule of law and individual rights and liberties as well as the ideals of a peaceful foreign policy.[29] In a similar vein, as was the case for the Syrian crisis, the Gülen movement did not share the AKP's position on the Mavi Marmara incident, when Israeli commandos killed nine Turkish citizens on May 31, 2010. The movement insisted on using peaceful means and diplomatic channels to lift the blockade and embargo on Gaza.[30] The Mavi Marmara incident proved to be an historic event that exposed the significant difference between the peaceful approaches of the Gülen movement and the AKP/Erdoğan, who had begun signaling a return to its factory settings, namely its political Islamist origin.

Before the AKP consolidated its power by garnering 49.83 percent of the vote in the June 12, 2011 general election,[31] Erdoğan and his party had managed to empower those who supported them unconditionally in media, business and civil society. Thus, the AKP/Erdoğan no longer needed the support of the genuine liberals, the Gülen movement and various democratic circles of the society and arrived at a crossroads. This period of time coincided with the day Erdoğan embraced once again the political Islamist agenda of his Milli Görüş (National Vision, a political Islamist movement founded by the late Necmettin Erbakan) years.[32]

Following these developments, a crisis over the National Intelligence Organisation (MIT)[33] on February 7, 2012 further strained relations between the Gülen movement and the AKP/Erdoğan. Erdoğan pinned the blame on the movement for this crisis which, he claimed, targeted the 'Settlement Process' for the Kurdish issue. The incident triggered the biggest gap to date between the AKP/Erdoğan and the Gülen movement.

Aziz Babuşcu, the provincial head of the ruling AKP's Istanbul branch, had clearly hinted on April 1, 2013 that the AKP under Erdoğan would abandon its liberal democratic path and return to its political Islamist roots and objectives.[34] The return of Erdoğan and his AKP to their political Islamist roots; their quest for a window of opportunity in the 2011 Arab uprisings for their own expansionist political Islamist agenda; the policy of intervening in the internal affairs of other countries, notably Egypt and Syria; the distancing of Turkey day by day from its EU membership aspirations, the rule of law and democracy; and their increasing involvement in massive corruption and international money laundering to secure financial resources for the illegal activities they had resorted to in order to achieve their political Islamist objectives led to growing criticism and the opposition of the followers of the Gülen movement together with other segments of society to Erdoğan and his government. The reaction of Erdoğan and the AKP to this criticism and opposition was the illegal profiling and dismissal of public servants alleged to have links to the Gülen movement. Erdoğan's words, "I can label you as a terrorist organisation with a prosecutor and three police officers,"[35] about the movement were uttered during these days. It was the point of no return.

Intending to inflict a fatal blow to the Gülen movement, the Erdoğan regime targeted the movement's raison d'être, its institutions in the field of education. The government took a decision on November 14, 2013 to shut down the 'dershanes,' preparatory schools for high school and university entrance examinations.[36] Businesspeople and educators affiliated with the Gülen movement were among the main actors in the education sector, and the movement's dershanes attracted tens of thousands of young people thanks to their high-quality education and record of success.[37] Erdoğan's children Bilal and Sümeyye as well as Berat Albayrak, Erdoğan's son-in-law and the current finance minister, were among the students of these schools.[38] By making the decision to close the dershanes without any assessment of the after-effects, Erdoğan inflicted severe damage on the Gülen movement.

International corruption, money laundering and bribery probes that implicated Erdoğan, his family and some of his cabinet ministers erupted into public view December 17/25, 2013. Prosecutors and police had been conducting the investigations since 2012. Erdoğan and the AKP pinned the blame for the investigations on prosecutors and police officers alleged to be close to the Gülen movement. Eventually, Erdoğan's tense and problematic relations with the Gülen movement were transformed into enmity. Erdoğan claimed the Gülen movement was behind the graft investigations.[39] The anti-corruption broadcasts of media outlets linked to the Gülen movement further heightened that animosity.

Despite concrete evidence, Erdoğan claimed that the corruption investigations were coup attempts against his government. By using the huge media network under his control, he managed to convince the AKP base in particular of his claims. The witch-hunt against the Gülen movement officially started as of December 2013, as was also stated by Erdoğan himself.[40] This witch-hunt evolved into a total persecution of the Gülen movement and its followers in the aftermath of the controversial July 15, 2016 coup attempt.

3.1. New target of the people who glorify death

It would have been painful but preferable for genocides and massacres to remain the shame of the past, to be read about only in history books. However, the popular culture that paved the way for the aforementioned calamities in Turkey has become stronger, providing the potential for new tragedies. President Erdoğan's sharp turn toward radical Islamist authoritarianism and populism in particular has increased this risk and danger. Mobilisation of this potential against a targetted ethnic or religious group is only a matter of time. Thanks to his efforts at polarisation and hate-mongering, Erdoğan has succeeded in bringing his radicalised followers to the verge of carrying out a massacre of adherents of the Gülen movement.

Since the December 17/25, 2013 graft probes, Erdoğan and his close circle have started to reference a "war of independence." War, blood, chaos and death have become the central topics of their speeches rather than peace, stability and life. The new Erdoğan wants people to sacrifice their lives, as opposed to the old Erdoğan, who had frequently referred to spiritual leader of early years of Ottoman State, Sheikh Edebali's culture of tolerance, saying, "Keep humans alive to keep the state alive."[41]

At one of his political rallies in Trabzon province, after inflaming the crowd with the promise of more blood and death, Erdoğan said: "There is dying like a man and there is dying like a woman. Let's die, but let's die like a man." These words sparked reactions among opposition circles.[42] Just as he had been doing for a long time, in a speech on the occasion of the anniversary of the Battle of Gallipoli, he continued to glorify death, saying, "Martyrdom is not a dreadful place for us but a place to be reached," adding, "This country needs martyrs' blood to become the motherland."

Erdoğan had previously used the Arab uprisings, the Palestinian issue and other real or perceived victimisations of Muslims around the world to radicalise and mobilise his followers, but he later started to employ 'local and national' arguments to generate a new radicalism. Media, education and religion are Erdoğan's three key weapons for radicalising people and turning them into militant masses that would easily offer their lives and blood. Like other examples in the Middle East, the Turkish nation has been attempted to be totally radicalised and mobilised under the cover of Islamisation and 'religiousification.'[43]

In such an atmosphere of hatred, former Ankara Mayor Melih Gökçek, striving to align with Erdoğan, pointed to Alevi citizens as targets and emphasised the necessity of the arming of the people.[44] Gökçek also hinted at a kind of 'genocide' for alleged members of the Gülen movement in an interview with the pro-Erdoğan *Türkiye* daily in June 2017. Admitting that the post-coup witch-hunt was aimed at annihilating all followers of the Gülen movement, Gökçek said: "Completely annihilating the Gülen movement in Turkey will take us 10 years. In order to finish off FETO completely, we need to transform an entire generation. Therefore, as the government, the political power and the municipalities, we have tried to fulfill the tasks given to us."[45]

Sedat Peker, a convicted crime boss who is a devoted supporter of Erdoğan, said during a visit to the Çengelköy Martyrs Cemetery in Istanbul on July 15, 2017 that "they should pray for our president, who they call a dictator. May God save him [Erdoğan], if his visit to this world ends even in natural ways, they will see what a dictator is. God willing, we will hang all those who were sympathetic to them [the Gülen movement], walked with them, stayed with them, on the nearest flagpole. We will hang them on the nearest tree."[46]

Peker also said on February 8, 2019 that "they are planning to call on their supporters to take to the streets following the elections [on March 31, 2019]. Their objective is to mix their supporters with members of terrorist groups and cause destruction across the country. Our police and military are strong, but the children of this country will also come to the defence of the streets. That is why those who have the means should acquire licenced firearms. We should absolutely be prepared."[47]

In fact, Peker's stance is parallel to that of Erdoğan. Telling the story of a citizen who was allegedly killed by coup plotters on July 15, 2016, Erdoğan gave the order to get ready. "This incident shows us something. This is an example for us... It means 'get ready'... If you'll notice, we did not put a full stop, we just put a comma,"[48] said Erdoğan, who was actually ordering his radicalised followers to kill and die.

It did not take long for Erdoğan and his close circle, who speak constantly about death and killing, to attract a mass of people who share their "ideals." Scenes that would cause bewilderment and fear in healthy societies have long been seen in Turkey. For instance, in Trabzon on December 22, 2013, just a few days after the December 17/25, 2013 graft probes were revealed to the public, Erdoğan was welcomed by his followers wrapped in burial shrouds with a banner that said, "We came with our shrouds, we are with you until death."[49] Similar scenes were seen in Istanbul,[50] Şanlıurfa[51] and Hatay[52] provinces on December 27, 2013, March 10, 2014 and March 22, 2014, respectively. Moreover, this radicalised group staged the same demonstration in Brussels on January 19, 2014 during a rally to welcome Erdoğan.[53]

Similar demonstrations with shrouds and banners that said, "We took to the road wearing our burial shrouds. We dug our graves and we came," were staged for then-Prime Minister Ahmet Davutoğlu in Konya province on March 19, 2014[54] and for Binali Yıldırım during his candidacy for mayor of Izmir. These scenes, which shocked the society, were repeated in Niğde[55] and in many other cities during protests of the coup attempt. The demonstrations in shrouds were followed by mock lynchings of Fethullah Gülen as a figure of hatred in city centers. In many cities, including Ankara,[56] Istanbul,[57] Izmir[58] and Bursa,[59] effigies of Gülen have been hanged from scaffolds accompanied by theatrical torture.

Such demonstrations of hatred are not the only manifestation of the radicalisation produced by Erdoğan and his ruling party. In many places, schools and workplaces that were close to the Gülen movement were looted. Countless restaurants and stores, which are required to provide service to everybody without discrimination, scornfully announced that they would not serve Gülen movement adherents. This atmosphere subsequently targeted other dissident groups and people, such as Kemal Kılıçdaroğlu, leader of the main opposition Republican People's Party (CHP), who was threatened with death.

On his social media account Bülent Gürpinar, leader of the pro-AKP Fatih Generation Youth and Education Association, threatened participants of the 'March for Justice' led by Kılıçdaroğlu. Gürpinar said they would teach a lesson to dissident groups under the leadership of Kılıçdaroğlu and wrote about his and AKP supporters' desire to become martyrs as had happened during the failed coup. Gürpinar shared a message on his Facebook account saying: "It is said that the justice marchers' entrance to Istanbul will be like July 15. Is that a coincidence? Of course not. Then, too, we will teach them a lesson like we did on July 15. We beg our God for martyrdom, let them [CHP supporters] think about what will happen." In a message the following day, Gürpınar wrote that they were only waiting for Erdoğan's 'Go out!' order to carry out their plans against the marchers.[60]

Previously, the 'March for Justice' had been targeted by a group led by Emrah Kavuz, a pro-AKP alderman of the Karabağlar Municipality in Izmir province. Once again, CHP leader Kılıçdaroğlu was threatened with death. In the video he shared, Kavuz says, 'We are just waiting for the word from our Reis [chief, meaning Erdoğan]. We are running for martyrdom and will kill with just a word from him. We'll do everything necessary," in the company of a group chanting "Allahu Akbar" and making the Rabia salute, a hand gesture widely used by Erdoğan.[61]

The incident with Kavuz is not an exceptional or individual initiative. Similar threats and demands for dying and killing have frequently been made by ministers, pro-AKP columnists and thousands of social media users. For instance, "These coup plotters will die like sewer rats in 1.5 to 2-square-meter cells," then-Economy Minister Nihat Zeybekçi said during a speech in the Civril district of Denizli province on September 1, 2016, adding: "We will punish them in a way to make them beg for death. They'll

never, ever, see a human face or hear a human voice. We know who's behind them, who fed them, who sent and who fashioned them." Later he
said, "We'll continue – without stopping -- to bring them to account until
we wipe them out, notably the traitor hiding in America [implying Fethullah Gülen] and will inflict revenge upon them for the martyrs' blood."[62]

Hüseyin Adalan, a columnist for the pro-Erdoğan *Yeni Söz* and
Milat newspapers, defended the necessity of murdering adherents of the
Gülen movement on his social media account and claimed that "slaughtering them, even their babies" was a religious duty. Adalan tweeted: 'I
promise God, slaughtering someone who pities a Gülenist is necessary.
The noble Turkish state should show its magnificent power. Slaughtering
the Gülenists, all the way down to their babies, is a necessity."[63]

Meanwhile, @_GizliArsivTR, which has almost 35,000 followers
and is one of Erdoğan's well-known Twitter trolls, called for the execution of Gülen movement followers, tweeting: "The best FETO member
is a dead one. Their murder is religiously permissible and is a must. For
the future of our state and our ummah, their executions are necessary."[64]
Another pro-Erdoğan Twitter troll named Ahmet Üstün (@ustunn_
ahmet) also called on the government to assassinate Gülen movement
sympathizers in the country and abroad.[65] In a similar move, journalists
Cem Küçük and Fuat Uğur, both supporters of Erdoğan, made a call for
the assassination of followers of the faith-based Gülen movement living
abroad in a live broadcast on the TGRT news channel.[66]

During a speech at an iftar (Ramadan) dinner at the Police Special
Operations Department in the Gölbaşı district of Ankara, Erdoğan said
about people who were arrested over their alleged involvement in the
coup attempt in 2016 that they would not be satisfied with the verdicts
given them by the courts. "None of these bloody murderers will be able
to escape the painful end awaiting them. Their immorality in the courts
will not be of any use to them as they are rotting in prison. If some of
them serve their sentences and leave prison, our nation will give them
the necessary punishment whenever they see them on the street. They
will spit in their faces, and they will drown in the saliva of the nation.
Our struggle will continue until there is no one left who hasn't paid the
price of his betrayal,"[67] said Erdoğan.

Like his father-in-law Erdoğan, then-Energy and Natural Resources Minister Berat Albayrak said he would strangle supporters of the

Gülen movement wherever he saw them. Claiming that members of the Gülen movement had been defaming Turkey, Albayrak said: "You probably see them in the countries you visit. In God's name, I would barely be able to contain myself if I were you. I would strangle them wherever I see them."[68]

Meanwhile, the pro-Erdoğan news website Haber7 called for an Ottoman-style solution for the execution of people linked to the Gülen movement. "This is an example of execution in the days when decisions were taken without losing time on investigations, interrogations and court proceedings for people who rebelled against the state," Haber7 tweeted, with a headline reading, "The ideal execution method for FETO was used by the Ottomans," along with an Ottoman miniature depicting the execution of people hung by hooks in their stomachs.[69]

Moreover, pro-Erdoğan media outlets have been doing everything possible to lay the psychological groundwork for a possible massacre that could be realized following a simple signal from Erdoğan, such as allegations aimed at members of the Gülen movement they have frequently repeated, for example, claiming that imprisoned Gülen followers will stage a revolt and break out of prison.[70]

After assuming full control of law enforcement and the judiciary (which will be discussed in detail in section 2.3.) under the pretext of the 2016 coup attempt,[71] Erdoğan started making concrete preparations to proceed to a different stage in his witch-hunt against sympathisers of the Gülen movement. Since the coup attempt, which he called "a gift from God," Erdoğan has constantly kept the issue of reinstating capital punishment on the agenda. Erdoğan and his partisans' willingness to bring back the death penalty, which has not been practiced in Turkey since 1984 and was officially abolished in 2004, demonstrates the regime's abhorrent view of the value of human life.

After the April 2017 referendum, Erdoğan said reinstating the death penalty would be his first act.[72] In a speech on the evening of the referendum, in order to reiterate to his partisans his feelings about bringing back capital punishment, Erdoğan said, 'Firstly, I will discuss the death penalty issue with Prime Minister Yıldırım and [MHP leader] Devlet Bahçeli.' Saying, "We can hold another referendum for the reinstatement of capital punishment,"[73] several times, Erdoğan excited his supporters, who cheered every time Erdoğan repeated the words. The idea of the death penalty for soldiers under arrest, Fethullah Gülen and his followers has become widely accepted in the society as the best method of punishment. By virtue of mobilised AKP organisations, crowds chant slogans such as "We want the death penalty" at every public rally.

However, İbrahim Kaboğlu, a professor of constitutional law, has said that even in the event of the reinstatement of capital punishment, it would be impossible to give death sentences to the alleged coup plotters. "It would be necessary to pass major constitutional amendments to be able to carry out the death penalty," he said, because Article 15 of the Turkish constitution does not permit retroactive punishment even in the case of a state of emergency. Another limiting factor is the European Convention on Human Rights (ECHR). Reinstatement of the death penalty would mean a violation of ECHR Additional Protocols 6 and 12.[74]

The ignorance of Erdoğan and his government of these basic facts is impossible, but by keeping capital punishment on the agenda, they have been preserving and inciting the social psychology against members of the Gülen movement. The results of public opinion polls are instrumental in showing the value of human life in Turkish society. According to a poll conducted by the pro-Erdoğan ORC pollster within the first 10 days after the coup attempt, 91 percent of respondents supported the death penalty for crimes of terrorism and treason.[75] Another poll carried out by the independent StreetBees survey platform in the same timeframe showed that 92 percent of AKP supporters and 58 percent of society in general supported capital punishment.[76]

On the other hand, the Erdoğan regime has been fabricating an epic victimhood myth through the July 15 coup attempt and has been inciting the society against adherents of the Gülen movement through the media and the use of public resources that are under the full control of Erdoğan. Erdoğan has been contributing to the same goals in person by reading inflammatory poems and giving long speeches to the crowds.[77] In one of his addresses Erdoğan said that July 15 martyr Omer Halisdemir's widow, while mourning her husband, said, "Will God also give us martyrdom?" Erdoğan added: "This is the way it is... I hope God gives us the same kind of martyrdom. We are ready to die at any moment for the sake of God's way, for the sake of our religion and nation. When we were embarking on this road, we said, 'We've put on our shrouds and are going out onto the road.'"

In a speech about the systematic mass agitation in the media, especially the visual media, concerning the July 15 failed coup and its martyrs, Erdoğan emphasised that this campaign strengthens the prospects
of the future. As if making a confession, Erdoğan said: "We remember
our martyrs. Our faith in the future is increasing and will increase as
we continue to remember them. Believing in martyrdom and living it…
It cannot be described but only experienced. That is very important. It
resides in our nation's history and will continue to reside there from here
on out."

The impact of such rhetoric on the crowds is displayed through
its actual consequences. For instance, Alaattin Küçük, whose son Oğu-
zhan Küçük, 22, was martyred by the outlawed PKK during his military
service, said when he learned of his son's death: "I'm not grieving over
this. If it wasn't inappropriate, I would laugh and dance. If I had a gun, I
would fire it in the air three times [to show my happiness]."[78]

Columnist for the T24 news website and veteran journalist Osman
Ulagay is among the intellectuals who draw attention to Erdoğan and
the AKP's obsession with death during election campaigns. In one of
his articles, after citing many examples, Ulagay said, "Imaginary gallows
are prepared; burial shrouds are worn; hopes for martyrdom are uttered;
salutes are given to the angel of death."

So indeed, for the last few years, Erdoğan has not talked about anything more than death, killing, jihad and martyrdom. For instance, upon
learning of the death sentence of ex-President of Egypt Mohamed Morsi,
Erdoğan said: "We donned our burial shrouds before embarking on this
road… If Morsi is put to death, although I don't believe he will be, he
will achieve the rank of martyr. If I suffer a similar fate, I hope my God
will grant this rank of martyr to me as well."[79] Only a day later, former
Prime Minister Davutoglu said, "You ignoramuses, as God is my witness, if we were to be granted martyrdom for the nation, for the country,
for God, we would not hesitate for a moment, we would salute the angel
of death."[80]

Ulagay analysed the goal of this inflammatory discourse: "Is it possible that this discourse, developed around the threat of death, to have a
goal other than depicting the people in the strongest and the most impe-
rious terms as victims and oppressed? The voters are called to defend the
victims and the oppressed against secret powers."[81] It can easily be said

that this rhetoric, devaluing human life, contributes to the conditions required for a possible genocide.

3.2. Systematic dehumanisation of the Gülen movement

"They are grave robbers! They are body snatchers. They are characterized by lies, deceit, subterfuge, dissension, conspiracy and slander. It is a treacherous terrorist organization. They have no morality! They have no decency! They have no love for the homeland, nation or flag! What an impostor he [Fethullah Gülen] is! They are slanderous! They are so lowly, so treacherous... They are viruses! They are cancers! They are malignant tumors! They are bloodsucking leeches! In terms of hypocrisy, they are well ahead of the Shia. They are a treacherous terrorist organization! As you already know, they are scoundrels and traitors! ..."[82]

Experts[83] underscore the fact that the more powerful and populous group needs to portray the potential victims as 'less than human,' 'subhuman' or 'inhuman' in the process leading up to genocide. The Erdoğan regime would have little trouble ensuring this situation since the phrases in the previous paragraph are just a few examples of at least 240 phrases of hate speech[84] by which Erdoğan has aimed at dehumanising followers of the Gülen movement. The defamation and hate speech, the impetus of which is Erdoğan himself, started right after the 2013 corruption and bribery scandals in which Erdoğan and his inner circle were caught red-handed. Since then, every person who is in one way or another related to the Gülen movement has become a target of hate speeches and hate crimes for a substantial part of the Turkish public and the state apparatus, which has successfully been transformed into a fascist regime by Erdoğan.

Starting in December 2013, Erdoğan increased the dose of defamation and hate speeches. Detailed research conducted by Stocholm Center for Freedom (SCF) revealed that Erdoğan himself used the 240 hateful phrases mentioned above to target the Gülen movement. In the research, gross insults, hate speech and efforts at dehumanisation and criminalisation by government ministers, AKP officials and the media, which is effectively controlled by the AKP, were not taken into account. It must be borne in mind that insults and expressions of hatred have been reiterated by Erdoğan on an almost daily basis. In addition, for a better grasp of the

sheer volume of hateful and defamatory speech against the Gülen movement, it must be remembered that the media, controlled by Erdoğan,
not only multiplies but also expands on the hate speech frequently and
repeatedly.

It is almost impossible to prepare an exhaustive list of examples of
how extensively and frequently Erdoğan's hate speech has been covered
by the Erdoğan-controlled media, along with numerous other allegations he has made. However, as a telling example, Google provides over
71 million results if the acronym "FETO" (Fethullahist Terror Organization) is searched (retrieved on February 9, 2019). Erdoğan, without
any legal basis, commonly uses this hateful expression to describe and
defame the movement.[85]

Another aspect of the issue is the hate crimes such as physical attack, boycott, character assassination, social lynching and torture triggered by the impunity of the people engaging in hate speech against
members of the Gülen movement. While those committing hate crimes
are not prosecuted, the victims who file criminal complaints with judicial authorities are regarded as criminals.[86] At this point, it is necessary
to highlight a serious contradiction.

Currently in Turkey, the most vigorously prosecuted crime is 'insulting President Erdoğan.' There are thousands of people, from prominent journalists Hasan Cemal and Nazlı Ilıcak to young pianist Dengin
Ceylan, from the tea boy at the *Cumhuriyet* daily to an ordinary high
school student, standing trial for allegedly insulting Erdoğan. More than
20,000 investigations were launched into Turkish citizens in 2017 on
accusations of insulting Erdoğan. In that year alone, in excess of 6,000
criminal cases were filed against people for allegedly insulting the president of Turkey.[87]

According to data released by the Ministry of Justice on June 29,
2017, chief public prosecutors, in 2,776 cases, had initiated criminal proceedings against 3,658 people for committing 4,098 crimes of [insulting
the president] in total as of that date.[88] Out of the 3,658 defendants, the
court convicted 1,080 individuals, 102 of them between the ages of 12
and 15, and 138 of them between 15 and 18.[89] The figures continued to
increase in the second half of 2017. Murat Aydın, the vice president of
YARSAV (the only internationally accredited Turkish law society), was
frustrated in his attempt to exercise his legal right to apply to the Con-

stitutional Court against the law on insulting the president.[90] The few acquittals in the many cases were not allowed to be covered by the media in order to continue the suppression of the public.[91]

Among the insults and demeaning expressions used on an almost daily basis by Erdoğan since 2013 to demonise members of the Gülen movement are "scumbags," "traitors," "rascals," "hashashi" (literally meaning drug addict, Hashashi is used in reference to the Order of Assasins in twelfth century), "blood-sucking vampires," "grave robbers," "malignant tumors," "impostors," "immoral," "agents," "dastardly," "subjects for sterilisation," "spies," "spy ring," "mob," "self-interested band," "rotten," "coup-plotter terrorists," "abusers of the religion," "instigators for foreign powers," "enemies," "more dishonest than an enemy," "indecent," "bewitched," "blood-shedding villains," "F-Type" (a kind of labeling to mean Fethullahists), "conspirators," "Fethullahist Terror Organization [FETO]," "instigation movement," "instigators," "betrayers," "band of betrayers," "thieves," "slanderers," "treacherous gang," "betrayer network," "system of betrayal," " hypocrites," "un-Islamic heretical faction," "bloodsucking leeches," "bloodsuckers," "blood lobby," "cancer cells," "chaos gang," "sinister base," "sinister core," "sinister circle," "subcontractor of dirty businesses," "pawns of a dirty plot," "filthy axis," "vicious structure," "characterless robots," "rotten," "conspirators," "global network of traitors," "collaborator of MOSSAD," "unchaste," "ungrateful," "parallel betrayal organization [PİÇ (this abbreviation in Turkish also means 'bastard')]," "blackmailers," "blackmailing gang," "heretics," "phony/phonies," "axis of evil," "sneaky," "sneaky viruses," "leeches," "filthy water mixed in milk," "pawns," "terrorist organisation," "terrorists," "vampires," "Mankurts" (people who have lost their connection to the values of the society they live in), etc... The Erdoğan-controlled media's coverage and repetition of these expressions many times over, as part of systematic black propaganda, will automatically lead to the degrading of any targeted group to a subhuman category in the eyes of the public.

On the other hand, one can easily notice a more gradual approach to insult and hate speech against members of the Gülen movement since Erdoğan himself and his inner circle were caught red-handed in the December 17/25, 2013 bribery and corruption scandal. "Extermination"[92] of the alleged members of the Gülen movement became Erdoğan's sole agenda item in 2014 when he assumed the presidency. Labelling the

Gülen movement as a 'parallel structure/state' in the aftermath of the corruption scandal was the mainstream discourse of Erdoğan, who accused the movement of betrayal by exposing the entrenched corruption.[93] This label was extensively circulated until Erdoğan finally succeeded in having the National Security Council (MGK), over which he presides, include on January 2, 2015 the Gülen movement in the National Security Policy Paper, commonly known as the 'Red Book,' as a 'Parallel State Structure.'[94]

Towards the end of 2015, on November 31, Erdoğan, during an interview with the aHaber TV channel, introduced a new expression to defame the Gülen movement: "illegal structure with a legal appearance."[95] However, Erdoğan, not satisfied with this vague expression, was determined to declare the Gülen movement a 'terrorist organization,' despite the fact that the movement not only has no record of involvement in any kind of violence but has also maintained a resolute stance against all kinds of violence and terrorism. It was finally time to label the Gülen movement, one of the most peaceful and pacifist civic groups, as FETO – the Fethullahist Terror Organization.[96] Every single label introduced by Erdoğan was echoed and reproduced in the national media, over 95 percent of which is directly controlled by Erdoğan.[97]

During his address at a political rally in Kırşehir province on May 27, 2016, Erdoğan said: "We took [at the National Security Council] a new decision yesterday. We called it an illegal terrorist organisation under the guise of legality. We recommend calling it the 'Fethullahist Terror Organisation.' We forwarded this recommendation to the government and are awaiting the cabinet's decision. We will succeed in designating them as a terrorist organisation."[98] He did exactly as he promised. Eventually, at the direction of Erdoğan, the Gülen movement was labelled "FETO" by the cabinet.[99] The other countless derogatory expressions paled in the face of this single phrase, which appears 71 million times in Google search as of February 2019.[100]

While putting newspapers featuring pictures of Erdoğan on the ground is regarded as a crime and high school students are being arrested for criticising Erdoğan on Facebook, Erdoğan's insults and hate speech targeting his opponents are considered within the framework of freedom of expression by the 'guided' Turkish judiciary. A blatant example of this double standard, which totally disregards the equality of people before the law, took place on February 22, 2017. Prof. Dr. Baskın

Oran, one of the academics who signed a 'peace declaration' protesting military operations in Turkey's Southeast,[101] was called by Erdoğan, among other names, "rascal, traitor, immoral, utter darkness, ignorant, repugnant, lumpen, pawn of the terrorist organisation, remnant of a [foreign] protectorate and tainted soul." Oran filed a defamation lawsuit against Erdoğan. The court declared, in its justification of its verdict, that "Erdoğan's statements ought to be considered criticism and the exercise of his right to put forward counter arguments." The court also declared that Erdoğan's offensive terms "are ordinary and should be regarded as natural in the normal course of life." By this decision the Turkish judiciary officially stated that Erdoğan can insult and use hate speech as much as he likes against anyone he deems a target.

Under the current circumstances, the absence of any arrest or detention warrant for Oran, who challenged Erdoğan in the courts, can be considered good fortune or a blessing since every other person who filed a defamation suit against Erdoğan due to his hate speech targeting the Gülen movement has been arrested. As a result, victims' rights and the ability to demand justice in the face of Erdoğan's insults and hate speech have effectively been terminated.[102]

At this point, it can be argued that Erdoğan's systematic and extensive defamation and hate speech against the Gülen movement not only constitute an important level in the witch-hunt (Erdoğan publicly declared: 'If it is a witch-hunt, then it is a witch-hunt. We will carry it out.'),[103] but also represent a critical milestone and psychological background for a possible genocide. Due to the non-stop propaganda through the media, Erdoğan exerts tremendous influence over AKP voters in particular and the public in general. Thus, Erdoğan's defamation and hate speech such as "leeches," "agents," "traitors," "double-dealers," "scumbags" and "hashashi" against members of the Gülen movement gain at least the tacit consent of the general public, but more importantly of the bureaucracy. The direness of the situation extends to putting up signs corresponding to those of Hitler's Germany on shop windows such as "FETO members are not welcome" and "Parallel [statists] cannot shop here"[104] and hanging banners in the streets reading "FETO members cannot enter."[105]

Relatively well educated and highly qualified Gülen movement sympathisers who were dismissed from the civil service and became unemployed after the confiscation or shuttering of their employers are even prevented from finding jobs in the private sector or establishing their own businesses since they were profiled by the Social Security Institution with "Code 36."[106] As a result, hundreds of thousands of people, while systematically segregated from the public, are becoming the victims of an economic genocide as well.[107]

Those individuals or segments of society who seek to take a reasonable approach towards members of the Gülen movement are also the subject of Erdoğan's threats. For instance, Erdoğan, in his address to neighbourhood heads (*mukhtars*) on October 26, 2016, said, "Whoever says that 'FETO' members are victimized is a traitor."[108] On the other hand, resorting to defamatory rhetoric and hate speech against the Gülen movement and its sympathisers has become a 'useful shield' covering any kind of wrongdoing.[109]

Even if such degradation and dehumanisation of a significant social group by black propaganda and systematic and extensive defamation and hate speech might not lead to genocide, this malignant campaign has already led to gross human rights violations such as widespread torture and ill treatment. SCF's report on torture,[110] published in June 2017, has called attention to this issue by asserting the following: "… torturers are motivated primarily by their perception of victims as 'traitors' and desire to punish them for being so. Some public officers who torture may resort to torture with the intention of proving their patriotism to their colleagues or with expectations of reward or promotion from their seniors. … In settings with widespread and systematic torture of those who are labeled 'traitors,' the public and security officers who disapprove of torture are suppressed, isolated and made pariahs."

According to the report, the labelling of the Gülen movement by Erdoğan's regime using religious justification provides the 'jihadist' motivation to the security officials carrying out the torture, who already have strong nationalist and patriotic inclinations. Thus, the people interrogated are not only seen as 'traitors' but also 'heretics' and 'enemies of the religion.' Subjected to intense propaganda and hate speech, security officials do not consider maltreatment and torture crimes since they do not see the people being tortured as human beings.[111]

When examining the 'jihadist' motivation of the torturers, one needs to call attention to statements of radical Islamist theologian Hayrettin Karaman, who issues controversial *fatwas* for Erdoğan. In one of his articles published in the aftermath of the July 15, 2016 coup attempt Karaman stated that "the minor crimes of soldiers, committed while fighting the enemy, are not to be punished."[112] With this remark, he gave moral/religious consent to the toleration of maltreatment and torture and the impunity of security officials engaged in such behavior against members of the Gülen movement who were detained and arrested in the post-July 15 period without any solid criminal charges or evidence. With reference to the movement, Erdoğan has stated many times directly or indirectly that "they are not Muslims, they are kafirs [infidels]." This might have also served as a motivation for security officials to torture members of the Gülen movement.[113]

The movement, with its hundreds of thousands of members and sympathisers, has effectively been alienated, antagonised and demonised by the hate speech that has gradually and systematically been used and expanded by the regime-controlled media. In addition, some segments of society that have the capacity to somehow react to injustice, unlawfulness and the violation of rights of people who have been marginalised and segregated have been effectively suppressed by threats and systematic intimidation.[114] In this respect Erdoğan declared, "Whoever says that 'FETO' members are victimised is a traitor."[115] As a result, the groundwork for a possible genocide against members of the Gülen movement is being completed.

Chapter IV

Tracing Genocidal Markers
in the Gülen Movement Crackdown

Article 2 of the UN Convention on the Prevention and Punishment of the Crime of Genocide[1] catalogs the acts that target and harm physically or mentally the group or groups that would be the victims of genocide. According to the convention, acts other than inflicting bodily or mental damage, such as aiming at national, religious, cultural or sociological values, are not considered within the framework of the crime of genocide. The first act mentioned in Article 2 is "killing members of the group." The act of killing is the most blatant and explicit indicator of genocide.

The second act of genocide described in Article 2 is "causing serious bodily or mental harm to members of the group." According to this clause, perpetrator(s) of genocide must cause serious physical or mental/ spiritual harm to members of the target group. Practices such as torture, physical or mental abuse, sexual violence, tyrannical or inhuman treatment and deportation are the archetypical acts mentioned in the article.

The third act of genocide in the article is "deliberately inflicting on the group conditions of life calculated to bring about its physical destruction in whole or in part." In this category of acts, even though the lives and physical integrity of the victims are not directly targeted, they are intended to be terminated through indirect means. Not only depriving the victims of nutrition, clothing, hygiene, housing, sanitation, etc., which are essential for survival, but also systematic exile, physical burden and over-exploitation at work, all of which seriously aggravate living conditions or make them impossible, are among the acts within the framework of this article.

The fourth act of genocide cataloged in Article 2 is "imposing measures intended to prevent births within the group." This method includes systematic acts such as, among others, enforcing contraceptive measures on the individuals, castration and the segregation of men and women.

The fifth act of genocide listed in the article is "forcibly transferring children of one group to another group." In this category of genocide acts, members of the target group who are under 18 years of age are forcibly separated from their families and eventually from the cultural values espoused by the group. As a result of this transfer, the children are forced to grow up in an environment controlled by other group in order to give them a new identity. All kinds of moral coercion such as psychological torment, pressure and fear of violence are considered among the acts implied in this article. Forcibly transferring the children of one group to another has a cultural aspect as well. Even though cultural groups are not included in the groups protected against the crime of genocide, this clause of Article 2 is intended to preserve the cultural identities of the groups in question.

The acts described in the body of genocide regulations and literature are those that are common in genocides that took place in the past. Logically, this does not and should not mean that potential perpetrators will never use other means or methods to terminate their targets. Along with this admonition, one should certainly underline the following point: According to its generally accepted legal definition, genocide does not have to be inclusive of all atrocities, pogroms and unlawful prosecutions listed in the genocide legislation or literature. On the contrary, even one of the acts perpetrated is considered sufficient for this act to be defined as a crime of genocide.

This chapter will focus on the acts and conduct of the Erdoğan regime, aimed at, as overtly and repeatedly stated, "exterminating"[2] and "annihilating"[3] the Gülen movement and to what extent those acts meet the criteria of the crime of genocide as well as the applicability of the convention to those acts.

4.1. The massive persecution against the Gülen movement

In the 10 stages of genocide as categorised by Gregory H. Stanton, the president of Genocide Watch, the "killing" or "extermination" stage occupies ninth place. All stages before this stage, namely classification, symbolisation, discrimination, dehumanisation, organisation, polarisation, preparation and persecution, are only preparatory to the "stage of extermination." However, this process is not linear. The fact that all the preliminary stages have been completed to a large extent reinforces the risk of the extermination stage of the genocide process and rings the alarm for the urgency of counteracting measures.

Regarding this point, which is to be elaborated on in the relevant section, it can be said here that the Erdoğan regime's systematic and deliberate campaign of extermination of the Gülen movement meets the requirements for eight out of the 10 stages set forth by Stanton. Denial, the 10th stage, is only subsequent to the extermination stage. While on the one hand, acts that fit into other stages of the mass persecution against the Gülen movement, which has hundreds of thousands of adherents, are ongoing, on the other hand, commencement of the ninth stage on a massive scale is only a matter of time. Actually, that stage has already started on an individual basis. The timing of this massive action, whose entire practical and psychological infrastructure has already been prepared, remains at the discretion of the Erdoğan regime, a regime that has the power to carry it out and has repeatedly declared its unequivocal intention and displayed its unwavering will to do so.

However, the fact that the genocide process for the Gülen movement has come to the verge of the ninth stage, that is, extermination, does not necessarily mean that the acts and actions in line with the previous stages will come to an end. As a matter of fact, it can well be said that even if the ninth stage were to be initiated, the acts and actions of the other stages would continue to the extent they are needed by the genocide perpetrators. For example, while the first stage of the genocide process, that is, classification, is still ongoing on the one hand, the extermination stage can very well start on the other. Therefore, the preliminary stages are absolutely prerequisite as a premise for the extermination phase. However, all these preliminary stages can still continue after the extermination process has begun.[4]

Just as in the Genocide Convention and the Rome Statute, in Article 76 of the Turkish Penal Code (TPC) acts that would constitute the crime of genocide are exhaustively recounted. Deliberate killing is at the top of the list. Deliberate killing means in this context the killing of group members. The killing of even a single member of a target group due to his/her group affiliation with a view to destroying a national, ethnic, racial or religious group entirely or partly through a plan is sufficient for the commission of the crime of genocide.[5] There is no need for the perpetrators who committed the crime of genocide to act in order to destroy the entire group. The killing of only a part of the group, say, its elite, is a crime of genocide. Even if the perpetrator has killed only one person, if it is known that it is part of a larger plan of destruction of the target group, then genocide has been committed.

According to Stanton, the crime of genocide contains two main components: intention and action. The component of intention can be proved directly by statements or instructions.[6] That said, the presence of the component of intention can be inferred from the systematic nature of the coordinated actions. In the event of a possible partial or general extermination of the members of the Gülen movement, there will be no doubt of the intention since both Erdoğan himself and his ministers have made scores of unequivocal statements to this end. The content of the secret orders that he gave or is likely to give in this matter can only be understood after they are transformed into action or after it is too late.

With his hate speech, Erdoğan seems to embody Arthur Koestler's famous aphorism, "Wars are not fought for territory, but for words. Man's deadliest weapon is language," by copying what Hitler and his henchmen gradually did to the Jews.[7] Some of Erdoğan's statements that can be construed as the intention of or incitement to genocide[8] are as follows:

Speaking before an AKP parliamentary group meeting on January 14, 2014, Erdoğan said: "The kind of *rottenness* that prevails is yet to be revealed. A *virus* infiltrated the body and *insidiously* spread. However, this body is not so weak as to submit itself to the mercy of those *insidious viruses*. We've seen this in history, too. We have seen how a structure called the *Assassins* tried to take over the state. Our state has proven to be impassable against those *infiltrations*. It will remain so."[9]

On September 22, 2014 Erdoğan said in a speech delivered at the Council on Foreign Relations (CFR) in the US: "We have started to take very determined measures against the *parallel structure*, which is a *threat* to national security. We see that this *dangerous organisation* is used by our opponents both in Turkey and abroad, in the US first and foremost, as a convenient *tool*. We observe that some media organisations and think tanks in the United States are under the influence of the *parallel structure*. This *organisation* would not hesitate to *backstab* even those who once used it. A *very dangerous organisation* .... *The ringleader* is the one who disrupted the unity and solidarity of our country."[10]

Speaking at an AKP consultation meeting in Afyonkarahisar on May 11, 2014, Erdoğan said: "They keep talking about the transformation of the fight against the *parallel structure* into a witch-hunt. Let it be known that if changing the jobs of those who *betrayed* this country is a *witch-hunt, we will conduct this witch-hunt*. You will inform us about who is doing this and where. I am calling on all my citizens to inform us, and we will take action. *We will sterilise this filthy water that leaked into the milk either through boiling it or dividing it into molecules.*"[11]

From Erdoğan's speech at a Religious Council meeting in Ankara on August 3, 2016: "I declare from this hall: Anyone heeding the delusions of the *charlatan in Pennsylvania* and *terrorist chieftain* from now on is responsible for what is going to happen to them."[12]

From Erdoğan's speech at an inauguration ceremony on the 15th anniversary of the founding of the AKP on August 14, 2016 in Istanbul: "These *vile people* by killing our 240 citizens and wounding many more made this nation pay the price. It is a binding duty for us *to root out FETO*."[13] ("FETO" is pejorative acronym to describe the Gülen movement.)

From Erdoğan's speech at a dinner given for martyrs' relatives on August 30, 2016: "Those who are still part of this *treacherous gang* are *traitors*. Those who put their minds under the order of a *charlatan* living in the US and *sell their soul for one dollar* have nothing to do with our history and culture or with us. The issue is no longer about gullibility."[14]

From Erdoğan's speech at an opening ceremony held in Rize on November 15, 2016: "We said we will break into *their lairs*. We said they would run away and we would chase them. *Traitor* members of FETO who escaped abroad will not be able to remain Turkish citizens. They should be the citizens of the countries to which they fled. *FETO* is a *terrorist organisation* just like the PKK, ISIL and the DHKP-C. Anyone in this organisation is a *terrorist*."[15]

From Erdoğan's speech at the inauguration ceremony of the high-speed train station on November 29, 2016 in Ankara: "I call on those in *FETO*. Keep in mind that you will crush the wall of this nation if you remain members of *FETO*. This nation will make you pay the price."[16]

Erdoğan in an interview with Israeli Channel 2 on November 22, 2016: "This has spread through the body just like a *cancer cell*. There is *metastasis* in progress now, and we need to *clean* this *metastasising cell*."[17]

"Genocide and its prevention both result from human choice and bystander indifference," said Richter, Stein, Bernea and Sherman in their co-written article, arguing that "Since the Armenian genocide, and the Holocaust, perpetrators have used dehumanizing metaphors to prepare their followers to overcome normative inhibitions that stand in the way of their becoming killers, rapists, and plunderers of members of potential victim populations. Today, one lesson from the Holocaust is that there are existential dangers associated with ignoring state sanctioned dehumanizing hate language."[18]

These authors underline that genocide can be prevented by stemming hate speech, which motivates the inciters and desensitises the masses. Approaching the issue from the perspectives of public health and preventive medicine, these writers qualify genocide as the leading reason of deaths by violence, saying that "if genocide—the ranking cause of violent death in the 20th century, 280 million—is predictable, it should be preventable." They also wrote: "Today, it is an oxymoron to refer to 'preventing' genocide once the killing, raping, expulsions and plundering begins. But can most genocides be prevented by preventing state sanctioned dehumanizing hate language and incitement? If the answer is yes, the stakes are enormous for genocide prevention everywhere in the world."[19]

Pointing out that the risk of genocide increases when hate speech coupled with incitement comes from the top down in the compelling, directive and peremptory environment of authoritarian regimes, they offer the following analysis: "The past century has taught us that when leaders of movements or governments in power use explicit pseudo medical and epidemiological metaphors, such as microbes, filth, cancer, typhoid, and rats, to dehumanize victim groups, it is prudent to regard such language as an urgent warning sign of imminent genocide, and the burden of proof is on those who deny their ominous portent. This burden of proof becomes heavier when perpetrators propagate notions of in-group exclusivity based upon myths of hygiene or purity, and when their incitement is accompanied by direction, instruction, supplying, informing, and supporting those who become the agents of genocidal actions."[20]

Erdoğan in his campaign against the Gülen movement is precisely at the aforementioned stage. Gülen movement members or those affiliated with the movement are not yet being killed in gas chambers or exterminated in crematoriums as in Hitler's 'death industry.' However, all conditions are ready for a similar disaster. After all, tens of people have already died in prisons[21] due to widespread and systematic torture,[22] inhumane treatment and poor medical care for those taken ill[23] because of pregnancy, infancy[24] or old age,[25] or the deliberately downgraded living conditions of prisons.[26]

A report titled "Suspicious Deaths and Suicides in Turkey" published in March 2017 pointed out the many incidents of ill treatment and torture during and after the mass arrests and detentions across Turkey following the July 15, 2016 coup attempt. The report stated: "In statements and criminal complaints made by defendants and their family members, widespread torture practices have been uncovered in detention centers and prisons. These practices range from verbal abuse and threats to physical violence that includes beatings, rape, exposure to icy water, strappado, sleep deprivation, denial of food and water, limiting access to fresh air, restricting exercise and forced alcohol and drug consumption. There have been serious allegations that many suspects died as a result of physical and psychological torture but described by authorities as suicides in what appears to be a cover-up. In some cases, prosecutors launched inquiries into suspicious deaths. Another question that needs to be addressed is why some people allegedly chose to commit suicide out of fear of likely detention before their arrest or after their release from detention."[27]

During the months following the coup attempt, 169,000 people were the subjects of investigations and then were detained on allegations of ties to the Gülen movement. At least 77,081 of them were arrested and put behind bars (excluding thousands of people who were released after their initial arrest) over their alleged links to the movement between July 15, 2016 and April 11, 2018, according to a statement made by Turkish Interior Minister Süleyman Soylu on April 18, 2018.[28] Findings that the suspects were exposed to pressure, ill treatment and torture during police operations, under detention and after arrest have been reflected in international reports.[29] In the days immediately following July 15, 2016 in particular, Turkey's state-run Anadolu News Agency (AA) and official state television station TRT published and broadcast images of detainees. The difference between the pictures pre-detention and during their transfer to courthouses clearly exposed the severe torture carried out in detention.[30]

According to an updated list compiled by SCF, as of January 25, 2019, a total of 126 people died under suspicious circumstances in prisons, while in detention and in the course of detention procedures, or allegedly committed suicide after being suspended from their jobs or out of fear of being detained in the wake of July 15, 2016.[31] At least 58 of the suspicious deaths occurred in prisons.[32] Since a proper flow of information is impossible due to censorship, publication bans and repressive government policies, it is not known whether there are more executions or similar suicide incidents.

Meanwhile, certain members of the Gülen movement who were killed under the influence of the climate created by smear campaigns and hate speech constitute another category. It is believed some of them were murdered due to feelings of hatred towards Gülen movement affiliates,[33] and some murders were committed with the expectation of acquittal by the judiciary, which is extremely tolerant of crimes committed against alleged members of the movement, while other murders that were committed for different reasons were portrayed in this context to enable the perpetrator to benefit from minimal punishment.[34]

As mentioned in section 3.1., during a speech made on July 16, 2017 in Istanbul, Sedat Peker, one of the leaders of the mafia and militia structures, terrorist organisations and crime networks with which Erdoğan has established relations or connections in recent years, daringly said that they "will hang them on the nearest trees."[35] Peker's mafia rhetoric is a result of the climate created by Erdoğan and his regime in Turkey.

Besides, Erdoğan himself had already stated that they would not confine themselves to sentences imposed, even by a judiciary totally under their control. "None of these blood-shedders will be able to escape the bitter fate awaiting them. If they complete their sentences and are released, our nation will punish them whenever they see them in the street. Our nation will spit in their faces, and they will drown in the nation's saliva. Our struggle will continue until not a single FETOist who didn't pay for their betrayal remains."[36]

4.2. Systematic physical and psychological damage

The main point to note with regard to the "serious physical or mental/

psychological damage to the members of the target group" that constitutes the crime of genocide is the necessity of the damage to be intentionally inflicted on the physical or mental/psychological integrity of the
members of the target group and that it be severe. These actions can be
in the form of injury to persons, torture, rape or threat of death.[37] Sexual
assault is also an act causing severe physical and mental harm.[38]

The acts in this category falling within the definition of the crime
of genocide are, in general, crimes within the scope of torture and ill
treatment. In Article 1 of the United Nations Convention Against Torture and Other Cruel, Inhuman or Degrading Treatment or Punishment
dated February 10, 1984, the concept and scope of torture are defined.
According to the convention, "The term 'torture' means any act by which
severe pain or suffering, whether physical or mental, is intentionally inflicted on a person for such purposes as obtaining from him or a third
person information or a confession, punishing him for an act he or a
third person has committed or is suspected of having committed, or intimidating or coercing him or a third person, or for any reason based on
discrimination of any kind, when such pain or suffering is inflicted by
or at the instigation of or with the consent or acquiescence of a public
official or other person acting in an official capacity."[39]

One of the important elements of Lemkin's definition of genocide
is, without doubt, the destruction of individual safety, freedom, health,
honour or even the life of the members of the target group. It should be
noted that there is a significant difference between a certain individual being subjected to torture and ill treatment and the fact that "these
criminal acts take place not because of the individual characteristics of
persons but because of the membership to the target group."[40] This latter
point also constitutes a characteristic of the crime of genocide.

The infliction of injury, torture, ill treatment, rape, sexual assault or
threat of death are also serious offences, no doubt, but they are individual criminal offences as named and defined in the relevant penal code.
However, similar crimes committed on the basis of mere membership in
a targeted national, ethnic, racial or religious group, after membership
is identified through profiling or some other means, falls directly under
genocide. Committing those crimes with this intention is sufficient in itself to judge that the crime of genocide has been perpetrated as set forth
in the academic and legal definitions of genocide.

In this respect, such crimes as torture, maltreatment, sexual assault, rape, injury and threat of death perpetrated by the Erdoğan regime on arrestees and detainees on the grounds of mere affiliation with the Gülen movement fall directly under the crime of genocide. Depriving people of their liberty through massive detentions and arrests can as well be considered within the same category. The victims of these crimes are targeted by Erdoğan's dictatorship because of their affiliation with the Gülen movement, a religious group with distinctive characteristics as explained in detail in Chapter 3. There is no personal reason why those individuals are targeted in the massive and collective punishment currently being carried out in Turkey against members of the Gülen movement.[41] Members of the Gülen movement have been suffering detention, arrest, seizure of property, torture, maltreatment and other torments as mentioned above simply because they are members of the movement and are labelled/stigmatised as such rather than having committing any individual crime.[42]

Moreover, Turkey, as set forth in the reasoning of Article 94 of the TPC, has committed itself to taking necessary precautions for the prevention of torture, acknowledging that torture is prohibited by international conventions to which it is a party. In addition, according to Article 5 of the Universal Declaration of Human Rights, "No one shall be subjected to torture or to cruel, inhuman or degrading treatment or punishment."[43]

Pursuant to Article 3 of the Convention for the Protection of Human Rights and Fundamental Freedoms dated November 4, 1950, "No one shall be subjected to torture or to inhuman or degrading treatment or punishment," and Article 2 of the United Nations Convention Against Torture and Other Cruel, Inhuman or Degrading Treatment or Punishment prescribes that "No exceptional circumstances whatsoever, whether a state of war or a threat of war, internal political instability or any other public emergency, may be invoked as a justification of torture. An order from a superior officer or a public authority may not be invoked as a justification of torture." In relation to torture, the obligation imposed on the parties to this convention is also valid for preventing "other acts of cruel, inhuman or degrading treatment or punishment which do not amount to torture." (Article 16)[44]

Turkey also ratified the European Convention for the Prevention of Torture and Inhuman or Degrading Treatment or Punishment dated

November 26, 1987.[45] Parallel to these international obligations, torture is forbidden in the Turkish constitution as well. "No one shall be tortured or persecuted; no one shall be subject to any punishment or treatment incompatible with human dignity." (Article 17, Paragraph 3) "No one shall be forced to testify against himself or produce evidence for self-incrimination." (Article 38, Paragraph 5)[46]

Article 94 of the TPC also states: "Acts which constitute torture attack the physical integrity and dignity of those who are subject thereto and disrupt their physical and mental health. On the other hand, the person subjected to torture may, under the influence of pain and suffering, make delusive explanations and confessions as his/her free will has been eliminated and their perceptive abilities impaired. Therefore, the torture aimed at forcing a confession or other evidence for a certain offence may as well have an obstructive effect on revealing the truth and realising justice. Thus, punishment of torture as a separate offence also serves the purpose of the criminal proceedings by helping reveal the material truth."[47]

A report titled "Mass Torture and Ill-Treatment in Turkey," published by SCF in June 2017, addressed widespread and systematic torture and ill-treatment incidents after the military coup attempt on July 15, 2016. The report argues: "A State of Emergency was declared a few days after the failed coup bid and the duration of detention was extended from four to thirty days under the State of Emergency Decree No. 667. The rights of people in custody to see their lawyers were restricted. This extended duration gave the police enough time to obscure evidence of torture. Erdoğan and government officials made remarks which encouraged police and security officers to proceed with unlawful treatment of suspects."[48]

With the same decree-law, the relevant articles of the European Convention on Human Rights (ECHR) and the International Covenant on Civil and Political Rights (ICCPR), to both of which Turkey is a party, which prohibit torture and ill treatment and protect the right to a defense, were suspended.[49] Under the state of emergency new laws were enacted to ensure that the security forces would not be prosecuted for the offences they committed. Article 9 of decree-law No. 667 issued on July 23, 2016 states that legal, administrative, financial and criminal liability shall not arise out of the actions of those who discharge their official duties under the decree-law.[50] Thus, the way was paved in Turkey for widespread and systematic torture and ill treatment, which are absolutely prohibited, even in a state of war, by international law.

Many suspects, once they were able to appear for their first hearing in court, testified that they had suffered oppression, torture, threats and ill treatment during long periods of detention but that their statements to this effect had not been reflected in their testimony. The police officers did not allow victims to annotate to their testimony that 'I suffered intimidation,' claiming that no complaint could be lodged against them or that they could not be prosecuted as set forth by the aforementioned decree-law. Lawyers were not allowed to make annotations, either.[51] In this time of widespread torture and ill treatment, doctors as well failed to observe the rules of the Istanbul Protocol,[52] which governs how people who allege torture should be examined. While some doctors drafted their reports without even seeing the victims, others who were willing to report the signs of torture exhibited by the victims were prevented from doing so by the police.[53]

When a high-ranking military officer testified in court that he had been tortured, the policemen who had tortured him, in order to prevent the incorporation of his testimony into the minutes of the hearing, put their guns on the table and threatened the judge, saying, "It would be very easy to take you into custody as well," the media reported.[54] Despite all efforts of the government and the police at a cover-up, it became obvious that many cases of torture and ill treatment occurred during the detention and arrest processes. Paradoxically, footage showing some alleged coup-plotting soldiers who had been tortured were broadcast for purposes of propaganda and intimidation by the state-run Anadolu News Agency (AA) and official state television station TRT.

Images of wounded and bruised generals and admirals in detention published by AA exposed widespread torture and ill treatment while also revealing the recklessness of the government and the police for engaging in that torture and ill treatment. Among the flag officers who were tortured was Gen. Akın Öztürk, one of the top 15 generals in the Turkish Armed Forces (TSK), who was shown as having been tortured and humiliated by the police while in custody. Öztürk appeared in the pictures with wounds and bruises on his body and a bandage on his ear due to a beating. Similar scars and bruises were also observed on other generals. Two different sets of photographs showing Öztürk's arrest and subsequent referral to court indicate that the torture he underwent was continuing.

Photographs and images published on social media by police officers who bragged of their torture of alleged coup plotters in detention document the widespread torture and ill treatment. In one of those cases, military members, handcuffed from behind and held in a sitting position, were threatened at police headquarters with death as well as the rape of their wives and daughters. The clothes and bodies of the tortured military members were soaked in blood, and traces of blood could be seen on the walls where they leaned.[55]

Among the most common methods of torture detected from the narratives of the suspects as reflected in court minutes were beatings, spraying with pressurized cold water, thrusting nightsticks into the anus, squeezing of the testicles, exposure to electrical shock, submersion of the head in a toilet, stress positions, deprivation of sleep, hogtying, strappado, threats of raping family members and others, all of which are incompatible with human honour and dignity. Some suspects died, lapsed into insanity or were psychologically traumatised because of the severe torture they had undergone.[56]

Regarding the widespread allegations of torture and ill treatment in the aftermath of July 15, 2016, the AKP government, instead of taking preventive measures, preferred to make remarks that could never be reconciled with basic human rights and freedoms and universal principles. Mehmet Metiner, chairman of parliament's Sub-commission on Prisons, announced that the sub-commission would neither visit the detainees in Gülen movement-related prosecutions nor investigate their allegations of ill treatment and torture.[57]

Then-Economy Minister Nihat Zeybekçi said in a televised speech to party members: "We will punish them [alleged members of the Gülen movement] in such a way that they will say, 'I wish I would die.' They will not see a human face or hear a human voice. They will die like sewer rats in 1.5 to 2-square-meter cells," in effect declaring that the regime would act with hatred and revenge.[58] The AKP government, through these and similar statements, sent a clear message that they would turn a blind eye to the crime of torture, thus encouraging public employees to perpetrate torture on detainees. During this period of time, cases involving complaints of torture and ill treatment were either closed or covered up due to the impunity afforded to state employees.

Meanwhile, at least 38,000 convicted criminals were released from prison under a partial amnesty to make room for alleged members of the Gülen movement.[59] Nevertheless, the population in prisons remains much higher than overall capacity.[60] A journalist incarcerated in Çorum Prison for more than a year is reported to have said that 45 inmates are being held in a 14-person ward. According to a close relative of a journalist arrested in Konya province, there are 40 people in a ward designed for eight inmates. According to reports prison wards have a single toilet, and inmates wait in line for an hour to use the facilities. Some inmates reportedly do not eat to avoid the necessity of using the facilities. The conditions in the overcrowded prisons are reportedly worsening with every passing day.[61]

Şaban Yılmaz, the director general of Prisons and Correctional Facilities, announced on November 14, 2018 that prison occupancy in Turkey exceeded capacity by some 40,000 inmates. Yılmaz stated that as of that date some 260,000 inmates were being held in Turkey's prisons, which have a capacity of around 220,000. Yılmaz also revealed that 743 mothers accompanied by their children were imprisoned, 519 of whom have been convicted. In addition Yılmaz said that of the 743 children accompanying their mothers in prison, 343 belong to the 0-3 year age group. He added that 57 people in 2017 and 44 people in 2018 committed suicide in prison.[62]

The AKP government, having already hampered international human rights organisations' review and scrutiny in Turkey, took various measures to prevent inspection of the deteriorating conditions in detention centers and prisons. In this context, it was revealed that the Security National Directorate had sent a classified letter to police units in all 81 provinces ahead of an official review by the European Committee for the Prevention of Torture, instructing them to eliminate any traces of torture in all detention centers.[63]

Moreover, unofficial interrogation and detention centers were revealed to have been set up throughout the country.[64] Suspects and detainees were systematically tortured in places such as sports halls and factory buildings where they were held in large groups and where supervision was impossible. In these centers, even the simplest human needs of inmates such as using the toilet were not met. A victim who suffered severe torture in detention told the media that 160 people held in a sports hall in Ankara suffered mass torture and had only one toilet and only two bathrooms assigned for their use. "Water was given out only two hours a day. We would wait to use the bathroom for days. I was interrogated 11 times without any lawyer," he said.[65] Some detainees who fell ill after drinking the water also said they suspected that they were given drugs with the water.[66]

One of the buildings unlawfully used for detention and interrogation was the historic Weaving Mill (Dokuma Fabrikası), built in Antalya in the 1950s. The government-controlled media reported that the factory, with a capacity of 500, was put into use because the police detention centers in all 19 districts of the city were full. More than 200 men and women were held in the factory for several days and allegedly subjected to intense interrogation and psychological and physical torture.[67]

Military officers arrested after the July 15, 2016 coup attempt revealed another reality during their trial, which started months after their arrest. They claimed that an interrogation room had been set up at the General Staff headquarters and that they had been interrogated there under duress and intimidation. Lt. Kübra Yavuz, who had previously worked at the headquarters, testified during her trial that she had been interrogated there under threat of execution.[68] After the mass detentions, it was claimed that in addition to interrogation rooms at police headquarters and stations, such rooms were also set up at the National Intelligence Organisation (MIT), the Office of the Chief of General Staff, the Police Academy and at the presidential palace's horse farm in Ankara's Bestepe neighbourhood. Senior military personnel such as Lt. Col. Levent Türkan, aide to then-Chief of General Staff Hulusi Akar, were allegedly questioned under torture at the presidential palace. Photos showing detained military personnel being tortured in mosques and masjids were also shared.[69]

According to information included in court minutes, one of the places where torture was most prevalent was the Special Forces Command (OKK) headquarters in Ankara. Defendants stated in testimony that methods of torture such as hogtying, waterboarding, electrical shock and submersion of the head in a toilet were widely used there. On March 2, 2017 military defendants in a hearing at the Ankara 14th High

Criminal Court related details of the horrific torture they had suffered.[70] The accused soldiers said Special Forces Commander Zekai Aksakallı kicked and cursed at them and personally gave instructions for their torture.[71] For example, 27-year-old infantry lieutenant Ahmet Müfit Küçük argued that nobody knew it was a coup, and that they acted on the orders of the officer in charge. "Had I known it was a coup d'état, I would have directly gone to the nearest police station and informed them. I was taken into custody at the OKK. They blindfolded me. I was also hogtied. Every passerby kicked me and swore at me. When I opened my mouth to speak, I was kicked in the head, and I fainted. Capt. Volkan in particular kicked me 40 or 45 times. I was punched countless times. I could not even remember my name when the prosecutor was interrogating me. I have never betrayed my homeland."[72]

One of the cases in which torture was most mentioned was the detention on April 26, 2017 of more than a thousand people accused of membership in the Gülen movement. According to accounts obtained from victims' lawyers, under the detentions that started in Ankara and were conducted throughout all 81 provinces, detainees were systematically tortured during interrogation. The State Waterworks Authority (DSI) sports arena on the Ankara-Eskişehir highway was used for this purpose. After the July 15 coup attempt, this hall had been allocated to the counterterrorism branch of the Ankara Police Department. It became clear that torture was conducted under the guise of 'interviews' in unlawfully set up interrogation rooms. It was noted that such methods of torture as spraying cold water under pressure on naked bodies, strappado, raping with nightsticks, beating, threatening and cursing were employed there. Male suspects, in addition to beating, were threatened with the 'raping of their spouses.' Female suspects were similarly threatened with rape and forced to become informants. The detainees were held in inhumane conditions. Everyone lay side by side on a tarp laid on the floor of the stadium. There is also information showing that a single toilet and a single pair of slippers were assigned to hundreds of detainees.[73]

The official complaints of suspects subjected to severe torture and ill treatment in custody or detention resulted in judicial decisions that would serve to encourage security personnel accused of torture. For instance, Abdullah B., arrested as part of an investigation carried out in Trabzon province into the Gülen movement, filed a complaint with the Trabzon Chief Public Prosecutor's Office claiming that he had been beaten, ill treated and threatened after being taken into custody with his two-months-pregnant wife. Prosecutor Eşref Aktaş ruled that 'there is no grounds for prosecution,' referring to Article 9 of decree-law No. 667 issued by the government.[74] Aktas argued that pursuant to the decree-law, police officers have no criminal liability for their actions during the discharge of their official duties and would not be prosecuted. Independent jurists found the decision, which ensures impunity for the commission of crimes of torture, 'terrible.'

Turkish media reported that people tortured while in police custody in Zonguldak province said they would file criminal complaints against the torturers, upon which the latter responded that they had been acting under the orders of the chief prosecutor himself and that nothing could be done to them under the state of emergency, quoting chief prosecutor Hüsnü Hakan Yağız as having instructed them, "Leave them able to at least stand on their feet." This information reported by the media has not been denied.[75] Unfortunately, some cases of torture went well beyond the criterion of "being able to stand on their feet," and deaths as well as injuries occurred during interrogations under torture. Teacher Gökhan Açıkkollu[76] and noncommissioned officer Onder Irmak died due to torture and ill treatment while in custody at the Istanbul Police Department.[77] At least 58 similar suspicious cases have been recorded.[78]

During the state of emergency not only was the permissible period of detention extended from four to 30 days, but the suspects were also barred from meeting with their lawyers during the first week, violating their right to legal counsel. Long periods of custody were used for psychological torture as well as for destroying traces of physical torture. Some suspects said that lawyers assigned by the bar association collaborated with the police and misled them. Others refused to undertake the defence of suspects who they had already labelled as traitors.[79]

President of the pro-government Lawyers Association Mehmet Sarı provocatively declared: "Under the Code of Criminal Procedure the state is required to appoint lawyer for the defendant. The right to a defense arises out of the fact that human beings are able to think. It is called human dignity in the Western literature. That said, it is necessary for coup plotters to first be human in order to benefit from human dignity. Since we do not accept them as human beings, we do not accede to their demands for lawyers."[80] With this stance adopted by bar associations on the right to a defence, it is no surprise that they remained silent in the face of complaints of torture and ill treatment as well.

One of the complaints of suspects regarding the detention process was the failure of forensic doctors, who they suspected of collaborating with the police, to report signs of torture during daily health checkups in spite of the clear provisions of the Istanbul Protocol,[81] to which Turkey is a party. In subsequent phases it was established that during the mandatory health checks, to be conducted with a view to preventing torture, even findings of severe torture were ignored and not covered in medical reports.

Chairman of the Contemporary Lawyers Association (ÇHD) Selçuk Kozağaçlı (he was also arrested and imprisoned in November 2017[82]), who had followed up on rights violations with ad hoc delegations, publicised their findings at the Ankara Bar Association's ordinary plenary. Kozağaçlı said all suspects including judges, prosecutors, police officers and ordinary citizens detained on charges of membership in the Gülen movement had been severely tortured. According to him some of the detainees were raped with hard objects, some of whom were hospitalised for surgery due to perforations to their intestines, and that torture was rife not only in detention centers but also in prisons. "Those who pray together in the justice hall masjids rape their friends in prison. They are pulling out their nails at the police stations and raping the prisoners. I saw people who had colectomies due to rape from hard objects inserted into their anuses. Eighteen people committed suicide. Prosecutors, police officers, district governors … Just think for a moment, how does a man get the idea of shooting himself in the head? If the bar association cannot even prevent torture in the courthouse itself…" Kozağaçlı said,[83] also giving details of the systematic torture to the press.

"Almost everyone in custody is being tortured. Whatever was done in the old days is being done right now as well. For example, men are bastinadoed. And because of the bastinado, many have sores on their feet. Physicians are taken to detention and torture centers for examinations. This is a criminal offence. Since the examinations are not conducted in examination rooms, we cannot ascertain the torture. Once taken into custody, everyone is put into a five-day period of detention without access to their lawyers. Hence, torture cannot be detected. We receive many applications all the same. Families cannot go to the press because a witch-hunt has already started. Torture is a crime and is never subject to the statute of limitations. We will not let it go," said Kozağaçlı. Kozağaçlı also noted that many women were under the threat of sexual assault.[84]

Head of the Istanbul branch of the Human Rights Association (IHD) lawyer Gülseren Yoleri is also among those who stated that torture was taking place in detention centers. "The torture of the old days has resumed. It's as if they hid the old torture devices like hangers and electrical cables, and now they have come out again," said Yoleri, also quoting what a female teacher who had applied to the IHD said: "We have nothing to do with FETO. We're just a conservative family. My husband has been fired from the civil service. I saw him on his fourth day in custody. There were scars on his face. When I asked 'What happened?' the police intervened, saying, 'If you ask anything, we will take you into custody, too. Do not talk, just look.' They threatened my husband as well, saying, 'If you say anything [about what happened in custody], you will serve 30 years...' My husband responded: 'Do not put me into custody. I am willing to serve 30 years.' He was very scared. I was also informally questioned there. I was threatened."[85]

Prisons whose conditions were deliberately allowed to deteriorate constitute another method of torture, ill treatment and inhuman and degrading treatment of members of the Gülen movement. One of the issues that the inmates who are able to have their voices heard complain of is the terrible conditions in the prisons. A letter from prison that *Sözcü* daily columnist Emin Çölaşan published in an article describes the prison conditions as follows:

"Twenty-two to twenty-three inmates are staying in a ward originally designed for eight to 10 people. A two-storey ward is 30 + 30, 60 square meters in total. There are beds upstairs. There is a bathroom and a toilet on the lower floor. There are 14 beds in the ward. In every instance eight or nine people sleep on the floor. Meals are eaten in shifts. Using the toilet, taking showers and doing laundry are huge problems. Epidemics like diarrhea are constant. The inmates cannot fit into the ground floor, so the television is watched and meals are eaten in shifts. You can imagine what kind of torment and torture it is to spend a night in a ward as large as a small hall in such hot weather where temperatures reach up to 44-45 degrees... It is already quite usual to wait in line to be able to have a shower or go to the toilet. Skin diseases proliferate due to excessive temperatures and a lack of hygiene. Imagine 23 people living in a 60-square-meter house with a locked door for months in extremely high temperatures. To say nothing of the fact that such activities as reading books and engaging in sports are forbidden."[86]

Sevim Halman, a member of the IHD Prison Commission and the aunt of prisoner Ali Gülmez, who was sentenced to life in prison, quotes from Gülmez as follows: "There is a prevailing mentality which holds that political prisoners 'deserve' all kinds of rights infringement. We are having a coup here. The inmates who are charged with FETO membership are suffering terribly from torture. We hear groans from the cells. We give them water, cigarettes and ice. An investigation has been launched into us because we are reacting to the torture. The female prisoners transferred from Sincan Prison to Silivri No. 9 send letters saying, 'Hear our voices.' They were subjected to strip searches while they were being transferred. They were beaten because they were objecting. Resmiye Vatansever and Deniz Tepeli said: 'Cameras face our bathroom. We hung curtains, but male guards came and removed the curtains. We have not received any response to our petitions.' They want support against sexual harassment."[87]

Members of the Gülen movement, subjected to intense torture and ill treatment, are suffering from severe psychological problems such as intense stress, depression and anxiety due to oppression, persecution, fear, anxiety and the uncertainty of their future. Hence, the number of suicides is on the rise. Incidents of suicide account for a significant part of the 126 suspicious deaths[88] after the July 15, 2016 coup attempt. It is estimated that suicides triggered by oppression and persecution are much higher than recorded due to fear of further oppression as well as censorship, or the shame the victim's relatives may feel because of cultural codes.

It has also been observed that widespread and systematic practices such as detention, arrest, collective punishment, torture, ill treatment, rape, sexual harassment, injury and murder targeting members of the Gülen movement have caused serious psychological breakdowns among group members. On the other hand, with conspiracy theories based on various stigmatisations such as the 'Parallel State Structure,' the 'Pennsylvania Organization,' 'Assassins,' 'FETO,' etc., the Gülen movement has been transformed not only into an object of hatred but also a subject of fear in the eyes of society. Therefore, both the members of the Gülen movement and various other opponents similarly labelled who are targeted with detentions, arrests, torture and ill treatment, insults, hate speech, persecution and other types of oppression are psychologically disturbed or devastated. Other segments of society are pushed into psychological depression, too. As a matter of fact, media outlets reported that some psychiatrists have initiated studies with a view to registering a paranoia called 'Gülenophobia' and a psychological disorder called the 'FETO Syndrome' in the psychiatry literature.[89]

Psychotherapist Çağatay Öztürk, who was interviewed by the *Sözcü* daily, said he had made application through universities in England to insert the term 'FETO Syndrome,' which he coined, in the psychology literature. "The psychological balance of the society has been disrupted," he said. He also said the 'FETO Syndrome' was spreading rapidly in the society and that people want to flee Turkey. "This syndrome means depression and crisis. In other words, it is a contagious disorder like some sort of recurrent depression. In fact, it is a state of emotion, and what you call emotion is infectious. This is why the FETO syndrome is spreading rapidly," he argued. Öztürk claimed that many people had come to him for help against this syndrome. "The point in common among these people is that they are planning to go abroad."

According to Öztürk, the 'FETO Syndrome' triggers moods in society such as a hidden depression called 'masked depression,' heavy depression called 'major depression' or other disorders that require medication, and anxiety caused by suspicion. Öztürk also gave examples of this syndrome: "A patient anxiously said that when he broke his leg, he preferred to go to a distant hospital, not to the one nearest to his home fearing that it could have a connection with FETO. Another patient changed his longtime grocery store because of the possibility that the market might be connected to FETO. Many people kept repeating that they were no longer watching news on TV channels they thought were connected to FETO. In short, this syndrome has disturbed the psychological balance of the society, leading to mood disorder in society."

The results of research carried out by SCF also revealed that the Erdoğan regime's policies of tension and fear, widespread human rights abuses, oppression and persecution have led to a serious and widespread emotional disturbance stemming from stress, depression and anxiety among Turkish society. According to the results of a survey conducted through self-reporting questionnaires on 358 people with an average age of 36, 86.3 percent of respondents experienced a high level of depression; 78.8 percent said they were trying to cope with stress; 72.1 percent claimed they were suffering from anxiety; 65.1 percent identified themselves as 'unhappy' to varying degrees; and 34.9 percent described themselves as 'happy' to varying degrees.[90]

It is estimated that the results of a similar research that would focus solely on members of the Gülen movement would give much more negative results than these figures. That said, it is obvious that widespread violations of fundamental freedoms and democratic rights, meddling in the private lives of the people, deterioration of the economy and increasing violence and terrorist acts under the Erdoğan regime have seriously damaged the psychology of Turkish society. The Ministry of Health confirms this. Consumption of anti-psychotic medication in Turkey has increased from 7,201,000 boxes to 12,158,000 boxes in the last five years, and mental health institutions are fully occupied.

While in 2012, 37,351,187 boxes, in 2013, 37,355,035 boxes and in 2014, 39,246,223 boxes of antidepressants were dispensed, this figure soared to 43,563,596 boxes in 2015 when authoritarianism was on the rise. In the first nine months of 2016, 33,648,916 boxes of antidepressant drugs were dispensed.[91] According to Ministry of Health data as of August 5, 2014, the number of applications to hospitals and clinics due to psychological problems increased to 9.2 million in 2013 from 3 million in 2009.[92] It is estimated that in recent years the number of people who use anti-depressants and seek psychological treatment is well above average among Kurds and Gülen movement members, who are specifically targeted by the Erdoğan dictatorship's oppression, persecution and killing.

4.3. Making life hell: Condemned to civil death

In the act of "deliberately inflicting on the group conditions of life calculated to bring about its physical destruction in whole or in part," which constitutes genocide as stated in the Genocide Convention and the Rome

Statute as well as Article 76 of the Turkish Penal Code (TPC), there is no direct attack on the victim's life or person. However, the imprisonment of group members in concentration camps and depriving them of the food, clothing, shelter and medical care necessary for life are examples of living conditions that can give way to suppression. In extreme situations, systematic exile may also constitute a crime of genocide[93] as thousands of Gülen movement members have had to seek shelter in other countries.[94]

It is possible to divide the deterioration of living conditions into two categories: physical and social. Physical destruction is visible and would include the burning of fields and harvests, the devastation of production facilities and houses and the slaughter of animals. The Erdoğan regime carried out physical destruction, for instance, by bombing the besieged cities of Sur, Nusaybin, Silvan, Cizre and many other Kurdish residential areas using tanks, artillery and heavily armed security forces for months.[95] One of the natural consequences of the physical deterioration of living conditions is, of course, social deterioration. It would be illogical to think that the living conditions of people who had to migrate due to the devastation of their homes or the physical destruction of their production and trade facilities did not change in social terms.

The persecution of Gülen movement members by the Erdoğan regime in this regard differs from the persecution of the Kurds. While the residential areas and living conditions of the Kurds were destroyed, forcing them to migrate, the persecution of Gülen movement members is more for the purpose of 'civil death,'[96] in addition to kidnapping,[97] arbitrary detention and arrest, torture, ill treatment and execution under custody. Cem Küçük, one of the propagandists in the Erdoğan regime's media who has exerted efforts to create anger and hatred against the movement, is the person who brought to Turkey's agenda the concept of 'civil death,'[98] which the European Court of Human Rights used in its decision in the case of conscientious objector Osman Murat Ülke in 2006.[99]

Unfortunately, the term 'civil death' is the most apt description of the vicious persecution that perhaps millions of people and their families and relatives have been subjected to since July 15, 2016. Not only have the social and economic assets of those who are thought to be members of the Gülen movement been plundered, they also have been deprived of the opportunity to find a job in both the public and private sectors or to work in a self-employed capacity.

In August 2014 Okan Özsoy, a prosecutor at the Istanbul Court-house, told Fatih Altaylı from the *Habertürk* daily that if necessary 500,000 people could be taken into custody in a witch-hunt. Özsoy brought to mind the hundreds of thousands of detentions during the military coup era of September 12, 1980 and said, "The state can do it again."[100] This figure, which was considered to be exaggerated at the time, has gradually become reality. In fact, the effects of the first year of the state of emergency, declared on July 19, 2016 on the pretext of the failed coup and extended every three months for two years, have been wide-spread in terms of people who have been detained or arrested or fled into exile. And eventually, Interior Minister Süleyman Soylu announced on February 13, 2019 that more than 500,000 people had been detained over alleged links to the Gülen movement.[101]

According to official figures, as of July 15, 2017, more than 130,000 civil servants had been dismissed on grounds of alleged connections to the Gülen movement.[102] Moreover, 32,080 public employees were sus-pended from their duties.[103] A total of 91,143 people, including 43,439 who were released under judicial supervision after they had remained in custody for days, had stood trial while free on bail as of May 2017. Addi-tionally, arrest warrants have been issued for at least 8,087 people.[104]

Amnesty International stated that purged public servants consisted of 33,500 teachers, 31,500 police officers, 13,500 military officers, 7,000 healthcare professionals, 6,000 academics and some 39,000 from other professional groups. On July 8, 2018, only 10 days before the state of emergency was terminated, 18,632 public sector workers were dismissed in the last decree issued under the state of emergency, the largest single mass dismissal of civil servants since September 1, 2016. Furthermore, a new law passed on July 25, 2018 allows for another three years the summary dismissal of public sector workers deemed to have links to 'ter-rorist' organizations or other groups posing a threat to national security – similar to those announced through state of emergency decrees.[105]

Interior Minister Soylu also announced on April 18, 2018 that the Turkish government had jailed 77,081 people (excluding those who were detained for a period of time and then released) between July 15, 2016 and April 11, 2018 over alleged links to the Gülen movement. Soylu also stated that the government conducted 20,409 operations in 2017 and that 20,478 people were arrested by the courts and put in pretrial detention as part of the government's post-coup witch-hunt across Turkey targeting alleged members of the movement.[106]

Defense Minister Hulusi Akar announced on October 27, 2018 that 15,153 military officers, including 150 generals and admirals, had been dismissed from the Turkish military since July 15, 2016.[107] According to other sources, 169 flag officers were purged and arrested on the pretext of involvement in the Gülen movement.[108] Stating that the dismissal process had not yet been completed, Akar said an algorithm developed by deputy chief of the Naval Forces Adm. Cihat Yaycı and referred to as the "FETO-meter" had accelerated dismissals from the Turkish military. Adm. Yayci developed an algorithm for profiling individuals for ties to the Gülen movement that has scrutinized some 800,000 people, former and active duty military members along with their spouses and children, to ferret out some 4,500 Gülen-linked officers in Turkey's Naval Forces.

Seventy main criteria and 249 sub-criteria form the basis of the software used in the profiling process in order to analyse in detail the individual data of the officers under scrutiny that was provided by several ministries and other institutions. An earlier report on the algorithm published in January 2018 by the pro-government *Sabah* daily had revealed that the data to be analysed would pertain to the officers' scores on several nationwide civil service-related tests, their spouses' workplaces and the schools of the officers' children, financial transactions at the Gülen-affiliated Bank Asya, use of the ByLock mobile messaging app and suspect and witness testimony as well as whether or not these officers had served on the interview or examination boards that confirmed new recruits during periods when Gülen movement members were considered to be influential within the institutions.[109]

While 4,238 of 14,661 judges and prosecutors have been sacked for their alleged links to the Gülen movement,[110] 2,431 members of the judiciary have been arrested. Of those, 2,280 were judges or prosecutors, 105 were members of the Supreme Court of Appeals, 41 were members of the Council of State, two were members of the Constitutional Court and three were members of the HSYK.[111] Furthermore, 555 lawyers had been arrested and 1,546 were under prosecution as of January 24, 2019. Two hundred sixteen lawyers have been sentenced to a total of 1,361 years in prison.[112]

According to a report released in July 2018 by SCF that compiled data related to purges and seizures in the education sector, the Erdoğan regime has jailed some 20,000 instructors and arbitrarily fired 34,185 public school teachers and 5,719 academics, including professors from state universities. They were branded as 'terrorists' and 'coup plotters' without any effective administrative or judicial probe and as such were marked for life.

The government also shut down 1,069 privately run schools, most of which were the nation's best performing science schools and were affiliated with the Gülen movement, and closed down 15 universities that were run by privately held foundations. Most of the shuttered institutions were transformed into religious schools that are designed to raise a new generation of Islamist supporters for Erdoğan's regime. As a result, 2,465 academics and 54,350 teachers instantly became unemployed. With the support staff who worked at these schools, the total number of people who lost their jobs has reached 65,214. The government also canceled the licences of 22,474 teachers, making it impossible for them to continue working as teachers in other institutions.[113]

Government agencies have not shared any specific figures; however, according to data compiled by BBC's Turkish service, at least 23,427 academics were dismissed from government and private jobs, lost their tenure/rights or lost their jobs due to the closure of their universities in the year following the coup.[114]

According to SCF's report 96,719 teachers and academics in total were purged from Turkey's public and private educational institutions. This number does not include the support staff that was hired to run schools and universities in administrative and other capacities. When all the closed institutions are taken into account, the total loss in value including fixed property and land is around $100 billion, one source estimated. The crackdown included foreign students who came to Turkey for study or Turkish students who were sent abroad on government scholarships. According to some estimates at least 20,000 of the dismissed teachers have been detained and arrested.[115]

The assets of at least 1,004 major companies with a value of TL 55.74 billion[116] as well as 4,887 small companies of an undetermined value have also been confiscated.[117] The list of major companies seized, which was updated on January 21, 2019, shows that 944 companies are

Fevzi Yazıcı, the Design Director of *Zaman* newspaper. He has been under arrest since July 27, 2016, on charges of being a member of Gülen Movement. *Zaman*, first taken over and then shut down by the government the same year, had won more than 100 awards with Yazıcı's creative work. *Zaman*'s building was occupied by the police on March 4, 2016.

In an effort to silence opposition, Erdoğan regime started to harass critical media since the corruption scandal in December 2013. They arrested many journalists and assigned trustees to change the management of media organizations like Bugün TV and Kanaltürk as early as October 2015. The government takeover of *Zaman* and *Today's Zaman* newspapers took place with police brutality wounding scores of peaceful protestors with rubber bullets, tear gas, and water cannon (March 4, 2016). *Zaman* was by far the top circulating newspaper of Turkey until the takeover.

Fadime Günay

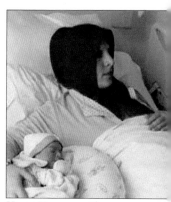

Havva Hamamcıoğlu

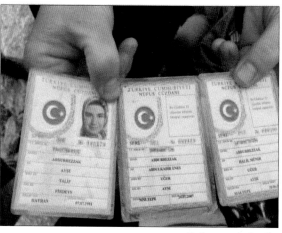

Abdurrezzak family

Judge Neslihan Ekinci

Countless tragedies marked the recent history of Gülen Movement members who tried to flee Turkey for their freedoms since 2016. On February 13, 2018, two families lost their lives when their little boat capsized as they were crossing the Evros River to Greece. After spending 11 months in prison, Uğur Abdurrezzak (39), an English teacher, decided to leave the country when he was released pending trial with his wife Ayşe (37), a Turkish language teacher, and their two boys: Abdülkadir Enes (11) and Halil Münir (3). On the boat with them were another couple: Fahrettin Doğan (30), a biology teacher, his wife Aslı (28), a chemistry teacher, and their baby boy.

Thousands of legal professionals were dismissed from their jobs and purged after the coup attempt in July 2016. Neslihan Ekinci, an expelled judge and the former deputy secretary-general of Turkey's top judicial body, spent 29 months in solitary confinement on coup charges. Her husband Judge Hüseyin Ekinci, a former rapporteur of Turkey's Constitutional Court, was also expelled and incarcerated right after the coup.

During the crackdown against the Gülen Movement, thousands of women have been arrested. Despite international and national law that provide exemptions for pregnant women and nursing mothers, hundreds of them were rounded up from delivery rooms on the day of birth or in the next few days while they were still in the hospital. Many were separated from their newborns for days and had to endure the pain of being unable to suckle them. Their alleged crimes range from fundraising for students to subscribing to a newspaper, organizing reading clubs, being a wife to a suspect who is not found, or having a copy of Fethullah Gülen's books.

Five children left alone in tears in front of Sincan Prison in Ankara after their mother was detained while they were visiting their father in prison. (January 23, 2017)

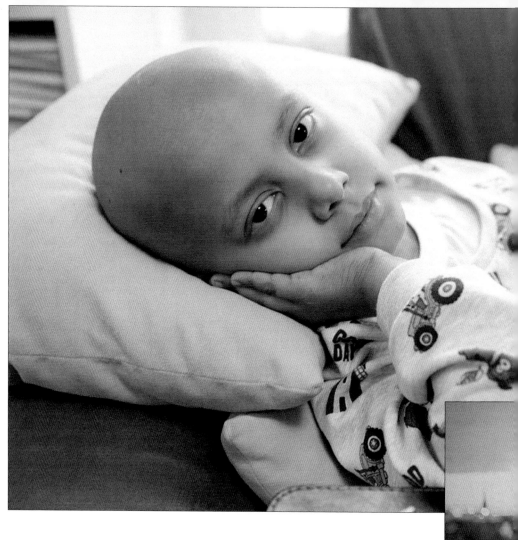

8-year-old Ahmet Burhan Ataç died on May 7, 2020, after almost a two-year fight to survive cancer which he developed under the ordeal they went through as a family. Both of his parents were arrested February 2018 because of their alleged membership to Gülen Movement. His father Harun Reha Ataç has been sentenced to nine years because he used to work at a Movement-affiliated student hostel. His mother (now sentenced to six years, three months in prison) was released pending trial after two-and-a-half months under custody. When she took Ahmet to a hospial first time in September 2018 for his shoulder pain, he was diagnosed already stage-4 bone cancer. Turkish government did not cooperate to lift the travel ban on the mother until the last minute so they could go to Germany for treatment. During these years, little Ahmet's father was allowed to see his dying child only for once and only two months before his last breath.

Dr. Haluk Savaş was a professor of psychiatry at Gaziantep University. Along with thousands of other academics, he was fired from his job and then arrested after the staged coup in July 15, 2016. Since he was diagnosed cancer a couple months later he was released from prison. It took a long time and campaigning to get his passport back although he was acquitted of charges. When he was finally able to go to Germany to seek hope for cure, it was already too late. Dr. Savaş was 54 years old when he died on June 30, 2020.

Gökhan Açıkkollu, 42, was a teacher until he was dismissed from his job and arrested following the July 15 coup attempt. He was tortured during his 13-day custody as a result of which he collapsed in his cell one night and died due to heart failure. The family was told that they could get the deceased for funeral on condition to be buried in "Traitors Cemetery" opened by Istanbul Municipality. Diyanet, the official body of government for religious affairs) refused to assign an imam to conduct funeral service. All charges against Açıkkolu were later dropped as he was found to be innocent one-and-a-half years later after which his family received a letter from the Ministry of Education reinstating him back to his job.

Fatih Kılıç, a teacher who was dismissed under post-coup emergency rule, has been missing since May 14, 2017. Many individuals have been abducted with illegal operations with a black transporter van since the coup attempt in July 2016.

still under the control of the state-run Savings Deposit Insurance Fund (TMSF).[118] However, Vice President Fuat Oktay said on November 1, 2018 that the TMSF had appointed trustees to 1,004 companies across 42 provinces as of October 25 over their alleged links to the Gülen movement.

The Erdoğan regime, which has been confiscating the private property of non-loyalist businesspeople without due process on unsubstantiated charges of terrorist links, has seized companies including Koza, Boydak, Dumankaya, Akfa, Orkide, Sesli and Naksan, which were among the 500 largest firms in Turkey.[119] Almost all the owners of these companies have either been arrested or forced by the Erdoğan regime to live in exile. In brief, the arbitrary seizure of companies and private properties owned by people affiliated with the Gülen movement has reached the volume of 'economic genocide.'

In addition, about 200 media outlets, the vast majority of whose journalists were close to the Gülen movement, have been shut down. The press cards of 900 journalists have been cancelled.[120] According to data compiled by SCF, as of April 26, 2019, while 191 journalists and media workers – two-thirds of whom are claimed to be members of the Gülen movement – were still under arrest, warrants for the arrest of 167 journalists living in exile were outstanding.[121]

Without doubt, those who have been victimised by the Erdoğan regime were not only people dismissed from public service. Tens of thousands of people including the self-employed, businessmen, entrepreneurs, students and housewives have been persecuted. Legal expert and academic Kerem Altıparmak stated that the world may never have witnessed such a mass purge of the public sector and that this process, devoid of any investigation or trial, is a real tragedy. Lawyers have expressed that the implementation of decree-laws in Turkey is a criminal sanction and should be subject to the protections afforded by criminal proceedings since tens of thousands of people have been dismissed from public service without any justification or right to defend themselves. In this case, it can be said that criminal convictions (extrajudicial execution) have been accomplished without any trial.[122] However, because of the fact that dismissal procedures from public service are similar to criminal law, the faults of the persons being fired must be evaluated. The Constitutional Court also decided that the total deprivation of rights, even in the case of persons who have been convicted by a court, contravenes the constitution. This state of affairs must be assessed in terms of those who have not been the subject of any criminal proceedings or investigation and who have not been given the right to defend themselves.[123]

In addition to dismissals carried out in the absence of any investigation, trial or right to defend, it is also a calamity to impose the stipulation included in Clause 2, Article 2 of Decree-law no. 672 of 'no further employment in public service, and no direct or indirect employment' for people who have been fired without the right to appeal. This provision implies that dismissed people and their families are condemned to lifetime unemployment and poverty and deprived of social security and health services. For instance, under this provision a judge or a professor of law cannot work as a lawyer, and a soldier or a policeman cannot provide private security services. Since they were designated as 'Dismissed on grounds of FETO membership' in social security records, in the case of a teacher, he/she cannot get a job at a private school or other private educational institution. An application made by an educational institution for the employment of a dismissed teacher was responded to by the Ministry of Education, which said it was impossible for dismissed teachers to be employed in study centers or private schools. The 'Dismissed on the grounds of FETO membership' record precludes those teachers from finding any jobs, even outside of their own profession.[124] It was claimed that those who were dismissed by government decrees were labeled with "Code 36" by the Social Security Institution (SGK) to prevent them from finding new jobs.[125]

A teacher who was dismissed said: "There has been social isolation, an alienation from society. Even my closest friends do not answer my calls. This is terrible for people who are completely innocent." Having said that there was no hope for finding a job, this teacher was offered a job without insurance "taking into consideration the current state" of applications received thus far. In the atmosphere of fear and oppression created by the Erdoğan regime among the entire society, there has been such extensive exclusion of people who have been labeled 'FETO members' that the victims even have difficulty finding a lawyer to defend their rights. One of the many who were dismissed by a decree-law is a teacher of seven years who completed his education in poverty and was a member of the left-leaning Egitim-Sen union. "I worked for this, I spent my

whole life on this, and today it is impossible to find a job related to my
profession, even with my education faculty diploma. There is also the
insurance issue. Health care costs need to be covered. In the end, I will
apply for a construction job. Nobody will ask about my qualifications or
diploma there," he said.[126]

More than 22,000 teachers whose licences have been cancelled due
to the fact that they were working at private schools closed for their affiliation with the Gülen movement have been unable to find a job any-
where.[127] The general health insurance scheme, which envisages that all
members of the community benefit from health services equally, effi-
ciently and effectively against the risk of illness, is not provided to people
dismissed under decree-laws. The insurance can be obtained by applying
to the district governor's office in the applicant's area of residence. Nevertheless, in many places the district governors refuse to accept these
applications due to the instructions given to them.[128]

While the possessions and houses of thousands of people have
been seized on the grounds of their alleged links to the Gülen movement, those whose houses have not been seized are prevented from rent-
ing them out. Due to the pressure exerted by President Erdoğan, who
said, "Report them; if you don't, you will be responsible," neighbours can
threaten anyone who wants to rent an apartment owned by Gülen-affiliated people, saying, "Do not rent from them, or we will denounce you."
If the current tenants know their homeowner is close to the Gülen movement, they do not have to pay their rent. Thousands of people preferred
to leave their homes rather than risk unlawful and arbitrary arrest. Their
houses also face the risk of looting. Commencing the execution of lien
attachment of houses because of non-payment of electricity, water and
telephone bills constitutes another dimension of the problem.

As can be seen, the problem of 'civil death' is not limited to people
who have been dismissed by decree-laws, nor is it restricted to the public
sector. Since the names of dismissed staff have been publicly announced
in lists attached to decree-laws in the Official Gazette, the way is paved
for victims to be stigmatised, to be declared putschists or terrorists, to
be excluded, to face discrimination and even social lynching. Namely,
they are said to be on some sort of blacklist and are abandoned to 'civil
death.'[129] Apart from administrative and legal hurdles, merely being so
labeled erects serious employment barriers for those who have been dis-

missed through decree-laws. Therefore, this method was preferred for the purpose of 'deliberately ruining the living conditions' of real or perceived members of the Gülen movement. The lists of names are believed to have been prepared a long time ago, and the staging of a coup attempt provided an opportunity to quickly implement these preparations for systematic dismissals.

On the other hand, the European Court of Human Rights (ECtHR) has established case law in cases from Eastern European countries, where mass dismissals following legal procedures took place after the collapse of the communist regime, ruling that this situation was a disproportionate intervention that led to discrimination because those who were labeled due to continuous stigmatisation would be prevented from enjoying a healthy relationship with society. In other words, despite the fact that the right to work and the right to enter into public service are not regulated by the European Convention on Human Rights (ECHR), owing to the fact that disproportionate interference in the person's work life hinders healthy relations with the society, the respect for private life and the right to freedom from discrimination provided under Article 8 and Article 14 of the ECHR, respectively, were still violated.[130] According to the ECtHR, the concept of private life protects the person's moral and physical integrity and ensures the development of the individual personality. Respect for private life also includes the right to establish and develop relationships with other people. Within this framework career and working life, which play a significant role in the development of relations with the society, are also involved in the concept of private life.[131]

In accordance with the ECtHR judgments, forcing people to live a life that can be described as 'civil death' does not comply with the criminal code in a democratic society.[132] Dismissal from public service by listing names in the decree-laws also constitutes a serious violation of the 'Basic principles of the Republic'[133] and the stipulation that 'Fundamental rights and freedoms may be restricted only by law and in conformity with the reasons mentioned in the relevant articles of the Constitution without infringing upon their essence. These restrictions shall not be contrary to the letter and the spirit of the Constitution and the requirements of the democratic order of the society and the secular republic and the principle of the proportionality,' provided under Article 2 and Article 13 of the Turkish constitution, respectively.

There is no doubt that depriving a person of all economic and social rights and consequently civil rights despite the lack of any tangible evidence linking that person to the coup attempt on July 15, 2016 infringes on the essence of these rights.[134] In addition, Article 15 of the Turkish constitution includes two major limitations to the restriction of rights and freedoms during a state of emergency: a) It should not be contrary to international law; and b) It should be proportionate to the exigencies of the situation.[135]

Article 70 of the Turkish constitution states: "Every Turk has the right to enter public service. No criteria other than the qualifications for the office concerned shall be taken into consideration for recruitment into public service." According to the second clause of Article 1 of the European Social Charter, "the contracting parties undertake to protect effectively the right of the worker to earn his living in an occupation freely entered upon." Therefore, 'civil death' measures contravene human rights law. Plans aiming at the exclusion of people from the private sector who have already been dismissed from the public sector are not based on legitimate grounds and are a serious and clear violation of international law.[136] Even in cases in which the absolute prohibition of returning to public service is legitimate, the prevention of all employment opportunities to a person is unacceptable.[137]

In addition, a state of emergency is not a period in which all measures can be taken freely, but rather additional measures can be taken to eliminate the risks of the state of emergency. The ECtHR provides this balance with the principle of proportionality, which 'strictly prohibits taking more precautions than [are] required by the exigencies of the situation.'[138] Taking into consideration the case law of the ECtHR and the reports of the Venice Commission, it is not difficult to say that the decree-law regulation is contrary to Council of Europe (CoE) standards.[139]

To recall, Lemkin's definition of genocide says: "Generally speaking, genocide does not necessarily mean the immediate destruction of a nation, except when accomplished by mass killings of all members of a nation. It is intended rather to signify a coordinated plan of different actions aiming at the destruction of essential foundations of the life of national groups, with the aim of annihilating the groups themselves. The objectives of such a plan would be disintegration of the political and social institutions, of culture, language, national feelings, religion, and the economic existence of national groups, and the destruction of the personal security, liberty, health, dignity, and even the lives of the individuals belonging to such groups."[140]

What Erdoğan's regime has been doing since July 15, 2016 falls within the scope of this definition. Erdoğan has deprived at least 160,000 people of their profession, one of the main determinants of their identity, personality, social status and role in society and the knowledge and experience they have accumulated during their lives simply due to their alleged membership in the Gülen movement through the pre-prepared profiling lists. This extent of oppression corresponds to that part of Lemkin's definition which says: "It is intended rather to signify a coordinated plan of different actions aiming at the destruction of essential foundations of the life of national groups, with the aim of annihilating the groups themselves."

The closure of 1,069 private schools and 15 universities known for their affiliation with the Gülen movement, which stands out for its educational activities both in Turkey and around the world, 848 private dormitories, dozens of media outlets and thousands of associations, foundations and unions corresponds to the "disintegration of the political and social institutions [and] economic existence" contained in Lemkin's definition: "The objectives of such a plan would be disintegration of the political and social institutions, of culture, language, national feelings, religion, and the economic existence of national groups." The seizure of more than 1,000 leading companies in Turkey is also synonymous with the "disintegration of economic existence" of group members and the previously mentioned "economic genocide."

In addition to the economic difficulties caused by the fact that 160,000 people have been dismissed from public service and are prevented from finding a job related their profession and that hundreds of companies in the private sector have been confiscated and tens of thousands of people have been labelled as members of a terrorist organization and subjected to investigation, custody, arrest and confiscation, the persecutions have also led to very serious social and psychological problems. In this respect, the arbitrary dismissals and seizures and the mistreatment and instant deprivation of the victims of their pensions, health insurance and other social security guarantees, which have relegated millions of people together with their families to a civil death, may have led to serious trauma and numerous suicides.

Even people who provide financial assistance to the families of victims who have been illegally arrested have been taken into custody and imprisoned. Thus, hundreds of thousands of victims have been systematically condemned to hunger.[141] All this complies with Lemkin's definition referring to "… the destruction of the personal security, liberty, health, dignity, and even the lives of the individuals belonging to such groups."

In January 2017, in the face of mounting political pressure, the government of Turkey set up the State of Emergency Inquiry Commission to review dismissals ordered by decree-laws. Out of approximately 125,000 applications made by dismissed individuals, the commission had issued decisions in only 36,000 cases as of October 5, 2018. Of these, the original decisions have been overturned in less than 7 percent (2,300) of cases. An Amnesty International report, which involved a review of the commission's procedures and 109 of its decisions as well as interviews with 21 dismissed individuals and their families, revealed that the commission is not set up to provide an effective remedy. It is deeply flawed by a lack of institutional independence, long waiting periods, the absence of safeguards allowing individuals to effectively rebut allegations and weak evidence cited in decisions upholding dismissals.[142]

4.4. Methods to prevent births not implemented yet, but…

There have been couples who have been taken into custody and imprisoned on the way to their weddings,[143] women who have been forced to give birth alone in a cell in unhygienic conditions by keeping them in prison in the last days of their pregnancy,[144] babies who have died in their mother's womb due to the ill treatment and adverse circumstances in prison[145] and women detained and arrested when they went to the hospital to deliver their babies as in at least 50 cases in 2017 alone.[146] However, it has not been determined that methods to prevent women from giving birth have been deliberately and systematically implemented due to their Gülen movement affiliations, nor has it been proven thus far that the Erdoğan regime has implemented deliberate, planned and systematic practices that could be called 'biological genocide,' such as castration of Gülen movement couples, obligatory birth control and separating men and women[147] except for instances of the arbitrary, long-term imprisonment of one or both of the spouses.

Nonetheless, it would be appropriate to mention here the existence of thousands of women, particularly pregnant women and women with children, who will suffer for years because of the trauma caused by the torture and ill treatment to which they have been subjected over their alleged links to the Gülen movement. According to official figures released by the Ministry of Justice in November 2016, 7,894 women were in prison, of whom 3,235 had been convicted. The number of female arrestees, which was 1,157 in March of the same year, grew threefold in the ensuing nine months alone.[148] It is not hard to imagine that this increase was caused by arrests without any concrete evidence due to Gülen movement membership.

Since the release of this data, no information on this issue has been shared by official sources. Nevertheless, it is estimated that some 17,000 women who have been jailed in the unprecedented crackdown have been subjected to torture and ill treatment in detention centers and prisons as part of the government's systematic campaign of intimidation and persecution of critics and opponents. Since there are only six prisons[149] across Turkey specifically allocated to female inmates, many women have been incarcerated in prisons built for men, where women have faced further difficulties in fulfilling their needs due to the smaller number of female guards.

Moreover, a total of 743 children were accompanying their mothers in Turkey's prisons as of November 16, 2018, according to a report released by the IHD. The mothers of a majority of the children have been arrested over their alleged ties to the Gülen movement, and most are in pre-trial detention and not yet convicted of a crime. The children in jail are mainly aged between 0 and 6 years, and insufficient and low-quality food is given to these children, who are forced to eat the same meals as the adults, according to the IHD. The report said that if there are 25 adults and three children in a prison ward, food is given to the 25 adults without taking the three children into consideration. As a result, mothers have to share their food with their children. According to the IHD report around 10,000 women including pregnant women and women who have just given birth as well as those with small children have been imprisoned due to alleged Gülen links.[150]

On the other hand, the poor conditions in overcrowded prisons have caused serious complications, especially for expectant mothers and women with newborn babies. They are deprived of the recommended diet, vitamins, medications, proper care and assistance during and after pregnancy. Many female detainees who require health services are unable to receive timely and adequate health care contrary to Rule 23.1 of the UN Standard Minimum Rules for the Treatment of Prisoners and the 2006 European Prison Rules, Recommendation Rec(2006)2, Rule 34.3. Furthermore, while they have not been allowed to go to hospitals due to difficulties in the availability of guards to accompany them, even if allowed to go, they have been handcuffed in violation of the relevant conventions of the UN and the principles of the European Committee for the Prevention of Torture and Inhuman or Degrading Treatment or Punishment (CPT).[151]

It has also been reported that under the state of emergency, women were kept in detention for up to 30 days in dire conditions and were separated from their babies, while women with newborns were only allowed to breastfeed their infants once a day in some cases. As an example, Mahmut Tanal, a CHP deputy and member of the Human Rights Commission in the Turkish parliament, said in a speech in parliament that a mother with a 2-month-old baby in Ankara's Sincan Prison was abused because the baby was prevented by authorities from breastfeeding for 17 days, in violation of Turkish law. He also said a month-old baby in the same prison was taken to a clinic for vaccinations without the mother and that the mother claimed the wrong vaccinations were given to her baby.[152] Moreover, NGOs brought to the attention of the OHCHR at least six cases of women who were detained while they were visiting their spouses in prison. They were either detained together with their children or forcibly separated from them.[153]

Emin Çölaşan, a columnist for the *Sözcü* daily, cited a letter from a female judge under arrest in one of his columns, which said: "At this moment, we, 21 inmates, are staying in a ward. Some of us are sleeping on the ground. There is no room to take even one step inside the ward. We have only one bathroom and one shower. We are facing poor physical conditions. We had to paint the toilet and bathroom ourselves. Using the library is forbidden. Disinfection was carried out due to cockroaches. The people who carried out the disinfection were masked, but we were not allowed to leave the ward. Our five-month pregnant friend passed out. There is also a three-month-old baby with us. Nobody is able to sleep at night since the baby is always crying. I cannot bring my three-year-old son to be with me in prison owing to the dire conditions of the ward."[154]

Although deliberate, planned and systematic practices on the part of the Erdoğan government to prevent births among Gülen movement members have not been observed, threats that exceed the limit are sometimes made by pro-Erdoğan columnists. One of them is Hüseyin Adalan, a columnist for the pro-government *Milat* and *Yeni Söz* dailies. He tweeted that it is a religious obligation to kill all followers of the Gülen movement, even their babies. Adalan shared the terrible message on Twitter and stated that 'It is *wajib* [a religious obligation] to kill [even] those who show mercy to members of FETO. The honourable state needs to reveal its power. It is *wajib* to slaughter the babies of FETO members."[155] He was not subjected to any legal action.

4.5. De facto separation and forcible transfer of children

One of the acts that are called genocide in the Genocide Convention and the Rome Statute, the basis of the ICC, even if committed in isolation, is the forcible transfer of children of the targeted group to another group. Since children ensure the continuation of a group, this kind of transfer is the second form of biological genocide. The concept of a child must be interpreted as a person under the age of 18 (Art. 6/1-b of the TPC). Such transfers must be permanent with the intention of destroying the group's existence. Transferring children to another group tears children from their social ties and alienates them from the identity, language, traditions and moral values of the group.

While the Erdoğan regime does not systematically implement any practices with that intention, a large number of children have been devastated because of the arbitrary arrest of their mothers and fathers.[156] On the other hand, one of the most frequent threats to Gülen movement sympathisers from pro-Erdoğan groups has been transferring their children to orphanages under regime control. Moreover, this crime, a different form of genocide, has been carried out in another form by interfering in the growth, education and socialisation environment of the children.

The jailed mother who sent a letter to journalist Çölaşan regarding her children's situation wrote: "I have been a judge for 10 years. I am in the 67th day of my imprisonment. I was arrested with my husband, who was a prosecutor. He was sent to another prison in a different city. There is no possibility for us to communicate or meet. We do not have any income due to our dismissals. Our property and money in the bank were confiscated. Our eight-year-old son was handed over to his uncle. Due to the dire conditions in prison, I cannot bring our three-year-old son with me. I have just one request: For families who have a child in need of care, both mother and father should not be jailed pending trial since the unity of the family disintegrates. At least, one parent should be released by the court pending trial..."[157]

Though the Erdoğan regime has not committed the crime of genocide as described in the beginning of this section—transferring children from Gülen-affiliated families to other families—by closing 1,069 private schools, 848 private dormitories and cancelling the licences of more than 22,000 teachers and rendering them jobless, the regime intentionally and in a planned manner is aiming at the result stated in the wording, "children who are transferred to another group are torn from their social ties and alienated from the identity, language, traditions and moral values of group."

Most of the 140,000 children who were studying at the closed schools have been exposed to economic problems or psychological trauma caused by the dismissal and arrest of their mothers and fathers. In addition, the children have for the most part been obliged to continue their education at religious imam-hatip schools, subject to the political Islamist indoctrination of the Erdoğan regime, which was caused by removing them from their former schools, where they were educated based on universal human values up until that time. Therefore, it can be claimed that the crime of genocide has also occurred at a certain level.

CHAPTER V

TEN STAGES OF GENOCIDE
A CHECKLIST FOR THE GÜLEN MOVEMENT CASE

In light of what has been presented above, and taking as a point of reference Genocide Watch President Gregory H. Stanton's formulation of 'The Ten Stages of Genocide'[1] in which he builds his argument upon the basic assumption that genocide stages are *predictable* and therefore *preventable*, we can easily determine the stage of genocide the Erdoğan regime has reached against its primary target, the Gülen movement. Arguing that genocide is a process with non-linear stages that can be stopped by some preventive measures, Stanton underlines that these stages (namely classification, symbolisation, discrimination, dehumanisation, organisation, polarisation, preparation, persecution, extermination and denial) may occur simultaneously.

5.1. Classification: The Erdoğan regime profiled the Gülen movement for years before taking action

At the stage of classification, in addition to hate speech, deliberate and systematic policies are pursued to polarize people into 'us' and 'them.' This is a sophisticated stage that involves profiling, listing, labelling, hate speech and hate crimes perpetrated against the target group, all occurring at the same time.[2] Hate speech and hate crimes generally arise from discrimination, and discrimination by itself is an all-out attack on the core values that constitute human rights. First of all, predefining and predetermining the target group that is to be subjected to the hate speech and hate crimes and then genocide would be necessary.

Purging tens of thousands of public officials from their jobs because of their alleged membership in the Gülen movement in the very first days following the controversial coup attempt on July 15, 2016 and issuing arrest and detention warrants for tens of thousands of people indicated that profiling and listing activities had been conducted long before that date. Therefore, it is not reasonable to dismiss the contention that the military coup attempt was plotted by Erdoğan and his cronies to use as a pretext to purge all of the pre-profiled public servants, particularly those in the military.

Erdoğan's dictatorial regime worked to identify alleged members of the Gülen movement by using unlawfully set criteria. With some slight differences in various news reports, the general criteria that presented even the most legitimate and normal practices of daily life as elements of a crime are as follows:[3]

- Having a subscription or renewing a subscription to the *Zaman* or *Bugün* dailies or other newspapers that were affiliated with the Gülen movement following the December 17-25, 2013 graft and bribery scandal;
- Registering children at private schools and other educational institutions that were close to the Gülen movement;
- Having an account at or conducting transactions through or depositing money in private lender Bank Asya, which was affiliated with businesses close to the Gülen movement;
- Attending meetings or activities organised by institutions and civil society organisations close to the Gülen movement;
- Visiting Fethullah Gülen in the US state of Pennsylvania;
- Continuing membership in associations affiliated with the Turkish Confederation of Businessmen and Industrialists (TUSKON);
- Serving in the management of or working for companies, universities, private schools and nongovernmental organisations affiliated with the Gülen movement;
- Using the ByLock smart phone messaging application;
- Being named in the testimony of witnesses or secret witnesses;
- Making donations to the Kimse Yok Mu humanitarian aid organization;
- Possessing books written by Fethullah Gülen;
- Canceling a subscription to the Digiturk TV platform after its exclusion of TV stations close to the Gülen movement;
- Carrying $1 bills or keeping them at home or at the office; and
- Visiting websites close to the Gülen movement.

It is clear that these criteria, which are in no way designed to determine a crime or a criminal, were used solely for the purpose of ascertaining people's affinity to the Gülen movement. Once determined as being close to the movement, without having committed any crimes or engaging in any unlawful activities, people were labelled as members of a terrorist organisation and subjected to criminal procedures.

However, in order for an act to qualify as a crime, the legislature must pass a law that does not contravene the constitution or the international conventions signed by Turkey. Yet this principle has been widely violated in the post-coup-attempt period. In this period, so-called 'Fethullahist Terror Organisation [FETO] membership' emerged as the most widespread crime in state of emergency law. Legally speaking, however, it is not possible to call the organisation 'terrorist' since a definitive judgement in this regard is yet to be made. Even if a legal precedent were to be established, every single act attributed to individuals must stand as a crime. Under the state of emergency, this rule was thoroughly disregarded. The Venice Commission found that the state of emergency practices in Turkey went far beyond "the measures."[4]

Moreover, as we mentioned previously in section 4.3, hundreds of thousands of former and active military personnel were scrutinized, including their family members, according to an algorithm referred to as the 'FETO-meter' to dismiss thousands of alleged Gülen-linked officers from the army.[5]

Schools, private educational institutions, Bank Asya, unions, associations and media outlets run by businesspeople close to the Gülen movement have all been targets of the Erdoğan regime's rage. Many of the organisations were seized before the controversial military coup attempt.[6] The employees of those organisations, the students of the schools and other educational institutions and their families; people who had an account or conducted transactions at Bank Asya; members of certain associations, unions, business organisations; subscribers of the *Zaman* daily or other dailies and magazines; and people who made donations to a specific charity organization were all suddenly accused of 'membership in a terrorist organisation.' None of these actions can be defined as a crime according to the Turkish constitution or the TPC.

Now let us take a look at the 'criminal acts' that have been used as pretexts by the government for labelling, detaining and prosecuting ordinary citizens.

5.1.1. Subscriptions to the Zaman newspaper

With a daily circulation of nearly 1 million, the *Zaman* newspaper was once Turkey's most widely circulated news publication.[7] On March 4, 2016 the Erdoğan regime confiscated *Zaman* and appointed partisan trustees to run the newspaper in a brazen violation of the Turkish constitution, which explicitly bans the seizure or confiscation of publication/broadcasting organs.[8]

Furthermore, the daily was shut down by emergency decree-law no. 668, issued on July 27, 2016,[9] shortly after the failed coup of July 15, 2016. Arrest warrants were issued for its editors, columnists, reporters and executives, resulting in the eventual detention of most of them.[10]

The problem is that there was no court decision as to whether or not the *Zaman* daily had links to terrorism. Moreover, even if there were such a decision, it could not be implemented retroactively and could not make former employees, subscribers and readers of the newspaper 'terrorists.' Hundreds of thousands of people have been labelled and thousands were put under arrest simply for subscribing to a newspaper that was sold at almost all newsstands, was subscribed to and paid for by credit card and was published under the guarantee of the law, the constitution and international law.[11]

5.1.2. Being a client of private lender Bank Asya

Bank Asya was the largest Islamic lender in Turkey and one of its biggest private banks.[12] It was popular for its sponsorship of Turkish football's League 1.[13] The bank, with 210 branches, 5,000 employees and around 1.5 million clients, was founded upon formal approval and operated under the supervision of independent regulatory bodies. Today, however, around 700,000 of its account holders are reportedly under investigation.[14] If any transaction record with Bank Asya is discovered, it is accepted as sufficient evidence of membership in a terrorist organisation in an indictment, and a conviction is rendered accordingly.[15]

According to current banking rules in Turkey, deposits of less than TL 100,000 are under state guarantee. In line with this obligation, the TMSF repeatedly announced that it would compensate depositors who had less than TL 100,000 in their accounts if Bank Asya were to go bankrupt.[16] Indeed, such statements confirm that depositing money in Bank

Asya was not a crime. Some 1.2 million clients had less than TL 100,000 in deposits – the state-guaranteed amount – in Bank Asya. Together with clients holding larger deposits or those who had other kinds of transaction records with the bank, such as loans, money orders and wire transfers, the number of people who have made any kind of transaction with the bank, more than 1.5 million, were denounced as potential criminals by the Erdoğan regime.

5.1.3. Labour union membership

Labour unions are among those organisations that people close to the Gülen movement had founded according to the rules and regulations in effect at the time.[17] Aksiyon-İş was established in the education sector but soon expanded to include other business sectors and became a distinguished confederation of unions representing the labor force in various sectors.[18] Since its foundation, the union had attracted the criticism of Memur-Sen, a pro-government union that acts like the AKP's sister institution.[19] Eventually, by means of decree-law no. 667, 19 unions, federations and confederations were shut down, their assets were confiscated[20] and their management and members faced arrest and detention.[21]

Overnight, the state that had been put under the tyranny of Erdoğan after July 15, 2016 declared that legally operating unions, the establishment of which the state itself had allowed, were criminal organisations and that their members, whose membership it had encouraged by paying their union dues, were terrorists. Membership in one of the unions has become sufficient grounds for criminal conviction.[22] The Cihan-Sen Confederation, consisting of unions that were established by public employees, had 22,104 members in July 2016 according to government data. Today, all of these members have been charged with membership in a terrorist organisation. The fact that the registration data have been collected from the Official Gazette clearly exposes the absurd contradiction.[23]

5.1.4. Membership in professional organisations and TUSKON

These organisations formed the bulk of 2,000 foundations and associations that were shut down in the wake of July 15, 2016. The members of a law association that was close to the Gülen movement were particularly targeted in an effort to deny the fundamental right of access to legal counsel to tens of thousands of people who were detained or arrested on unwarranted charges in the course of the witch-hunt, which was accelerated following the attempted coup. At least 555 lawyers have been arrested since July 15, 2016, and 1,546 were under prosecution as of January 24, 2019. Moreover, 216 lawyers have been sentenced to a total of 1,361 years in prison.[24] Following lawyers, healthcare professionals were among the most widely targeted occupational groups.[25] Thousands of doctors across the country were accused of membership in health associations affiliated with the Gülen movement that provided free health care services to the needy in African countries and of cooperating with these associations.[26]

The Turkish Confederation of Businessmen and Industrialists (TUSKON) was an umbrella organisation for 211 business associations across Turkey and 150 associations operating in other countries. TUSKON was shut down just a few days after the attempted coup. Many of its members were arrested and its substantial assets were seized. Now treated as a terrorist organisation,[27] TUSKON was the most highly respected and most active businessmen's association in Turkey just a few years ago,[28] with then-Prime Minister Erdoğan and his ministers for economy and trade attending its general assembly meetings.[29]

5.1.5. Possession of books written by Fethullah Gülen

Following the July 15, 2016 coup attempt, one of the charges used for substantiating arrest warrants and indictments was possession of 'organisational documents.' The term refers, first of all, to books or other published materials by US-based Turkish Muslim scholar Fethullah Gülen and promotional publications distributed by the *Zaman* daily to its readers. With government decree-law no. 668, dated July 27, 2016, these publications, which needless to say cannot be claimed to have been promoting terrorism and/or violence, were declared 'banned publications' without any legal ruling.[30]

Even before the issuance of the decree-law as well as in its aftermath, books and magazines put out by publishing houses listed as shuttered in the decree-law were treated as criminal evidence and a basis for arrest warrants and indictments.[31] Fearing prosecution for owning such books[32] and magazines that had been perfectly legal in the past (since they bore the Ministry of Culture's seal of approval and were held in public library collections), many people were panicked and tried desperately to find a solution. Some people were caught with books that had not been criminal evidence before promulgation of the decree-law. Dozens of headlines appeared in the media proclaiming 'Lawyer arrested while burying books,'[33] 'Architect arrested while burning books,'[34] 'Teacher arrested while throwing books in the garbage,'[35] and the like. The police even collected some of these banned books from dumpsters and arrested people if their fingerprints were found on them.[36] Adding to the nonsense, even biology, chemistry, mathematics and physics textbooks and test books as well as other relevant teaching materials from publishing houses that were close to the Gülen movement were banned,[37] and hundreds of thousands of these textbooks were burned.[38]

5.1.6. Cancellation of Digiturk subscriptions

One of the most arbitrary and absurd reasons for arrest in the wake of the July 15 coup attempt was the cancellation of Digiturk subscriptions. Digiturk,[39] which had previously been a subsidiary of the Çukurova Media Group, was seized along with the Akşam daily and Show TV and brought under the control of the government.[40] Other media organs of the group were handed over to businessmen affiliated with the AKP. The Akşam and Güneş dailies were transferred to Ethem Sancak, who later became a member of the AKP's executive board.[41] Digiturk remained under the control of the TMSF for quite a long time. Then it was dubiously sold without a public tender to a Qatari business group with close ties to Erdoğan.[42]

Digiturk was one of the leading actors in silencing the media that opposed Erdoğan. Firstly, TV networks close to the Gülen movement and then Kurdish TV stations were targeted. On the one hand Erdoğan ordered public monopoly Turksat, which controls the satellite broadcasting sector, not to provide service to TV stations airing dissenting views, and on the other he requested that the Digiturk broadcasting platform exclude them from its list of channels. Erdoğan's "request," which was incompatible with freedom of the press and freedom of expression as well as commercial law, was immediately enforced. The civilian and political opposition protested this arbitrariness. In addition to the censored stations, advocacy groups and journalist associations made statements underlining the unlawfulness and arbitrariness of this action.[43] Campaigns to boycott Digiturk were initiated.[44]

This initiative was supported by the main opposition CHP's present and former leaders, Kemal Kılıçdaroğlu and Deniz Baykal, respectively.[45] Even such a purely civil, democratic and lawful boycott was considered evidence allegedly underpinning the terrorist organisation accusations levelled against the Gülen movement after July 15, 2016. Cancelling Digiturk subscriptions was one of the acts put under investigation. Information provided by Digiturk on the status of subscriptions was considered adequate to warrant arrest.[46]

With such unlawful and arbitrary punishment processes and practices, a significant portion of the society has been labelled by preposterous accusations and stigmatised as terrorists and traitors just because of their affinity or sympathy with the Gülen movement. Everything has been done to ensure their isolation by singling them out as an alien class among the community and turning them into objects of hatred by the people. At this point, it can be said that the act of classification is ongoing in the process of targeting the Gülen movement for genocide.

5.2. Symbolisation: Labeling the 'Gülen movement' as 'FETO'

Concurrent with the classification process, symbolisation has also been initiated. In effect, any label or epithet used in hate discourse functions, in one way or another, as symbolisation. As we have discussed in detail in section 2.3., the Erdoğan regime followed a progressive and systematic path of symbolisation and thus implemented a gradual roadmap to reverse the considerable respect accorded to the Gülen movement and its members across diverse segments of society.

Initiating his process of genocide against the Gülen movement by labelling it as 'the illegal organisation with a legal appearance'[47] Erdoğan, soon labelled the movement as the 'Parallel State Structure,' and eventually 'FETO – the Fethullahist Terror Organisation'[48] was coined as the final label. The Cabinet declaring the Gülen movement to be the 'FETO' terrorist organisation was also realised upon instructions from

Erdoğan.[49] For this label alone, when searched on Google, over 71 million results were found on February 9, 2019, as mentioned before.[50]

Although not compelling all Gülen movement members to bear or wear a special sign, colour or uniform (as Hitler did to the Jews), the Erdoğan regime has been planning a similar practice on a smaller scale since July 2017.[51] According to this plan, among all the prisoners and detainees in the country, only those alleged to be members of the Gülen movement are to be obliged to wear a distinctive uniform.[52]

The Erdoğan regime's gradual method of symbolising the movement, which was put into action after the eruption of the December 17/25, 2013 graft and bribery scandal, managed to encapsulate the once widely respected movement in the 'FETO' label and symbol. To stigmatise possibly the most peaceful movement in the world as 'FETO,' the regime aggressively employed national media outlets, an estimated 95 percent of which are under the direct control of the Erdoğan regime, according to a recent IPI report.[53] The incessant black propaganda continued day and night, and the movement has been made an object of hatred under the "FETO" label, which symbolises its members en masse as the enemy in the eyes and subconscious of the public.

5.3. Discrimination: How it was justified and widely implemented for the Gülen movement

All types of crimes perpetrated against individuals or groups and/or their property motivated by prejudice on the basis of race, religion, language, ethnicity, sexual orientation, gender, age, physical or mental disability or other grounds are called 'hate crimes.'[54] Just like hate speech and hate crime, genocide inherently arises from discrimination, and discrimination by itself is an all-out attack against the core values that constitute human rights. To comprehend the risks posed by discrimination-induced hate crimes, consider what happened in the 20th century: The slaughter of 6 million Jews in World War II and the mass killings of 250,000 people in the former Yugoslavia and 800,000 people in Rwanda in the first half of the 1990s as a result of war and ethnic cleansing are the most substantial instances of destruction caused by discrimination.

Today, discrimination continues apace in different forms. The UN Human Rights Committee, in its General Comment No.18 adopted at the Thirty-seventh Session of the Human Rights Committee held on November 10, 1989, produced the following definition of discrimination, referring to Article 1 of the International Convention on the Elimination of All Forms of Racial Discrimination and to Article 1 of the Convention on the Elimination of All Forms of Discrimination against Women: "... the Committee believes that the term 'discrimination' as used in the Covenant should be understood to imply any distinction, exclusion, restriction or preference which is based on any ground such as race, colour, sex, language, religion, political or other opinion, national or social origin, property, birth or other status, and which has the purpose or effect of nullifying or impairing the recognition, enjoyment or exercise by all persons, on an equal footing, of all rights and freedoms."[55]

The Council of Europe (CoE) does not differ from the Human Rights Committee in this definition. Indeed, Article 1 of Protocol No. 12 to the Convention for the Protection of Human Rights and Fundamental Freedoms gives a similarly broad definition of discrimination and regulates the general prohibition of discrimination.[56] As Amnesty International puts it, "Discrimination ... systematically denies certain people or groups their full human rights just because of who they are or what they believe. Torture too, in this regard, feeds off discrimination. All torture involves the dehumanisation of the victim, the severing of all bonds of human sympathy between the torturer and the tortured. This process of dehumanisation is made easier if the victim is from a despised social, political or ethnic group. Discrimination paves the way for torture by allowing the victim to be seen not as human but as an object, who can, therefore, be treated inhumanely."[57]

Conceptualised firstly in the US in 1969 as 'crimes of prejudice'[58] hate speech and hate crimes on the basis of discrimination started to take a larger place in the legislation of European countries. Notably in Germany, the description of 'prejudice crimes,' which have been accepted as 'politically motivated crimes' since 2001, has been used more broadly for crimes in this context.

Regardless of its definition as a crime in the penal codes of various countries, any statement or behavioural pattern that leads to the victim's impression that he/she is perceived with bias, prejudice or hatred is a statement or act based on hatred. The manifestations of this crime can be observed as physical assault, threat of assault, property damage, harassment, written or verbal misconduct, hateful and offensive graffiti, threatening attitudes, bullying and offensive jokes.

The Organisation of Security and Co-operation in Europe (OSCE) defines all crimes originating from prejudices, biases, stereotypes[59] and intolerance towards certain groups in the society as hate crimes. Such crimes, in effect, carry the potential of dividing societies and creating vicious circles of violence and vengeance.[60] Accordingly, a strong response should be given to such crimes. For that matter, the OSCE participating states have adopted a series of decisions to obligate fighting against such hate crimes.[61] The participating states committed to "Consider enacting or strengthening, where appropriate, legislation that prohibits discrimination based on, or incitement to hate crimes motivated by, race, colour, sex, language, religion, political or other opinion, national or social origin, property, birth or other status."[62]

Article 2 of the Universal Declaration of Human Rights;[63] the International Covenant on Civil and Political Rights; the second paragraph of Article II of Part II, which contains the general provisions of the International Covenant on Economic, Social and Cultural Rights;[64] Article 14 of the amended text of the European Convention on Human Rights (the Convention for the Protection of Human Rights and Fundamental Freedoms, Rome, 4.XI. 1950) by the 11th Protocol;[65] Protocol No 12 (Rome, 4.XI.2000) to the Convention for the Protection of Human Rights and Fundamental Freedoms (the European Convention on Human Rights);[66] Article E of Part V of the amended European Social Charter (Strasbourg, 3.V.1996);[67] and Article 21 of Chapter III (titled "Equality") of the European Union Declaration of Fundamental Rights[68] are the significant human rights texts codifying the measures against crimes of discrimination.

Members of the Gülen movement are subjected to discrimination at the hands of the state in Turkey, a country with a troubled record of discrimination and hate crimes. When it comes to members of the movement, even the most basic principles of law are ignored, and the requirements of the most fundamental human rights and freedoms are overlooked. Concepts such as equality before the law, equality of opportunity, freedom of enterprise, freedom of thought and expression, freedom of belief, freedom of the press, protections for those employed in public jobs and the right to enjoy public services have all become meaningless for Gülen movement members. Take the legal protections for those employed in the public sector, for instance. Although applicable to all civil service employees, when it comes to members of the Gülen movement, these protections are cynically ignored by the regime, citing 'infiltration,' 'taking over' or the 'parallel structure.'

As far as members of the Gülen movement are concerned, every act that can be performed by an ordinary person in the course of daily life can easily be turned into a crime and thus treated within the scope of the penal code. When exercised by Gülen movement members, the constitutional right to establish media outlets and thus to publish newspapers, magazines and books as well as engage in TV and radio broadcasting is simply put into the context of crimes of 'terrorism' and 'treason,' and thus scores of media outlets were shut down, 191 journalists were arrested and arrest warrants were issued for 167 more without proving even a hint of violence or illegality.[69] Subscription to these publications, reading those books, a subscription or cancelling a subscription to a satellite TV provider (Digiturk) are all considered a terrorist crimes requiring harsh penalties.

The natural rights of people in all developed, democratic countries with a powerful civil society, such as establishing organisations and engaging in activities within the limits of the law, are considered the activities of a terrorist organisation and punished as such in the case of Gülen movement members. The instances amply mentioned throughout this book, namely the lawlessness, the criminalisation of lawful activities and the false accusations, investigations and detentions launched against more than 500,000 people, the arrest of about 80,000 people, the seizure of companies and media institutions and confiscation of their assets, the denial of citizenship services within the country and abroad, the revocation of passports, the abductions in the country and abroad,[70] the arbitrary detentions and arrests, the tens of thousands of people put under judicial supervision by obliging them to regularly check in at police stations, travel bans, denial of the right to work in a job providing state insurance after dismissal from public service, cancellation of all licences and documents relating to one's profession and so many other arbitrary and unlawful practices that we have difficulty even counting them, are all included within the scope of discrimination committed by the state.

The Erdoğan regime can now easily perpetrate all types of discrimination through the successfully created social perception towards members of the Gülen movement and enjoys strong approval among the public opinion it has so skillfully manipulated.

5.4. Dehumanisation: Demonised by the state, media and society

Erdoğan's dictatorial regime had already managed to otherise, demonise and antagonise Gülen movement followers by means of a systematic hate speech campaign led personally by Erdoğan even before the aforementioned classification and symbolisation had been fully realised. The dehumanising discourse produced by Erdoğan and his team like a generator of hatred has been repeated millions of times through the media to the extent that members of the Gülen movement were denied their humanity. As explained in detail in section 3.2., they have become identified as animals, parasites, viruses, germs and diseases.

More than 240 examples of dehumanising hate speech, including "immoral," "spies," "rascals," "espionage organization," "gang," "self-seeking gang," "rotten," "coup perpetrator terrorists," "exploiters of religion," "agents of external forces," "enemies," "bloodthirsty murderers," "troublesome movement," "troublemakers," "malignant tumors," "traitors," "treacherous organisation," "hashashi," "thiefs," "treasonous gang," "treasonous organisation," "treasonous network," "treasonous system," "perverted non-Islamic sect," "blood-sucking leeches," "bloodsuckers," "blood lobby," "cancer cells," "shadowy headquarters," "shadowy center," "shadowy organisation," "subcontractors of shady businesses," "pawns of a shady conspiracy," "vicious center," "vicious structure," "characterless robots," "putrid," "conspirators," "global treasonous organisation," "Mossad collaborators," "dishonourable," "grave robbers," "parallel treason gang [PİÇ - the initials mean 'bastard']," "blackmail network," "blackmailers," "they are perverted," "sly," "sly viruses," "leeches," "sewage that taints the milk," "stooge," "terrorist organisation," "terrorists," "vampires," "Mankurt [unthinking slave]," and etc.,71 which are a prerequisite and a required condition for every potential genocide, have not only been able to make large segments of society enemies of the targeted Gülen movement but have also ensured that the voices of the Gülen movement in the face of the persecution are not heard by the masses, have functioned to intimidate members of the movement and finally have laid the groundwork for their total annihilation.

As is known in the crime of genocide, the perpetrator is engaged not only in the extermination of current members of the targeted groups but also in actions aiming at the eradication of future generations. The perpetrators usually plan and premeditate in detail the genocide they will commit. Genocides do not take place for reasons that are out of the perpetrators' control. To the contrary, perpetrators put several methods into practice to facilitate the act of genocide. They primarily use the tools of mass communication under their control against the target group, and they 'dehumanise' the victims, in other words, inculcate in people's minds the idea that they do not possess human traits.[72]

As the dehumanisation campaign waged by the dictatorial Erdoğan regime targeting the Gülen movement has been extensively explained above, the subject will not be reexamined below in detail. However, in addition to the said efforts, suffice to say that the endeavours to portray the Gülen movement and its members as non-Islamic in the eyes of supporters who have been radicalised by Erdoğan's regime and media also have an important place. Upon Erdoğan's order the Directorate of Religious Affairs (Diyanet), one of the most highly functional organs of the Erdoğan regime, declared the Gülen movement a 'non-Islamic perverted sect' (firak-ı dalle)[73] in the Extraordinary Religious Council and published in July 2017 a biased report that was full of slander and distortions. Such declarations had the same purpose: to portray the Gülen movement outside the fold of Islam.[74]

Expressions referring to Fethullah Gülen, such as a 'secret Christian' and even a 'covert cardinal,' 'working against Islam together with the Vatican,' 'betraying Islam through inter-religious dialogue activities' and 'undermining the essence of the religion,' were often employed in the Erdoğan regime's black propaganda campaign to disgrace the Gülen movement in the eyes of the public. Gülen's visit to Pope John Paul II at the Vatican in 1998,[75] his several meetings with Christian and Jewish spiritual leaders in Turkey[76] and the Gülen movement's significant interfaith dialogue activities, especially during the 1990s, constitute the main grounds for all these unjust accusations. In a speech during a visit to Pakistan Erdoğan expressed his discomfort with Gülen's activities in this area, saying: "He can easily establish inter-religious dialogue with the Vatican. How can dialogue be possible between religions? How can we suggest a dialogue between Islam and other religions? Is it possible? But this person dares to suggest that."[77]

As in hundreds of similar articles in the Erdoğan-controlled media, Tamer Korkmaz, a columnist for the Erdoğanist *Yeni Şafak* daily, claimed the Gülen movement had been working on behalf of the "Crusader-Zionist front" and wrote: "Jerusalem was surrounded by the Crusader army, on July 7, 1099 and captured on July 15, 1099! Gülen, the head of FETO, who wanted to occupy Turkey in the name of the Crusader-Zionist front states with the July 15, 2016 coup attempt, stated in a conversation in Pennsylvania on August 20, 2016 that 'The occupation of your country by the Crusader is not dangerous!'"[78]

Erdoğan's ultra-nationalist political ally, Nationalist Movement Party (MHP) leader Devlet Bahçeli, who supported Erdoğan in establishing a fascist regime, connected the Gülen movement to the Crusader armies and said: "Taking the order for the occupation of Turkey from the barbarians who commanded the last Crusade, FETO moved into action on the evening of July 15. They were disguised in the camouflage of honourable Turkish troops. They served the falsehood by the exploitation of religion, they were aligned with infidelity. They were inscribed in the national memory as the most despicable, the lowest of the low, the most nefarious of living creatures."[79]

A radical, pro-Erdoğan Islamist columnist for the *Yeni Akit* daily, Ali Karahasanoğlu, alleging that the Gülen movement was in cooperation with the Vatican, wrote: "If they cooperate with the Vatican and organise any kind of mischief to silence the voice of the oppressed and deter the unbowed Muslim stance that Turkey is trying to build... The pit you will fall into, you have already fallen to the lowest level... The treason you will attempt, you have already attempted... Don't you see that the infidels are with you arm-in-arm... Atheists are side-by-side with you... All the Muslims of Turkey are against you..."[80]

The defamatory allegation that Fethullah Gülen, a Muslim scholar, is a 'secret cardinal' is part of the black propaganda that Erdoğan's regime and media frequently refer to. More than 82,000 results were displayed on April 27, 2019 when 'Secret Cardinal Gülen / Gizli Kardinal Gülen' was searched on Google. This defamatory expression, previously

used only by neo-nationalist circles, has been used continuously by Erdoğan and his media in recent years. In fact, trying to demonize Gülen
by accusing him of being a "Christian" or "cardinal" exposes the view of
Christianity and Christians in the minds of the neo-nationalists and the
Erdoğan regime. The claim about Gülen being a 'secret cardinal' was first
alleged in an article titled "The Secret Cardinals of the Pope" written by
the late columnist Aytunç Altındal for the *Cumhuriyet* daily on March
18, 1996.[81]

Especially after the December 17/25, 2013 corruption and bribery
scandal, Erdoğan has tended to spout extremist neo-nationalist rhetoric
as well as political Islamist discourse. Thus, he has endeavoured to keep
alive the anti-Western and anti-Christian sentiment already existing in
the nationalist-conservative masses in the country. The Gülen movement
has been accused of 'betrayal of Islam' and 'undermining the essence of
the religion' by means of interfaith and intercultural activities in these
black propaganda campaigns, which have been carried out to discredit
the Gülen movement in the eyes of the masses, who have been indoctri-
nated with anti-Western and anti-Christian propaganda, also found in
many indictments drafted by Erdoğanist prosecutors.[82]

Erdoğan and his media attribute negative implications to Christianity and the Gülen movement and want to create a negative perception
of both in the eyes of the masses. It seems that Erdoğan and his media
have opted for a strategy to reinforce these negative perceptions by pre-
senting Christianity and the Gülen movement as being in cooperation
and connected to each other. By means of the intense propaganda of
Erdoğan and the media under his control, the hostility against interfaith
dialogue activities in Turkey has skyrocketed. A striking example happened during a national holiday on April 23, 2017 (National Sovereignty
and Children's Day), when a primary school student, who sat symbol-
ically for a day in a minister's chair, made this short statement: "Our
Alliance of Civilizations Initiative has reached a leading position in the
context of intercultural and interfaith dialogue." The student's teachers
were immediately suspended.[83] But even that was unable to appease the
rage of Erdoğan's media.[84]

At this point, the Erdoğan regime has completed the dehumanisation phase, which is a sine qua non of genocide, and the Gülen movement has been given an irreparable image in society.

5.5. Organisation: Turkish state aligned with jihadist and ultranationalist gangs and militias loyal to Erdoğan

As can be seen in the examples of the Holocaust, Bosnia and Herzegovina, Rwanda and Darfur, genocide is always organised. Special army units or militias are trained and armed for this purpose. Criminally inclined segments of the society such as violent individuals, mafias, gangs and terrorist groups are organised and armed. Check and balance mechanisms and judicial and parliamentary supervision are rendered non-functional, and a state apparatus is created in which power is centralised. Supervisory structures such as the media and civil society lose their vitality. As mentioned in section 2.3., the security apparatus, consisting of soldiers and policemen, is transformed into a partisan militia power.

The preparations for this transformation were accomplished while the Gülen movement was being dehumanised and antagonised. The Erdoğan regime dismissed tens of thousands of policemen[85] and arrested thousands of them,[86] closed police schools and academies and expelled all the cadets[87] and transformed the police force into an ideological party apparatus and partisan armed militia in official uniforms by opening four-month courses.[88] After the controversial coup attempt on July 15, 2016, the same – and even more – was carried out in the Turkish military, when thousands of officers including 169 generals were purged and incarcerated.[89] Military colleges and academies were shifted to a partisan line. Efforts were made to redesign the Turkish Army, an institution with a thousand-year tradition, according to political Islamist codes.[90]

While all these developments were taking place, as mentioned in section 2.3.3., militia forces such as SADAT and the Ottoman Hearths (Osmanlı Ocakları) were established, and a systematic, sinister relationship between the Erdoğan regime and radical Islamist terror organisations such as IBDA-C and Turkish Hizbullah were developed.[91] Organised crime networks and mafia structures, as in the case of Sedat Peker, have also been boosted under the support and protective shield of the Erdoğan regime and turned into strike forces that can be used to carry out any unlawful acts for the dictatorial regime.[92] In addition, it is commonly alleged that a significant number of international armed jihadist groups organised by the Erdoğan government to fight against the Assad regime in Syria have also been deployed in Turkey for the same nefarious purpose.[93] On the other hand, Erdoğan's affinity for jihadist elements in the Mideast, the Caucasus and the Balkans is no secret.

Genocides are carried out by armed militias usually organised by regimes, as in the case of the Janjaweed militia in Darfur.[94] Such types of informal structures, terrorist organisations and gangs, operating in a decentralised fashion, play a dominant role in genocides. Governments opt to achieve their aims through such structures in order to deny their responsibility for the crimes of genocide. SADAT, the Ottoman Hearths, Hizbullah and even the IHH bear a striking resemblance to these kinds of organisations. Erdoğan's personal interest in organised criminal gangs, mafia organisations and in particular armed jihadist organisations operating in Syria, ISIL and al-Qaeda-affiliated terrorist organisations in Turkey and the indulgent approach of the regime, paving the way for criminal and terrorist structures,[95] can be interpreted as preparing the enforcers of a potential genocide.

Moreover, Erdoğan's regime has radicalised supporters of the ruling AKP, especially the party's youth organisations, through an intense campaign of propaganda and provocation in the media he controls as well as by means of the education system, of which religious imam-hatip schools are now the main actors.[96] Erdoğan, who has turned the police and the army into partisan militia forces by filling them with ul-tranationalist and radical Islamist elements, can also easily transform his masses of supporters into the perpetrators of massacres, rapes, pogroms and genocide whenever he wants, through intensive and extensive agitation and manipulation.[97] He demonstrated on the night of July 15, 2016[98] how easily he could do that against the Gülen movement[99] and by some limited actions against the Kurds on October 6-7, 2014.[100]

·   Just as in all autocratic regimes, which are most successful in organising fanatical hate groups, Erdoğan's dictatorial regime has also prepared all kinds of organisational infrastructure with the potential and capacity to carry out a full-fledged genocide against any target group that he points out. It would not be merely prophetic to assert that the Gülen movement, for which all preparations for annihilation have been completed, will be the first among the possible social groups that he will target.

5.6. Polarisation: Erdoğan's continuously working magic formula

The Erdoğan regime has caused the disintegration and polarisation of the public for the sake of its own consolidation of power.[101] Erdoğan has accomplished this not only through his inner circle's hate-filled political narrative but also by means of constant and highly polarising propaganda, disseminated among the society through social and conventional media.[102] The problem is, while Erdoğan unites and consolidates his support base, consisting of about 50 percent of the population (if MHP supporters are included, the proportion approaches 60 percent) against the common enemy, or enemies (!), the rest of the population, namely the opposition groups,[103] which are considered an enemy by the former, maintain their religious, ethnic, sociological or ideological ground to the detriment of acting in solidarity and forming a common front.

By controlling the mass media, along with almost all information and news mediums, Erdoğan keeps the public under nonstop bombardment of one-sided information and takes every measure, such as censorship, blackouts, closure of media outlets, the arrest of journalists and intellectuals and the beating up by thugs of writers-columnists-cartoonists in order to prevent alternative information, ideas or viewpoints from reaching the general public. In this constructed terrorist atmosphere, the opposition, moderates and democrats have been silenced by threats and intimidation. As Hitler did at the outset, respected writers and thinkers Ali Bulaç, Şahin Alpay, Ahmet Altan, Mümtaz'er Türköne, Ali Ünal, Nazlı Ilıcak and Mustafa Ünal, among others, and numerous academics and human rights defenders and the like have been detained and put in prison. By doing so, the Erdoğan regime aimed at intimidating and terrorising other journalists, intellectuals and rights activists.[104] Small opposition groups were discouraged from taking to the streets and were intimidated by the political rallies of the ruling party, which were attended by hundreds of thousands of people.[105]

His former colleagues, particularly Bülent Arınç and Abdullah Gül, who presumably had the potential to act more moderately, were first disbanded and then defamed on social media and in the conventional media.[106] In addition, they were intimidated further by the arrest of their close relatives.[107] All those who could play the role of a bridge among the various segments of the society were forced to choose a side. If the side taken was not the 'desired' one, they were either sidelined or put in prison.[108] The entire social and political stage has been left exclusively to those militant extremists who polarise the public by hate speech and intimidate the opposition. Anybody who is courageous enough to voice the slightest criticism is immediately labelled as a 'betrayer,' 'traitor,' 'enemy' or 'terrorist' and is exposed as a person who deserves to be eliminated.[109]

Under such circumstances, the Gülen movement was not only erased from civil society, the bureaucracy, the education sector, the business world, the arts, the media and other spheres of public life but was also deprived of the ability to express itself in defending its rights and freedoms. Thus, the movement, as all of its assets had been confiscated, was set as a target by the Erdoğan regime. And the supporters of the regime have been prepared by propaganda, lies and slander to unwaveringly applaud possible acts of annihilation against members of the Gülen movement, or even worse, to take part in such heinous acts. As a result, another milestone on the path to genocide has successfully been passed by the Erdoğan regime.

It is due to this extreme polarisation that the majority of Turkish society has not displayed any reaction to the injustice, unlawfulness, arbitrariness and cruelty that the Erdoğan regime employs against the Gülen movement. Furthermore, the society endorses such policies. One should not doubt that those segments of society, groomed carefully to do so, are going to be willing perpetrators of a possible genocide.

5.7. Preparation: Final touches before a possible genocide

Up to the extermination phase of a possible genocide, all other stages are accepted as preparatory. However, what is meant by preparation is quite distinctive. At this stage, there is a multifaceted preparation for genocide. While the state apparatus is being restructured to carry out the genocide, foreign relations are also adjusted accordingly since genocide is not something that can easily be dared and carried out in a country that has intertwined economic and political relations with the international community. Likewise, genocide cannot take place in a country possessing a justice system that does not permit impunity, which also has a transparent bureaucracy and participatory decision-making processes, a pluralist and vibrant civil society, a pluralist media, strong opposition parties, a respected and powerful parliament where the opposition is freely represented and a public that is fully aware of its rights as citizens and courageous and willing enough to hold the authorities accountable.

As is clearly the case in Turkey, most of those features of a democratic state were destroyed in the early stages of the possible genocide. In light of the developments in recent years, it can easily be seen that Turkey's national regulations, laws and judicial mechanisms, which used to be for the most part compatible with universal standards, have been swept away one by one.[110] Legitimate, transparent and participatory decision-making processes have effectively been replaced by arbitrary mechanisms.[111] It can be said that today a pluralist civil society, effective parliament, strong opposition, pluralist media and conscientious and courageous public do not exist in Turkey.

The sociopolitical progress and democratic achievements that Turkey has made, particularly in the last three-four decades, have been shattered in the last few years.[112] As a result of the anti-democratic steps taken by the AKP government, Turkey's sociopolitical fabric and foreign relations have been tailored to accommodate one or more genocides. In this regard, while Turkey is becoming more and more introverted,[113] the principles of universal law have totally been abandoned and the country has been distanced from the domain of international law, of which it has formally become a part through dozens of international conventions, acts and agreements.

The Erdoğan regime, consequently, has destroyed step by step all the potential mechanisms of the international community and international organisations that have the potential to deter it from such madness. This overarching strategy of Erdoğan included his efforts to maintain bilateral relations with Western countries by blackmail and bluff; overreactions in the face of even low-volume warnings by Council of Europe (CoE), European Union (EU), European Parliament (EP) and UN mechanisms; and his incessant threats targeting Western institutions, by which Turkey is still considered an ally, by showing exaggerated eagerness for membership in organisations such as the Shanghai Cooperation Organisation (SCO) that have no concern about human rights or democracy.[114]

While those steps were being taken in international fora, members of the Gülen movement were blacklisted on the grounds of use of the By-Lock mobile phone messaging application,[115] membership in designated unions, subscriptions to certain newspapers and magazines and ownership of accounts at Bank Asya as well as appearing in the registers of certain private schools, on the list of Digiturk subscribers who cancelled their subscription and on MIT blacklists. Moreover, Erdoğan's efforts to build private armed groups and militias and train them should also be considered within the framework of this stage. The ever-increasing allegations regarding the AKP's arming of its loyal supporters prove the worries of a possible genocide to be right.[116]

The preparatory stage is also the stage in which the last moves are made in terms of indoctrinating the public by using the target group as a source of fear and hatred. This is when the masses are made to believe the argument, "If we do not terminate them, they will terminate us." That is why Erdoğan constantly likens the actions taken against alleged members of the Gülen movement to a "war of independence."[117] If December 17/25, 2013 is regarded as the start of the path towards a possible genocide, the initiatives taken against the Gülen movement since 2013 comprise everything that precedes a genocide.

Preparations for genocide, by their very nature, are engineered clandestinely. Therefore, this work has been able to cover only those that have appeared in the media. There is no verifiable information as to whether the blacklists have been drafted with the intention of using them as death lists or if any other extermination lists have been drawn up in light of these blacklists. Nevertheless, one can find numerous news items in the Erdoğan-controlled media[118] and in the official statements of Cabinet ministers[119] that assassinations of well-known members of the Gülen movement who are forced to live in exile might be carried out by special units established in the police force and MIT.[120] Moreover, pro-government journalists[121] and AKP deputies frequently call on MIT to kill journalists living in exile who worked for media outlets that were close to the Gülen movement[122] and even the families of alleged members of the movement.[123]

Erdoğan himself repeatedly stated he would never end his campaign against the movement, saying "[Gülen movement members] are paying with life imprisonment and aggravated life imprisonment. They will all pay. Of course, there are still some who escaped the sword [kılıç artığı]. They will also be caught sooner or later."[124] "Kılıç artığı" is a Turkish term that refers to enemies who somehow escaped execution by the sword during the Ottoman and early Republican eras, mainly used in reference to non-Muslims such as Armenians and people belonging to the Alevi sect of Islam in Turkey.

However, there is no current concrete information on any work carried out in establishing ghettos or concentration or extermination camps into which to gather members of the Gülen movement, aside from the sport complexes, stables and abandoned factories where hundreds of detainees were kept in inhumane conditions. However, it can easily be asserted that the prisons, where in some cases up to 40 detainees have been packed into wards meant for eight people, have been used for the above-mentioned purpose.[125] Also, life sentences and aggravated life sentences given to about 2,000 people, including numerous renowned journalists, for their alleged coup involvement and alleged affiliation with the Gülen movement can be seen as another method.[126]

5.8. Persecution: Time for 'Genocide Emergency Alert'

The persecution stage, the last stage of genocide before extermination according to Stanton, corresponds precisely to the calamitous process in which alleged members of the Gülen movement are aggrieved, extensively and systematically, under Erdoğan's dictatorial regime in Turkey. The victims were already detected, labelled, profiled and listed based on their affiliation with the Gülen movement.[127] They were dismissed from public jobs, their properties were seized, the schools and the institutions where they worked were closed down[128] and they were exposed to all forms of discrimination. They were also isolated completely from the society by preventing them from setting up their own businesses or finding jobs. The number of deaths that have continuously increased under torture and inhuman treatment has reached the level of a massacre.[129] Thus, we have come to the critical stage where genocide experts believe that a 'Genocide Emergency Alert' must be declared because at this stage the final technical and practical preparations are being made, disguised as 'ethnic cleansing' and 'purity.'[130]

Having been detailed in other chapters, in particular Chapter IV, the persecution of Gülen movement members will not be repeated here.

It will just be enlarged upon with a few reminders exemplifying the inhuman treatment inflicted on these people. For instance, women who are pregnant or who just gave birth and their unborn or newly born babies are also targets of unlawful and arbitrary operations. As a result of this treatment, in clear violations of the TPC and international conventions, the number of women detained and handcuffed to their hospital beds by police officers immediately after giving birth has exceeded 50, indicating how the Erdoğan regime knows no boundaries against members of the Gülen movement.[131]

Subsequent to torture videos proudly shared by security officers on social media and photos showing people drenched in blood published in the press, the real scale of torture was revealed only after prisoners started to see their families and lawyers. Hundreds of people were subjected to various kinds of torture, such as strappado, rape with bottles, drenching with ice water and beating, while many others are still being tortured in prisons.[132] Laid bare by Amnesty International, the details of mass torture after July 16, 2016, the torture centers and the names of the torturers were revealed in prisoner accounts. Yet, this is just the tip of the iceberg.[133]

Another method of oppression employed by the Erdoğan regime, which was not mentioned in the report, is 'sippenhaft.' Sippenhaft, a common method of punishment in all dictatorships, disregards the principle of individual criminal liability, which is a fundamental principle even in the most primitive of judicial systems.[134] The Erdoğan dictatorship has employed this inhumane, collective method of punishment -- guilt by association -- hundreds of times. They have detained and arrested innocent people in place of the subjects of arrest warrants in order to force those being sought to surrender. Moreover, the spouses, children or parents of arrestees have been detained[135] with the aim of convincing people to sign pre-drafted testimonies in lieu of their original testimonies.[136] One of most cruel practices has been placing children whose parents have been arrested in state custody instead of entrusting them to the care of their relatives. This has mainly been the case with the children of civil servants such as judges, prosecutors and teachers. In addition to this, some children, including infants, were left to starvation or death as there was no one to look after them.[137]

Although members of the Gülen movement have not been forced to wear distinguishing clothing, symbols or colours as in state-sanctioned genocides, such as that in Nazi Germany, preparations have been underway to force detained suspects to wear identical uniforms merely because of their affiliation with the Gülen movement.[138] Similarly while not being coerced to live in ghettos or concentration camps, after the seizure of more than 1,000 companies, 4,887 institutions and the properties of thousands of Gülen movement members, their living conditions have dramatically deteriorated and they have been condemned to dire poverty in cities.[139] People who wanted to move overseas due to their untenable situation at home were prevented from doing so by the confiscation of their passports or the refusal of their requests for a passport.[140] Furthermore according to a report by the Netherlands International Statistical Institution (ISI), Turkish consulates have refused to issue passports for dozens of newborn babies and provide consular services to hundreds of people and have seized the passports of scores of people who are allegedly affiliated with the Gülen movement.[141]

The number of suspicious deaths and suicides under detention has now reached 126,[142] amounting to the scale of a massacre. Erdoğan partisans have become accustomed to the idea of genocide or massacre through the terrifying coverage in the pro-regime media. The theory of genocide deems the killing of even one member of a group with the intention of destroying the entire target group to be genocide. Tens of people arrested merely on suspicion of membership in the Gülen movement have been killed under heavy torture since July 15, 2016.

Erdoğan's regime has today reached the last stage before extermination in its possible genocide of the Gülen movement. All the signs of such a genocide have already appeared. As it will be too late when the extermination starts, international organizations and powers must act immediately. In line with the maxim, "If genocide is predictable, it is also preventable," whatever is necessary must be done today to prevent the approaching genocide. Once collective killing, annihilation, raping, looting and exiling start, speaking about preventing genocide would be an oxymoron.[143]

5.9. Extermination: Not such a remote possibility

Since perpetrators do not see members of the target group as human beings, they prefer to call the process of destruction 'extermination' instead of killing. They argue that they 'cleanse' by 'extermination,' purifying society of disease, animals, viruses, microorganisms, cockroaches, leeches, enemies and traitors.

In the Convention on the Prevention and Punishment of the Crime of Genocide, "partial or total destruction" of the target group is a required condition for recognition of the crime of genocide. In other words, the convention does not require the entire destruction of the target group and finds partial extermination sufficient to define the crime committed as genocide.[144] As was previously explained, the condition for "partial destruction" is met even by the killing of a single person merely due to membership in the targeted group with the intent to annihilate the group. The purpose and the intent of the perpetrators are more important than the number of victims in accusing the perpetrators of committing genocide.

According to genocide experts, the perpetrator contemplates and plans in detail the genocide he will carry out. In other words, genocides have never happened for reasons beyond the control of the perpetrator. It is striking that the perpetrator employs several methods to make genocide possible. For example, mass media is used against the target group, and the dehumanisation of the victims is realized by convincing the masses that they do not possess human traits.[145] Campaigns to desensitise the masses to massacre will be important after the decimation: The phenomenon of 'desensitisation' argues that the crime which was committed is exaggerated and includes attempts to cover up the seriousness of the crime.[146]

The Erdoğan regime's process of genocide targeting the Gülen movement has finally arrived at the extermination stage. It could even be said that extermination has already begun in that dozens of people have been individually executed under severe torture simply because of their alleged affiliation with the Gülen movement.

However, the point that should not be forgotten here is that the legal definition and description of genocide is not just mass murder; it includes "serious physical or mental/psychological damage to the members of the target group." Severe damage to physical and psychological integrity includes injury, torture, rape, threat of death and sexual assault etc... It is even possible to add massive detentions and arrests in the form of arbitrary and collective punishment that triggers mental disorders such as stress, depression and anxiety, leading to the emotional disorder of millions of people.

In such a case, it is not necessary to wait for the Erdoğan regime to implement a general and widespread extermination of the Gülen movement to recognise that the crime of genocide has been committed. The process is at a very critical stage in which competent and responsible national and international authorities must act immediately to prevent a possible genocide, of which concrete evidence is obvious, with even the extermination phase put into action at an individual level. At the United Nations World Summit in 2005, all member states voted to adopt a historic resolution, 'Responsibility to Protect - R2P' unanimously, emphasizing the fact that in the event of the signing countries failing to raise the alarm, serious human tragedies that would be impossible to repair would occur. "... the idea that sovereign states have a responsibility to protect their own citizens from avoidable catastrophe – from mass murder and rape, from starvation – but that when they are unwilling or unable to do so, that responsibility must be borne by the broader community of states." [147]

It seems unlikely that the Turkish state represented by the Erdoğan dictatorship, which could be the perpetrator of a possible genocide, will protect its citizens against genocide, war crimes, ethnic cleansing or crimes against humanity in accordance with international law. Let alone providing protection and security, the state apparatus, represented by the Erdoğan regime in our example, even has the potential of becoming the main perpetrator of a possible genocide. As such, it is absolutely necessary for the international community to consider intervening and assuming responsibility without delay, exercising all the rights bestowed by international law, including sanctions and use of force, within the framework of the UN Charter.

5.10. Denial: Already underway

Genocide perpetrators deny committing this crime during the act and afterwards. However, persistence in denial despite concrete evidence is also regarded as the most reliable evidence that persecution and massacres aimed at genocide will continue. Moreover, denial tactics and methods are generic and predictable in genocide cases. Arguing that genocide or mass murder never happened; minimising the numbers by raising doubts about the massacre statistics; preventing access to archives and witnesses of genocide; intimidating or killing witnesses; destroying the evidence by burning corpses and archives; attacking those who pursue the facts and disgracing them; claiming deaths were caused by hunger, migration or disease; accusing the victims of massacres; accusing out-of-control forces of massacres; arguing that what happened was not a genocide but a civil war and reciprocal; arguing that the massacres consisted only of legitimate self-defence; and urging victims to forget the dark past for the sake of the future by saying that peace and reconciliation are more important than blaming people for genocide can be counted among them.[148]

There is no doubt that they will continue to deny the genocide in order to complete it, just as former Justice Minister Bekir Bozdağ,[149] the ruling AKP's deputy chairman Leyla Şahin Usta, who had sued Turkey at the ECtHR over a headscarf ban and who also serves on the Turkish parliament's Human Rights Commission,[150] and other officials have begun to deny the widespread and systematic torture, the severe persecution being carried out and the gross violations of human rights. The discourse of Erdoğan, his ministers and bureaucrats that no one was harmed during the state of emergency,[151] that there are no journalists in prison[152] and that Turkey is ahead of even Western countries in terms of democracy,[153] the rule of law[154] rights and freedoms,[155] despite the latest edition of The Economist Intelligence Unit's Democracy Index, which ranks Turkey 110th among 167 countries,[156] is directed toward this purpose. While the process of genocide targeting members of the Gülen movement continues at full speed towards ultimate extermination, the Erdoğan regime's efforts at denial have already begun.

CONCLUSION

The cruelty of man to his fellow man is as old as the history of mankind. Mass killings, ethnic cleansing, massacres and genocide, which are still present today, continue to cause irrecoverable injuries to the collective conscience. Although there were some intellectual efforts to prevent massacres and genocides after World War I, it was only in the 1990s that the international law against the crime of genocide produced some legal results and penalties.

What is more important than the prosecution and punishment of the crime of genocide is its prevention by early recognition of the process that leads to it. Experts working on genocide emphasize that some conceivable mechanisms could be established on the subject. Gregory H. Stanton, one of the prominent experts, describes the process that leads to genocide step-by-step as "predictable" and "preventable" and formulates it in 10 stages.

The scientific approach developed by Stanton has been integrated with M. Hasan Kakar's studies in this book and applied to widespread and systematic prosecutions aimed at members of the Gülen movement in Turkey. The clear picture that emerged as a result of this work reveals that all the crimes and acts contained in the academic descriptions and legal definition of the crime of genocide have already been carried out against members of the Gülen movement by the Erdoğan regime.

As of today, millions of people have been victimised by the campaign of persecution conducted against the Gülen movement, which the Erdoğan regime accelerated after the controversial military coup attempt of July 15, 2016. More than 160,000 people have been dismissed from their civil service jobs and deprived of their and their families' subsistence. Tens of thousands of people in the private sector have suffered a similar fate. Prevented from starting any kind of business or working elsewhere, they were sentenced to poverty and 'civil death.'

More than 500,000 people of all ages, because of their daily activities, which are non-criminal acts according to law and a part of the natural routine of life, have been taken into custody and many more have been subjected to investigation. At least 77,000 people have been incarcerated. In excess of 110 (some claim about 200) media outlets have been closed. As of April 26, 2019, at least 191 journalists and media workers were still in Turkish jails. Thousands of journalists have been left unemployed, and hundreds of them have been forced into exile.

Thousands of educational establishments, including 15 private universities, were closed and their assets were confiscated. Some of them were transferred to Erdoğan supporters. In the process more than 23,000 academics have been directly affected, with the remaining universities transformed into mentally and spiritually hollow shells. Even according to official figures, over TL 55 billion worth of assets and more than 1,000 major companies were usurped. All the assets of thousands of people, 4,887 institutions and foundations were confiscated.

Widespread and systematic torture has re-emerged in Turkey. Thousands of people were severely tortured either in police custody or in prison. At least 126 people died under suspicious circumstances or committed suicide because of psychological and physical pressure or torture. At least 26 sympathisers of the Gülen movement were kidnapped in broad daylight through mafia-like tactics, and the whereabouts of most of them are still unknown.

The increasingly widespread witch-hunt, systematic and widespread hate speech, ongoing persecution and massacre of Gülen movement members have made conditions in Turkey ripe for a deliberate, planned and systematic genocide. The Erdoğan regime, along with millions of volunteers, has made significant progress in the direction of 'uprooting' the Gülen movement and has made its actual implementation only a matter of time. All the indicators in Turkey show that the risk of a systematic genocide increases with every passing day and that this risk has become a clear and present danger. This alarming situation requires the urgent mobilisation of all international institutions and powers that bear responsibility for the prevention of such a process before graver consequences are realized.

Despite some serious limitations, the most comprehensive and functional definition and description of genocide to date is found in Article 2 of the Convention on the Prevention and Punishment of the Crime of Genocide. As has been mentioned in this book, the realisation of just one of the five acts clearly described in the article is legally sufficient for the act to be defined as a crime of genocide. Genocide, described as systematic "acts committed with intent to destroy, in whole or in part, a national, ethnical, racial or religious group," is in the process of full implementation in Turkey against the Gülen movement, which constitutes a sui generis religious/social group with its distinguishing characteristics.

Kakar, known for his work on genocide, argued that there are some preconditions for the possibility of implementation of genocide in a country. In Chapter 2, it was discussed in detail to what extent the historical, sociological, cultural and conjectural conditions in Turkey meet these preconditions. In this context, the crimes committed against Armenians, Assyrians, Alevis, with events of poll/property tax, September 6-7 incidents in 1955, massacres in Maraş, Çorum, Sivas, and ongoing brutality against the Kurdish people show the violent track record of the political culture in Turkey and the value it gives to human life.

Along with his own dangerous radical Islamist ideology, Erdoğan has allied with the ultranationalist and neo-nationalist/Eurasianist ideologies. Thus, he has established a sui generis despotic regime based on these three pillars and succeeded in creating an agitated society nourished by racial, sociological and religious superiority discourse and ideology. As was explained in section 2.2, the extremist statements of these three lines of thought do find a place for themselves in Erdoğan's rhetoric, which sees people of a different race, civilisation, religious understanding and even different ideologies and lifestyles as enemies who are inferior and need to be destroyed. Radical Islamism, ultranationalism and Eurasianist neo-nationalism, which constitute the poisonous pillars of this fascist regime and constantly glorify death and killing, are known for radicalising their socio-cultural hinterland with a sharper discourse. The current regime in Turkey consists of a combination of these three ideologies, each one of which is already dangerous in the extreme and today sees members of the Gülen movement as the main target to be destroyed.

The fact that the more powerful majority group viewing potential victims of genocide as less than human or inhuman is interpreted as a significant sign of a process leading to a possible genocide. This is also the area in which Erdoğan's regime is most effective. As was explained in detail in section 3.2, the Erdoğan regime has not hesitated to use hate speech targeting the Gülen movement members to depict them as inhuman thousands of times. According to the findings, the number of expressions comprising obvious hate speech against the Gülen movement voiced by Erdoğan alone exceeds 240. Due to Erdoğan and his regime's systematic and widespread dehumanising hate speech, members of the Gülen movement have become objects of hatred who have been otherised, demonised and hostilised to the point that they are not perceived as human beings by the society any more. Even the extreme discourse such as 'malignant tumors,' 'We will sterilize them,' 'blood-sucking leeches,' 'cancer cells,' 'sneaky viruses,' 'dirty water mixed with milk,' 'vampires' and such that Erdoğan and his media use repeatedly about Gülen movement members are real alarm bells that require the international community to be vigilant against a coming genocide.

On the other hand, just as during the rule of the Committee of Union and Progress Party in the Ottoman era under which crimes against Armenians took place and Hitler's Germany, where the Holocaust was perpetrated, Erdoğan has succeeded in becoming uncontrollable by concentrating all power in his hands and has fulfilled a requirement for genocide infrastructure by establishing a centralised autocracy in Turkey. As explained in section 2.3, Erdoğan, who has rendered the system of checks and balances totally non-functional despite the fact that it is a vital requirement of both the Turkish constitution and binding international conventions, has abolished the constitutional democracy and has been able by usurping power to exercise arbitrary authority not delegated by law. Using this power without any limitations, he has succeeded in converting the state apparatus into an illegal maverick, the judiciary into a sledgehammer to crush his opponents and the police force in total and military forces to a great extent into his partisan militia.

Among the conditions of the process leading to genocide mentioned by Kakar, Erdoğan has also created armed militia elements consisting of malicious domestic and foreign individuals and criminals. As explained in section 2.3.3, Erdoğan, who has developed an ominous relationship with jihadist and radical Islamist terror groups in the Middle East, has integrated extensions of radical Islamist terror organisations such as Hezbollah, IBDA-C, al-Qaeda and ISIL into his regime. Additionally, by creating or collaborating with mafia structures as in the case of Sedat Peker, by creating militia forces as happened with SADAT and the Ottoman Hearths, and by arming his party members, Erdoğan has fulfilled another prerequisite of a possible genocide. A striking example was as recent as May 2020 as this book was getting its final editorial touch-ups when Sevda Noyan, a writer and a staunch supporter of Er-doğan said on a TV show that she had a list of her neighbors and would "take" those who are anti-government or pro-coup in the event of a new coup attempt in the country." Noyan said she and her family were unpre-pared on July 15, 2016, but now they are "equipped":

> "My family can take [kill] approximately 50 people. We are equipped very well in this respect, both materially and spiritually. We stand by our leader [Erdoğan], and let me say, we won't allow him to be taken down. Those [aiming for a coup] should watch out. There are three to five such people in our apartment complex. My list is ready."[1]

The acts listed in paragraph 5 of Article 2 of the Convention on the Prevention and Punishment of the Crime of Genocide are aimed at harming the group targeted for genocide, physically and/or psychologi-cally. As was discussed throughout Chapter IV, when studied carefully it can be seen that the Erdoğan regime's preparations for annihilating the Gülen movement seem to fit very well with the definition of genocide in Article 2 of the convention. However, it is worth noting that not all of the acts in this definition are necessary to define the crime committed as genocide. From the wording of Article 2, "genocide means any of the following acts [listed in the article] committed with intent to destroy, in whole or in part, a national, ethnical, racial or religious group."

As mentioned in section 4.1, the "killing of members of the group" in the genocide definition coincides with the ninth stage of Stanton's "stages of extermination" in the genocide process, which is divided into 10 stages. All stages before this stage are only preparations for the "ex-termination stage" in terms of the process of genocide. It is obvious that eight out of these 10 stages have been carried out in the process of geno-cide directed against the Gülen movement in Turkey. While the acts cor-responding to each stage of the Gülen movement's annihilation contin-ue, according to the findings of this research, it is just a matter of time to systematise the ninth stage, which has already begun with more than 126 suspicious deaths, in police detention and in prison. The timing of the implementation of a full-fledged genocide, for which the practical and socio-psychological infrastructure has already been prepared, is left to the convenience of the Erdoğan regime, which has repeatedly declared its intention on the issue.

Moreover, as stated in section 4.2, the predominant part of the persecution carried out by the Erdoğan regime against members of the Gülen movement corresponds to the act of "causing serious bodily or mental harm to members of the group" in Article 2 of the convention. Members of the Gülen movement have been subjected all the acts that are considered criminal acts under this article including torture, rape, death threats and sexual assault solely because of their affiliation with the targeted group. As can easily be seen, the acts in this category that fall within the scope of the genocide offence are generally qualified as torture and ill treatment. One of the important elements of Lemkin's definition of genocide is the destruction of individual security, freedom, health, honour and even life of the members of the group that is targeted for genocide.

In this respect, the Erdoğan regime's threats of torture, maltreatment, sexual assault, rape, wounding and killing, which target tens of thousands of people who have been taken into custody and deprived of their freedom by arrest solely for their affiliation with the Gülen movement, fall under the scope of the crime of genocide because there is no particular reason for targeting individuals who have been persecuted as part of the mass or collective punishment of Gülen movement members in Turkey. The victims have been targeted by the Erdoğan regime simply because of their affiliation with the Gülen movement. The members of the Gülen movement have been branded, labeled and subjected to treatment such as detention, arrest, seizure of property, torture, ill treatment and many other similar persecutions not because they are guilty of a crime but due to their ties to the movement.

As was analysed in detail in section 4.3, it can be seen that members of the Gülen movement have been completely exposed to "deliberately inflicting on the group conditions of life calculated to bring about its physical destruction in whole or in part." All actions cited in Lemkin's definition of genocide, such as "a coordinated plan of different actions aiming at the destruction of essential foundations of the life of national groups, with the aim of annihilating the groups themselves. The objectives of such a plan would be disintegration of the political and social institutions, of culture, language, national feelings, religion, and the economic existence of national groups, and the destruction of the personal security, liberty, health, dignity, and even the lives of the individuals belonging to such groups," have targeted members of the Gülen movement. As has been stated in this book, deliberate and systematic crimes committed by the Erdoğan dictatorship such as mass detentions and arrests, the confiscation of the properties of thousands of companies and individuals, media organisations and institutions, mass dismissals of people from public service, condemning them to a "civil death," correspond to the acts that constitute the offence of genocide according to the genocide definition.

As was underlined in section 4.4, although the Erdoğan dictatorship has not been acting deliberately in planning to systematically prevent births among members of the Gülen movement, some threats exceed the heinous practice of "imposing measures intended to prevent births within the group." For instance, the idea of the murder of infants is sometimes expressed by pro-Erdoğan journalists and his political cronies. As a matter of fact, about 17,000 (this figure is an estimate) women, most of them married, have been imprisoned solely for their affiliation with the Gülen movement. For the time being, except for the arbitrary, long-term imprisonment of one or both spouses, there are no deliberate, planned or systematic practices of the Erdoğan dictatorship against couples affiliated with Gülen movement in the form of 'biological genocide' such as the segregation of men and women, sterilization or forced birth control.

One of the acts that are treated as genocide in the convention even in the case of being executed in isolation is "forcibly transferring children of the group to another group." Children who are transferred to another group are torn from their social ties and alienated from their identity. As was explained in section 4.5, although the Erdoğan regime has not systematically practiced this type of activity, many children have been left behind due to the arbitrary arrest of both of their parents. Furthermore, one of the most frequent threats to Gülen movement members by pro-Erdoğan groups is taking children from their parents and giving them to orphanages controlled by the regime.

On the other hand, this crime of genocide is carried out in a different form by interfering with children's upbringing, education and socialisation environments. Aiming to produce a result similar to ripping children from their social ties and alienating them from their identity and the language, traditions and moral values of the group, the Erdoğan regime closed more than 1,060 private schools and 848 private student dormitories, cancelled the professional licences of more than 22,000 teachers, thus rendering them unable to teach, in a deliberate and planned manner. More than 140,000 students have been torn from their schools, where they used to be educated according to a set of universal humanitarian values, and have been forced to continue to study where the political Islamist indoctrination of the Erdoğan regime prevails. Therefore, it can be asserted that even this part of the genocide crime has also been committed at a certain level.

This book's findings reveal that the process of genocide conducted by the Erdoğan regime targeting Gülen movement members has completed the stages of classification, symbolisation, discrimination, dehumanisation, organisation, polarisation, preparation and persecution as detailed by Stanton. It has also been observed that the stage of extermination has already begun on an individual level. The stage of denial has also started as in the cases of people who were killed under torture because of their Gülen movement affiliation.

All five conditions Kakar lists in the process of a possible genocide in a country are present in today's Turkey under the rule of Erdoğan's regime, which is involved in a genocidal process targeting the Gülen movement. Moreover, at least two of the five acts described in Article 2 of the Convention on the Prevention and Punishment of the Crime of Genocide as the crime of genocide have been realized completely and three of them have been realized to various extents. If we elaborate on the Erdoğan regime's systematic, widespread and deliberate persecution of members of the Gülen movement, we can easily assert that it constitutes the crime of "Killing members of the group," as is mentioned in Article 2 of the Convention, *partially*; the crime of "Causing serious bodily or mental harm to members of the group," *completely*; the crime of "Deliberately inflicting on the group conditions of life calculated to bring about its physical destruction in whole or in part," *completely*; the crime of "Imposing measures intended to prevent births within the group," *partially*; and the crime of "Forcibly transferring children of the group to another group," *partially*.

It is important to remember that Article 2 of the convention begins with the words, "In the present Convention, genocide means any of the following acts committed with intent to destroy, in whole or in part, a national, ethnical, racial or religious group, as such: ..." and the fact that just one of these acts is legally sufficient to define the crime as genocide.

Although the act of extermination of the Gülen movement, or their 'uprooting' in the words of Erdoğan, meet the academic and legal definition and description of genocide in many ways, the most destructive dimension of genocide, physical extermination, has not yet been implemented systematically or widely. However, as mentioned earlier, the realisation of extermination is just a matter of time. Elihu D. Richter, Yael Stein, Alex Bernea and Marc Sherman pointed out in their article that "The lessons of the Holocaust empower us to address prevention of hate language and incitement when they are used against all populations, without waiting for the consequences."

Therefore, genocide experts like Stanton have underlined that genocides should be 'preventable' if they are 'predictable' and also mention the impossibility of preventing genocide after the start of killing, rape, deportations and looting. These scholars conclude from the evidence of several 20th-century genocides that "hate speech and incitement together increase risks for genocide, especially when they come from the top down in authoritarian regimes with their environments of coercion, direction and instruction." While acknowledging that "not all incitement leads to genocide," and that "genocide may occur without evidence of incitement," they advise that when political leaders "use explicit pseudo-medical and epidemiologic metaphors, such as microbes, filth, cancer, typhoid, and rats, to dehumanize victim groups, it is prudent to regard such language as an urgent warning sign of imminent genocide ...."

In the case of the Erdoğan dictatorship and its target group, namely the Gülen movement, unfortunately this stage has long passed. Erdoğan, by targeting the Gülen movement, has for quite some time been using hundreds of hate expressions including viruses, cancers, tumors, vampires, leeches, bloodsuckers, bacteria and microbes. However, since the systematic and widespread physical extermination process through killings has not begun, it is not yet too late.

Therefore, a genocide openly targeting members of the Gülen movement is not only predictable, it can also easily be seen with its concrete signs and thus should be preventable. In order to prevent this genocide, for which all the socio-political and psychological conditions and infrastructure have been prepared, with the stage of execution just inches away, it is vital that all international humanitarian institutions and political organisations such as the UN, EU, Council of Europe (CoE), OSCE and even NATO act without delay, develop measures within the framework of "Responsibility to Protect" (R2P) and implement them immediately.

NOTES

Introduction

1. *Investigation of December 17, 2013*: An investigation that was initiated as a result of a number of allegations in September 2012 and February 2013 and which became public knowledge on December 17, 2013, when public prosecutor Celal Kara's detention instructions and the relevant courts' search warrants were executed by the Istanbul Police Department's Organized Crime and Financial Crimes Units, on charges of "bribery, misconduct, bid rigging and smuggling" leveled against some businessmen, bureaucrats, a bank director and four Cabinet ministers and their children. *Investigation of December 25, 2013*: An investigation launched by prosecutor Muammer Akkaş into 96 people including Bilal Erdoğan, the son of Recep Tayyip Erdoğan, on charges of "establishing and leading an organization with the purpose of committing crimes, bid rigging and bribery." Over time, both investigations were covered up, and the members of the judiciary and the police force who took part in these investigations were first dismissed and then imprisoned.

2. M. Hassan Kakar, *Afghanistan: The Soviet Invasion and the Afghan Response, 1979–1982*, University of California Press, 1995.

Chapter 1

1. "The aggressor ... retaliates by the most frightful cruelties. As his armies advance, whole districts are being exterminated. Scores of thousands, literally scores of thousands, of executions in cold blood are being perpetrated by the German police troops upon the Russian patriots who defend their native soil. Since the Mongol invasions of Europe in the sixteenth century, there has never been methodical, merciless butchery on such a scale, or approaching such a scale. And this is but the beginning. Famine and pestilence have yet to follow in the bloody ruts of Hitler's tanks. We are in the presence of a crime without a name." See *Prime Minister Winston Churchill's Broadcast To The World About The Meeting With President Roosevelt*, (British Library of Information, August 24, 1941), accessed April 26, 2019, https://www.ibiblio.org/pha/timeline/410824awp.html

2. In 1933 Raphael Lemkin, a Polish law professor who narrowly escaped the Nazi occupation of his homeland, made a presentation to the League of Nations conference on international criminal law in Madrid for which he prepared an essay on the act of barbarism as a crime against international law. Lemkin's paper urges international leaders at the Madrid conference to enact laws against the destruction of religious or ethnic groups, which he called crimes of "vandalism" and "acts of barbarism." If only his proposal to the Madrid conference in 1933 had been accepted, Lemkin believed, a number of problems raised by the Nuremberg trials would have been prevented. See Dan Eshet, *Totally Unofficial: Raphael Lemkin and the Genocide Convention*, Facing History and Ourselves Foundation, p. 30, accessed April 26, 2019, https://www.facinghistory.org/sites/default/files/publications/raphael_lemkin.pdf

3. The term "genocide" was conceived in 1944 by Raphael Lemkin in his book ti-
    tled *Axis Rule in Occupied Europe: Laws of Occupation, Analysis of Government,
    Proposals for Redress.*

4. Lemkin 1944, p.79.

5. Murat Belge, "Genocide Kavramı," *Radikal*, 2 Haziran 1998.

6. "Soykırımın Zaman Çizelgesi," https://www.ushmm.org/wlc/tr/article.php?-
    ModuleId=10007095

7. See *United Nations General Assembly Resolution 96 (I), The Crime of Genocide,*
    (1946), https://www.armenian-genocide.org/Affirmation.227/current_catego-
    ry.6/affirmation_detail.html

8. Göktepeoğlu 2014, pp. 797-838.

9. This debate is still continuing among genocide experts. For a critical review see
    Kuper 1994, pp. 31-46.

10. Chigas 2000, pp. 245-265.

11. Horowitz 1977, pp. 35-37.

12. Rummel 1997, pp. I-VIII.

13. Başak 2003, p. 71.

14. 'Justifier l'injustifiable: Ideologie en Genocide in Rwanda (1994)," *Vrede en
    Veiligheid*, vol. 33, no.3 (2004), pp. 342-58.

15. Chalk and Jonassohn 1990, pp. 94-113.

16. Thornton 1997, pp. 310-315.

17. Kuper, "Theoretical Issues Relating to Genocide: Uses and Abuses," p. 34.

18. Morsink 1999, pp.1009-60.

19. Read 2006.

20. See *Convention on the Prevention and Punishment of the Crime of Genocide.*
    Adopted by the General Assembly of the United Nations on 9 December 1948,
    https://treaties.un.org/doc/publication/unts/volume%2078/volume-78-i-
    1021-english.pdf

21. Aktan 2001, p. 7.

22. See *Convention on the Prevention and Punishment of the Crime of Genocide,*
    https://www.ohchr.org/en/professionalinterest/pages/crimeofgenocide.aspx

23. See "Rome Statute," https://www.icc-cpi.int/nr/rdonlyres/ea9aef-
    f7-5752-4f84-be94-0a655eb30e16/0/rome_statute_english.pdf

24. For a Turkish translation of the convention, see Doğru 1998, p. 250.

25. Turhan 2004.

26. It is worthwhile for the reader to have a translation of the relevant provisions of
    the code before proceeding to a fuller analysis.

    ARTICLE 76 (1) The commission of any of the following acts, against any
    member of an ethnical, racial or religious group with the intent to destroy such
    group, in whole or in part, through the execution of a plan shall constitute
    Genocide:

    a) Intentional killing;

    b) Causing serious harm to the physical or mental integrity of persons;

c) Forcing the group to live under conditions calculated to bring about its physical destruction in whole or in part;

d) Imposing measures intended to prevent births within the group;

e) Forcibly transferring children of the group to another group.

(2) Any person who commits genocide shall be sentenced to a penalty of aggravated life imprisonment. However, where the offences of intentional killing and intentional injury are committed in the course of genocide, there shall be an actual aggregation of such offences, in accordance with the number of victims identified.

(3) Legal entities shall also be subject to security measures in respect of these offences.

(4) There shall be no prescriptive period in respect of these offences. See Koca 2010a, pp. 255-283, 2010. http://istanbul.dergipark.gov.tr/download/article-file/7042

27. Çolak 2005, p. 207.

28. Akün 2004, p. 66.

29. Başak 2003, p. 95.

30. Olgun Değirmenci, "Uluslararası Ceza Mahkemelerinin Kararları Işığında Mukayeseli Hukukta ve Türk Hukukunda Soykırım Suçu (TCK md. 76)," *Türkiye Barolar Birliği Dergisi*, vol. 70, 2007, p. 77.

31. Koca 2010b, p. 22.

32. Tezcan et al 2006, p. 49.

33. Arıcan 2009, p. 113.

34. Akün 2008, pp. 24-37.

35. Koca 2010b, p. 22.

36. Tezcan et al 2006, pp.73-74.

37. Kocaoğlu 2010, p. 145.

38. Jorgensen 2001, p. 290; Obote-Odora 2002, p. 397; Önok 2003, p. 151.

39. Dadrian 1974, pp.123-136.

40. Levin 1973, p. 20.

41. Tezcan et al 2006, p. 49.

42. Ibid.

43. Ibid.

44. Turhan 2005, p. 4.

45. Alpkaya 2002, p. 125.

Chapter 2

1. Ayşe Hür, "1937-1938'de Dersim'de neler oldu?" *Taraf*, December 16, 2008, accessed on April 26, 2019, http://web.archive.org/web/20140116082822/http://www.taraf.com.tr/ayse-hur/makale-1937-1938de-dersimde-neler-oldu.htm

2. "8 things to know about the mass killings of Armenians 100 years ago," *CNN*, April 27, 2015, accessed on April 26, 2019, http://edition.cnn.com/2015/04/23/

world/armenian-mass-killings/index.html ; Sophia Jones, "100 Years Ago, 1.5 Million Christian Armenians Were Systematically Killed. Today, It's Still Not A 'Genocide,'" *The WorldPost*, March 23, 2015, accessed on April 26, 2019, http://web.archive.org/web/20160312203433/http://www.huffingtonpost. com/2015/04/23/armenian-genocide-controversy_n_7121008.html

3. Walker 1980, pp. 200-203.

4. Jennifer Hyde, "Polish Jew gave his life defining, fighting genocide," *CNN*, December 10, 2008, (accessed on April 26, 2019), http://edition.cnn.com/2008/ WORLD/europe/11/13/sbm.lemkin.profile/

5. Caleb Lauer, "For Turkey, denying an Armenian genocide is a question of identity,"*Al Jazeera*, April 24, 2015, (accessed on April 26, 2019), http://web.archive. org/web/20160225100349/http://america.aljazeera.com/articles/2015/4/24/ for-turks-acknowledging-an-armenian-genocide-undermines-national-identity.html

6. Monroe 2012, p. 13.

7. "Assyrian Genocide," (accessed on April 26, 2019), http://combatgenocide. org/?page_id=1058

8. Yonan 1999.

9. "İsveç de Ermeni tasarısını kabul etti, elçi çağrıldı," *Zaman*, March 12, 2010.

10. Ayşe Hür, "1937-1938'de Dersim'de neler oldu?" *Taraf*, 16 Aralık 2008.

11. Ibid.

12. Uzay Bulut, "Remembering the victims of the Kurdish massacre of 1937," *Jerusalem Post*, May 24, 2015, (accessed on April 26, 2019), https://www. jpost.com/Opinion/Remembering-the-victims-of-the-Kurdish-massacre-of-1937-403963

13. "Dersim 1937-1938: Ayıptır, zulümdür, cinayettir," *NTV Tarih*, December 2009, p. 59.

14. Aygun 2009.

15. Yaşar Taşkın Koç, "Dersim'deki çocuk katliamının belgeleri," *Sabah*, January 11, 2012, (accessed on April 26, 2019), http://www.sabah.com.tr/gundem/2012/01/11/dersimdeki-cocuk-katliaminin-belgeleri?paging=4

16. Barutçu 1977, p. 263.

17. In the summer of 1942, Istanbul newspapers published news articles and cartoons linking non-Muslims in general and Jews in particular with acts of theft, black marketeering, profiteering and excess profit. Some of the headlines compiled by Rıfat N. Bali: "That'll teach profiteers. A Jew in Izmir was sentenced to five years in prison." (*Tasvir-i Efkar*, July 1, 1942); "The scam of the three Jews. They sold harmful (deleterious) substances instead of lemon salt." (*Tasvir-i Efkar*, July 4, 1942); "Merchants hiding goods, two Jewish business owners were transferred to the national protection court." (*Cumhuriyet*, August 14, 1942), "The issue of 150 wagon-loads of paper. It is necessary to prevent the game of the Jews who brought the paper from Romania." (*Tasvir-i Efkar*, August 21, 1942), "Thanks to stockpiling carbide, a Jewish merchant made more than 40,000 lira in additional profit." (*Tasvir-i Efkar*, August 28, 1942); "Two cunning Jewish children! They were stealing money from the collection box when pins were distributed for the benefit of the Air Association." (*Cumhuriyet*, August 31, 1942), "Two Jewish hoarders were caught," (Tasvir-i

Efkar, September 9, 1942); "A Jew who sells heroin." (*Tasvir-i Efkar*, September 15, 1942); "The known Jewish merchant, Simon Brod, was arrested yesterday." (*Tasvir-i Efkar*, September 18, 1942); "Jewish chicanery. As if skimming excess profit was not enough, he offered a bribe." (*Tasvir-i Efkar*, September 20, 1942); "The rise in rents was caused by the Jews." (*Tasvir-i Efkar*, October 8, 1942); "A covetous Jew was selling colored water instead of grape juice." (*Tasvir-i Efkar*, October 20, 1942).

18. Ökte 1951, p. 47.

19. Hamit Erdem, "Varlık Vergisi (1942) ya da Sermayenin Türklere Nakli," *Avlaremoz*, November 12, 2016, (accessed on April 26, 2019), http://www.avlaremoz.com/2016/11/12/varlik-vergisi-1942-ya-da-sermayenin-turklere-nakli-hamit-erdem/

20. See Resmi Gazete's (Official Gazette) issue on November 11, 1942, (accessed on April 26, 2019), http://www.resmigazete.gov.tr/arsiv/5255.pdf

21. Ayşe Hür, "1942 Varlık Vergisi Kanunu," *Radikal*, May 10, 2015, (accessed on April 26, 2019), http://www.radikal.com.tr/yazarlar/ayse-hur/1942-varlik-vergisi-kanunu-1353243/

22. Erdem 2016.

23. Hür 2015.

24. Erdem 2016.

25. Ayhan Aktar, *Varlık Vergisi ve Türkleştirme Politikaları*, (İletişim Yayınları, Istanbul, 2014), p. 204.

26. Erdem 2016.

27. Hür 2015.

28. Ibid.

29. Erdem 2016.

30. For more information see Şule Toktaş, "1950'ler İstanbul'unda Gayrimüslim Azınlıklar ve Nüfus Hareketleri: Türkiye Yahudi Cemaati (Non-Muslim Minorities and Population Movements in Istanbul of the 1950s: Turkey's Jewish Community)", *Eski İstanbullular Yeni İstanbullular (Old Istanbullites New Istanbullites)*, (İstanbul: Osmanlı Bankası Arşiv ve Araştırma Merkezi, 2009) pp: 97-114, (accessed on April 26, 2019) http://www.academia.edu/5028256/1950_ler_Istanbul_unda_Gayrim%C3%BCslim_Az%C4%B1nl%C4%B1klar_ve_N%C3%BCfus_Hareketleri_T%C3%BCrkiye_Yahudi_Cemaati_Non-Muslim_Minorities_and_Population_Movements_in_Istanbul_of_the_1950s_Turkey_s_Jewish_Community_

31. Dilek Güven, "6–7 Eylül Olayları (1)," *Radikal*, November 4, 2005, (accessed on April 26, 2019) http://web.archive.org/web/20051104130033/http://www.radikal.com.tr/haber.php?haberno=163380

32. de Zayas 2007, pp. 137-154.

33. Güven, "6–7 Eylül Olayları (1)," *Radikal*, November 4, 2005.

34. Ibid.

35. Can Dündar, "Gizlenen örgütün başındaki adam: Sabri Yirmibeşoğlu - Özel Harp'çının tırmanış öyküsü," *Milliyet*, January 8, 2006, (accessed on April 26, 2019), http://web.archive.org/web/20090212231436/http://candundar.com.tr:80/index.php?Did=2667

36. Ayşe Hür, "6-7 Eylül 1955 yağması ve 1964 sürgünleri," *Radikal*, September 6, 2015, (accessed on April 26, 2019), http://www.radikal.com.tr/yazarlar/ayse-hur/6-7-eylul-1955-yagmasi-ve-1964-surgunleri-1428641/

37. Koçoğlu 2001, pp. 25-31.

38. Hür, "6-7 Eylül 1955 yağması ve 1964 sürgünleri," *Radikal*, September 6, 2015.

39. Güven, "6–7 Eylül Olayları (1)," *Radikal*, 4 Kasım 2005.

40. Hür, "6-7 Eylül 1955 yağması ve 1964 sürgünleri," *Radikal*, September 6, 2015.

41. Koçoğlu, *Azınlık Gençleri Anlatıyor*, pp. 25-31.

42. Hür, "6-7 Eylül 1955 yağması ve 1964 sürgünleri," *Radikal*, September 6, 2015.

43. Abdullah Kılıç, Ayça Örer, "Maraş katliamı MİT planıydı," *Radikal*, Deçember 22, 2011, (accessed on April 26, 2019), http://www.radikal.com.tr/turkiye/maras-katliami-mit-planiydi-1073231/

44. Ibid.

45. "12 Eylül Belgeleri," *Belgenet*, July 31, 2012, (accessed on June 17, 2017), http://www.belgenet.com/12eylul/12syonetim.html

46. Bülent Şık, "Sevgili dayım," *Radikal*, July 22, 2012, (accessed on April 26, 2019) http://www.radikal.com.tr/radikal2/sevgili-dayim-1095040/

47. Kılıç, Örer, "Maraş katliamı MİT planıydı," *Radikal*, December 22, 2011.

48. "Çorum Olayları," *Ana Britannica*, 1987, Vol. 6, p. 517.

49. *Meclis Araştırması Komisyonu Raporu*, (TBMM, November 2012), (accessed on April 26, 2019), https://www.tbmm.gov.tr/sirasayi/donem24/yil01/ss376_Cilt2.pdf

50. "MİT'in 'Kanlı 1 Mayıs' belgeleri mahkemede," *Radikal*, January 15, 2013, (accessed on April 26, 2019), http://www.radikal.com.tr/turkiye/mitin-kanli-1-mayis-belgeleri-mahkemede-1117029/?ismobile=1

51. Sivas katliamı kurbanlarını anıyoruz," *CNN Türk*, July 2, 2009, (accessed on April 26, 2019), http://web.archive.org/web/20160304132235/http://www.cnnturk.com/2009/turkiye/07/02/sivas.katliami.kurbanlarini.aniyoruz/533360.0/index.html

52. Celal Başlangıç, "Bir Mazlum'un 'feryad-ı isyan'ı," *Radikal*, April 29, 2002, (accessed on April 26, 2019), http://web.archive.org/web/20151208063042/http://www.radikal.com.tr/haber.php?haberno=36176&tarih=29/04/2002

53. "Bu kadarını biz bile beklemiyorduk," *Sabah*, July 2, 2011, (accessed on April 26, 2019), http://www.sabah.com.tr/gundem/2011/07/02/bu-kadarini-biz-bile-beklemiyorduk

54. "Osmanlı'dan devralınan sorun," *Al-Jazeera Türk*, December 26, 2013, (accessed on April 26, 2019), http://www.aljazeera.com.tr/dosya/osmanli-dan-devralinan-sorun

55. Nurcan Baysal, "Bu Kürtler ne istiyor!" *T24*, March 17, 2015, (accessed on April 26, 2019), http://t24.com.tr/yazarlar/nurcan-baysal/bu-kurtler-ne-istiyor,11488

56. Vahap Coşkun, "Demokratikleşme ve PKK," *Taraf*, September 25, 2012, (accessed on April 26, 2019), http://www.duzceyerelhaber.com/haber-detay.asp?id=8330#.WXoYsYiGPIU

57. Hasan Aksay, "Erdoğan'ın savaşına hayır! Barış Süreci korunmalıdır!" *T24*, July

26, 2015, (accessed on April 26, 2019), http://t24.com.tr/yazarlar/hakan-aksay/erdoganin-savasina-hayir-baris-sureci-korunmalidir,12387

58. Koray Düzgören, "Kürt şehirleri yıkılıp yeniden yapılacak," *Artı Gerçek*, April 12, 2017, (accessed on April 26, 2019), https://www.artigercek.com/kurt-sehirleri-yikilip-yeniden-yapilacak

59. *Report on the human rights situation in South-East Turkey (July 2015 to December 2016)*, Office of the United Nations High Commissioner for Human Rights, February 2017, (accessed on April 26, 2019), http://www.ohchr.org/Documents/Countries/TR/OHCHR_South-East_TurkeyReport_10March2017.pdf

60. "BM raporu: Güneydoğu'daki operasyonlarda 2 bin kişi öldü, ciddi insan hakları ihlalleri var," *Sputnik*, March 10, 2017, (accessed on April 26, 2019), https://tr.sputniknews.com/haberler/201703101027576310-bm-raporu-guneydogu-daki-operasyonlarda-iki-bin-kisi-oldu-ciddi--insan-haklari-var/

61. *Report on the human rights situation in South-East Turkey (July 2015 to December 2016)*, Office of the United Nations High Commissioner for Human Rights, February 2017.

62. Rüştü Demirkaya, "BM raporu: Kürt illerinde kıyamet yaşandı," *Artı Gerçek*, March 10, 2017, (accessed on April 26, 2019), https://www.artigercek.com/bm-raporu-kurt-illerinde-kiyamet-yasandi/

63. Ibid.

64. Ibid.

65. Bülent Keneş, "15 Temmuz'dan 15 Temmuz'a: Erdoğan Soykırımın Hangi Aşamasında?" *TR7/24*, July 15, 2017, (accessed on April 26, 2019), http://www.tr724.com/15-temmuzdan-15-temmuza-erdogan-soykirimin-hangi-asamasinda/

66. "Gömlek kavgası," *Milliyet*, May 22, 2003, (accessed on April 26, 2019), http://www.milliyet.com.tr/2003/05/22/siyaset/asiy.html

67. Zeynep Gürcanlı, "Türkiye AB ilişkileri nereden nereye," *Sözcü*, November 24, 2016, (accessed on April 26, 2019), http://www.sozcu.com.tr/2016/gundem/turkiye-ab-iliskileri-nereden-nereye-1527681/

68. "Getting off the train," *The Economist*, February 4, 2016, (accessed on April 26, 2019), https://www.economist.com/news/special-report/21689877-mr-erdogans-commitment-democracy-seems-be-fading-getting-train

69. Bülent Keneş, "İslamî olana karşı siyasal İslamcılık," *Zaman*, Januart 26, 2014, (accessed on April 26, 2019), http://bulentkenes.blogspot.se/2014/01/islami-o-lana-kars-siyasal-islamclk.html

70. Fehim Taştekin, "Maliki ile flört, Kürtlerle dans," *Al-Monitor*, November 14, 2013, (accessed on April 26, 2019), http://fares.al-monitor.com/pulse/tr/originals/2013/11/turkey-juggles-baghdad-erbil.html

71. İrfan Aktan, "Barış Süreci Kronolojisi," *Hafıza Merkezi*, July 19, 2015, (accessed on April 26, 2019), http://hakikatadalethafiza.org/baris-sureci-kronolojisi/

72. "Eurasianism" in Turkey espouses an anti-Western approach in foreign policy and ultranationalist sentiment in domestic politics. The Eurasianists demand Turkey to leave NATO and end its bid for EU membership. They contend that Turkey's interests lie outside the Western world and that Turkey should join the Russia- and China-led "anti-imperialist" camp. According to leading Eurasianist, Doğu Perinçek, who is chairman of the Vatan Party "The Turkish na-

tionalists would befriend China and Russia in order to get rid of the US." See: Colakoğlu, Selçuk. (2019). "The Rise of Eurasianism in Turkish Foreign Policy: Can Turkey Change its pro-Western Orientation?" MEI, April 16, 2019, https://www.mei.edu/publications/rise-eurasianism-turkish-foreign-policy-can-turkey-change-its-pro-western-orientation (accessed on June 4, 2020).

73. "Ufuk Uras: Erdoğan, Ergenekon'la uzlaştı," T24, December 21, 2015, (accessed on April 26, 2019), http://t24.com.tr/haber/uruk-uras-erdogan-ergenekon-la-uzlasti,321258

74. Serpil İlgün, "İslamcı, milliyetçi, ulusalcı koalisyonu bir arada tutan tek faktör; Kürt düşmanlığı," Evrensel, Demokrat Haber, 7 Kasım 2016, (accessed on April 26, 2019), http://www.demokrathaber.org/siyaset/islamci-milliyetci-ulusalci-koalisyonu-bir-arada-tutan-tek-faktor-kurt-dusmanligi-h75054.html

75. Kemal Can, "Referandumda AKP MHP İttifakı: Yeni İktidarın İlk Seçimi," Özgürüz, January 30, 2017, (accessed on June 18, 2017), https://ozguruz.org/tr/2017/01/30/referandumda-akp-mhp-ittifakiyeni-iktidarin-ilk-secimikemal-can/

76. Oray Eğin, "Ulusalcı-İslamcı ittifakı," HaberTürk, July 5, 2017, (accessed on April 26, 2019), http://www.haberturk.com/yazarlar/oray-egin/1552512-ulusalci-islamci-ittifaki#

77. For example, in his book Din Yok, Milliyet Var (There Is No Religion but Nationality) Ruseni Barkur writes: "Our holy book is our nationalism, which protects knowledge, continues existence, embraces happiness, raises Turkishness and unifies all Turks." See "Atatürk ve Din Yok, Milliyet Var Safsatası," Belgelerle Gerçek Tarih, (accessed on April 26, 2019), http://belgelerlegercektarih.com/2013/04/02/ataturk-ve-din-yok-milliyet-var-safsatasi/ ; Mahmut Esat Bozkurt, who was a former minister of justice, said during a discussion in parliament on the 1921 Constitution: "They (non-Muslims) have resigned from the citizenship of this country, and they have resigned by betraying us, by pulling a gun on us. They are ungrateful children of Ottoman history and have no more rights in this country." He said in 1930: "My opinion and belief are that the land itself is Turkish. Those who are not native Turks have a right in the Turkish homeland. That is, to be a servant, to be a slave." See Nazım Alpman, "Türklerin üstünlüğü," Internet Haber, December 12, 2004, (accessed on June 19, 2017), http://www.internethaber.com/turklerin-ustunlugu-1213446y.htm ; CHP deputy Sukru Kaya also spoke about the supremacy of Turkishness in a speech he made in parliament during the inclusion of the "six arrows" in the constitution and said: "The history of humanity began with the Turks. If the Turks hadn't existed, perhaps history would not exist and certainly civilisation could not have started. ... How dark history would be without the Turks. You can predict and imagine how miserable and disheveled humankind would be without the Turks. A history without the Turks would be dark and chaotic."

78. Ertuğrul Kürkçü, "İsmet Paşa'nın izinde," Radikal, February 3, 2013, (accessed on April 26, 2019), http://www.radikal.com.tr/radikal2/ismet-pasanin-izinde-1120169/

79. Alpman, "Türklerin üstünlüğü," Internet Haber, December 12, 2004.

80. Kürşat Tecel, "Türk Sorunu Ve Türk Milletinin Kürt Milliyetinden Üstünlüğü!" KTÜ Vakfı, January 28, 2013, (accessed on June 19, 2017), http://www.ktuvakfi.org.tr/turk-milletinin-ustunlugu/

81. Murat Belge, "Irkçılığın son şekli," Radikal, June 26, 2007, (accessed on April

26, 2019), http://www.radikal.com.tr/yazarlar/murat-belge/irkciligin-son-sek-li-818067/#

82. Hasan Cemal, "İslamofobi... İslamofaşizm...," *T24*, October 25, 2016, (accessed on April 26, 2019), http://t24.com.tr/yazarlar/hasan-cemal/islamofobi-isla-mofasizm,15730

83. Tayfun Atay, "İslamofobi, İslamofaşizm ve AKP," *Radikal*, January 9, 2015, (accessed on April 26, 2019), http://www.radikal.com.tr/yazarlar/tayfun-atay/isla-mofobi-islamofasizm-ve-akp-1268295/

84. Perihan Mağden, "Kemalist Nasyonalistler ile İslamofaşist Erdoğanistler el ele yıkıma gidiyor," *Nokta*, June 20, 2016, (accessed on April 26, 2019), http://t24.com.tr/haber/perihan-magden-kemalist-nasyonalistler-ile-islamofasist-erdo-ganistler-el-ele-yikima-gidiyor,346120

85. See Yaşlı 2017.

86. According to Yaşlı, an authoritarian regime that is liberal in economy, is natio-nalist-religious in the social domain and feeds from nationalism and Islam in the political domain is envisioned. It is an actual party-state regime in which the power is concentrated in one center, namely in the (Erdoğan's presidenti-al) palace and in the hands of one man endowed with absolute authority and power; the separation of powers does not exist; and the executive branch cont-rols both the legislative and judiciary bodies. Yaşlı says the hegemony of the Islamist regime flavoured with nationalism is being built over religion, and the consent of the masses to this new order is assured by religious rhetoric. See "Can Semercioğlu, "Fatih Yaşlı: Şeriat anayasada yazmayacak ama fiilen uy-gulanacak," *Diken*, October October 28, (accessed on April 26, 2019), http://www.diken.com.tr/akademisyen-fatih-yasli-seriat-anayasada-yazmayacak-a-ma-fiilen-uygulanacak/

87. See Toni Johnson and Mohammed Aly Sergie, "Islam: Governing Under Sha-ria," *CFR*, July 25, 2014, (accessed on April 26, 2019), https://www.cfr.org/back-grounder/islam-governing-under-sharia

88. See Jay D. Fluckiger, *Surviving the Taliban: The Incredible, True Story of a Con-vert*, (Cedar Fort. Inc., December 2011).

89. See Joby Warrick, *Black Flags: The Rise of ISIS*, (Doubleday, 2015).

90. Bülent Keneş, "Instrumentalization of Islam: Hayrettin Karaman's Role in Erdogan's Despotism," *Politurco*, May 30, 2018, (accessed on April 26, 2019) http://www.politurco.com/instrumentalization-of-islam-hayrettin-kara-mans-role-in-erdogans-despotism.html

91. Cuma hutbesinde skandal!" *Sözcü*, April 16, 2014, (accessed on April 26, 2019), http://www.sozcu.com.tr/2014/gundem/cuma-hutbesinde-rusvet-san-suru-487747/

92. "AKP ayet ve hadisleri sansürledi," *Gerçek Gündem*, June 20, 2014, (accessed on June 18, 2017) http://www.gercekgundem.com/akp-ayet-ve-hadisleri-san-surledi-51758h.htm ; See also "AKP ayet ve hadisleri sansürledi," *Sözcü*, June 20, 2014, https://www.sozcu.com.tr/2014/gundem/akp-ayet-ve-hadisleri-san-surledi-537477/. "Diyanet İşleri Başkanlığı 'rüşvet' hutbesi," *Odatv*, December 21, 2014, (accessed on April 26, 2019) http://odatv.com/diyanet-2004te-hazir-ladigi-bu-hutbeyi-bugun-okutabilir-mi-2112141200.html

93. Hayrettin Karaman, "Yolsuzluk başka hırsızlık başkadır," *Yeni Şafak*, Decem-ber 21, 2013, (accessed on April 26, 2019), http://www.yenisafak.com/yazarlar/

hayrettinkaraman/yolsuzluk-baka-h%C4%B1rs%C4%B1zl%C4%B1k-baka-d%C4%B1r-2006694

94. Hayrettin Karaman, "Türkiye'nin dostları ve düşmanları," *Yeni Şafak*, December 19, 2013, (accessed on April 26, 2019), http://www.yenisafak.com/yazarlar/hayrettinkaraman/turkiyenin-dostlar%C4%B1-ve-dumanlar%C4%B1-44456

95. Samuel Osborne, "Salman Rushdie: Iranian state media renew *fatwa* on Satanic Verses author with $600,000 bounty," *The Independent*, February 21, 2016, (accessed on April 26, 2019), http://www.independent.co.uk/news/people/salman-rushdie-iranian-state-media-renew-fatwa-on-satanic-verses-author-with-600000-bounty-a6887141.html

96. "Bangladeshi Atheist Activist Taslima Nasrin Relocates to America After Death Threats," *Huffington Post*, April 6, 2015, (accessed on April 26, 2019), http://www.huffingtonpost.com/2015/06/04/-taslima-nasrin-relocates-to-us_n_7507716.html

97. Karaman, "Türkiye'nin dostları ve düşmanları," *Yeni Şafak*, December 19, 2013.

98. "15 Temmuz hukuksuzluğunun bilançosu: Asker, polis, hakim, savcı, vali, kaymakam 50 bin tutuklu, 155 bin gözaltı," *TR7/24*, May 28, 2017, (accessed on April 26, 2019), http://www.tr724.com/15-temmuz-hukuksuzlugunun-bilancosu-50-bin-tutuklu-155-bin-gozalti/

99. "Interior minister says more than 500,000 detained, 30,000 arrested over Gülen links," *Turkish Minute*, February 14, 2019, (accessed on April 26, 2019), https://www.turkishminute.com/2019/02/14/interior-minister-says-more-than-500000-detained-30000-arrested-over-gulen-links/

100. "Turkish gov't jailed 77,081 people since controversial coup attempt in 2016 over alleged links to Gülen movement," *Stockholm Center for Freedom (SCF)*, April 18, 2018, (accessed on April 26, 2019), https://stockholmcf.org/turkish-govt-jailed-77081-people-since-controversial-coup-attempt-in-2016-over-alleged-links-to-gulen-movement/ ; "Turkey orders detention of 222 people over Gülen links in one day," Turkish Minute, January 15, 2019, (accessed on April 26, 2019), https://www.turkishminute.com/2019/01/15/turkey-orders-detention-of-222-people-over-gulen-links-in-one-day/

101. William Armstong, "What a TV Series Tells Us About Erdogan's Turkey," *New York Times*, May 14, 2017, (accessed on April 26, 2019), https://www.nytimes.com/2017/05/14/opinion/erdogan-tv-show-turkey.html?mcubz=0 ; 'Kurgu tarih' dizileri, Erdoğan'ın Türkiyesi hakkında ne söylüyor?", *Gazete Karınca*, 16 Mayıs 2017, (accessed on April 26, 2019), http://gazetekarinca.com/2017/05/kurgu-tarih-dizileri-erdoganin-turkiyesi-hakkinda-ne-soyluyor-william-armstrong/ . For how this TV series is perceived in the Muslim world, see "Dangerous Delusions – Ertugrul Mania," by Pervez Hoodbhoy in *Dawn*, June 6, 2020 (accessed June 8, 2020), https://www.dawn.com/news/1561638?fbclid=IwAR1PXBnNJhyipw3uN89Bz-OU5b8TTEcQ11h8VKDZPCK0G5hQLE-FYg201ws8.

102. Örmeci 2014.

103. According to Volkan, the relation between leaders and societies, under normal circumstances, is like a main road with two-way traffic. During these times, the administrative traffic continues amid the conscience and reactions of the society in the face of political developments and the efforts of leaders to manipulate the society. However, in times of crisis, the traffic becomes one-way. This means

that the leaders enter a one-way relationship with the society. See Vamık Volkan, "Some Psychoanalytical Views on Narcissistic Leaders and Their Roles in Large-group Processes," (accessed on June 20, 2017), http://www.vamikvolkan.com/Some-Psychoanalytic-Views-On-Narcissistic-Leaders-and-Their-Roles-in-Large-group-Processes.php.

104. Örmeci 2014.

105. Post 1991.

106. Cengiz Alğan, "15 Temmuz ve Yenikapı: Toplumsal özgüven inşasında zirve," *Serbestiyet,* August 21, 2016, (accessed on April 26, 2019), http://serbestiyet.com/yazarlar/cengiz-algan/15-temmuz-ve-yenikapi-toplumsal-ozguven-insasinda-zirve-712758

107. "Erdoğan'dan 'önemli' açıklama: Tankın egzoz borusunun içine tıkamak suretiyle..." *Sendika.org,* July 16, 2017, (accessed on April 26, 2019), http://sendika63.org/2017/07/erdogandan-onemli-aciklama-tankin-egzoz-borusunun-icine-tikamak-suretiyle-433687/

108. "Erdoğan halka özgüven yükledi," *Milat,* January 9, 2017, (accessed on June 20, 2017), http://m.milatgazetesi.com/erdogan-halka-ozguven-yukledi-haber-102681

109. Armstong, "What a TV Series Tells Us About Erdogan's Turkey," *New York Times,* May 14, 2017.

110. Yaşar Ayaşlı, "Psiko-tarih neye yarar?" Sendika.org, February 22, 2016, (accessed on April 26, 2019), http://sendika63.org/2016/02/psiko-tarih-neye-yarar-yasar-ayasli-330763/)

111. Armstong, "What a TV Series Tells Us About Erdogan's Turkey," *New York Times,* May 14, 2017.

112. Lale Kemal, "Erdoğan'ın kibri ve özgüven patlaması," *Taraf,* June 5, 2013, (accessed on April 26, 2019), http://www.duzceyerelhaber.com/lale-kemal/16088-erdoganin-kibri-ve-ozguven-patlamasi

113. Levent Gültekin, a Turkish journalist who until recently was aligned with Erdoğan, said in an interview he gave to the *Özgür Düşünce* daily what he heard from a bureaucrat: "In order to secure his position, he is putting the whole country's life in danger, including his own electorate. I can't give you a name, but a high-level bureaucrat went to say goodbye to Tayyip Bey [Erdoğan] when he retired. When Tayyip Bey told the bureaucrat about some of his plans, the bureaucrat said, 'If you do just half of what you say, you will start a civil war in this country.' Tayyip Bey answered, 'I don't care if a civil war takes place, we will crush them.' Therefore, we have a leader who would dare to lead the country into a civil war." Author's note: I can only link this interview to a secondary source because the digital archive of the *Özgür Düşünce* daily was destroyed after it was closed by the Erdoğan regime. For the entire interview see Hüseyin Keleş, "İç savaş çıkar' diyen bürokrata Erdoğan'dan yanıt: Çıksın, ezer geçeriz," Özgür Düşünce, Cumhuriyet, June 13, 2103, (accessed on April 26, 2019), http://www.cumhuriyet.com.tr/haber/kultur-sanat/550248/_ic_savas_cikar__diyen_burokrata_Erdogan_dan_yanit__Ciksin__ezer_geceriz.html

114. "100 bin topladığınız yerde 1 milyon toplarım," *Vatan,* June 1, 2013, (accessed on April 26, 2019), http://www.gazetevatan.com/-100-bin-topladiginiz-yerde-1-milyon-toplarim--542907-gundem/

115. "Erdoğan: 'Türkiye'nin yüzde 50'sini zor tutuyoruz," *Milliyet,* June 3, 2013, (ac-

cessed on April 26, 2019), http://www.milliyet.com.tr/basbakan-4-gun-yok/siyaset/detay/1717873/default.htm

116. "Turkey's descent into arbitrariness: The end of rule of law," *Stockholm Center for Fredoom (SCF)*, April 2017, (accessed on April 26, 2019), https://stockholmcf.org/wp-content/uploads/2017/04/Turkey's-Descent-Into-Arbitrariness-The-End-Of-Rule-Of-Law.pdf

117. World Justice Project, *World Justice Project: Rule of Law Index 2019*, March 2019, (accessed on April 26, 2019), https://worldjusticeproject.org/sites/default/files/documents/WJP_RuleofLawIndex_2019_Website_reduced.pdf

118. "15 Temmuz'dan sonra 4 bin 238 hakim ve savcı ihraç edildi," *Milliyet*, May 11, 2017, (accessed on April 26, 2019), http://www.milliyet.com.tr/15-temmuz-dan-sonra-4-bin-238-gundem-2448679/

119. Alican Uludağ, "Erdoğan atamaları yaptı; Cumhuriyet'e soruşturma yürüten savcı HSK üyesi oldu," *Cumhuriyet*, May 19, 2017, (accessed on April 26, 2019), http://www.cumhuriyet.com.tr/haber/turkiye/744244/Erdogan_atamalarini_yapti..._Cumhuriyet_e_sorusturmayi_yuruten_Savci_HSK_uyesi_oldu.html

120. A press release published on the ENCJ's website states, "It is a condition of membership, and for the status of observer, that institutions are independent of the executive and legislature and ensure the final responsibility for the support of the judiciary in the independent delivery of justice." It was also indicated that "ENCJ has become concerned that the procedures adopted by the HSYK indicated that this condition was no longer satisfied." See "ENCJ votes to suspend the Turkish High Council for Judges and Prosecutors," *ENCJ*, December 8, 2016, (accessed on April 26, 2019), https://www.encj.eu/node/449; "Avrupa HSYK'nın statüsünü askıya aldı," *Hürriyet*, December 10, 2016, (accessed on April 26, 2019) http://www.hurriyet.com.tr/avrupa-hsyknin-statusunu-askiya-aldi-40302364

121. "In Turkey, the lack of institutional independence of the judiciary, the chilling effect of the mass dismissals of judges that took place under the state of emergency and the diminished quality and experience of the new members of the judiciary appointed following these purges are serious threats to the rule of law and the structural independence of the judiciary. As things stand, the HSK lacks the institutional guarantees that would allow it to withstand political influence and may act as a vehicle of executive and legislative interference in the work of individual judges." See "The Turkish Criminal Peace Judgeships and International Law," *International Commission of Jurists (ICJ)*, February 2019, (accessed on April 26, 2019), https://www.icj.org/wp-content/uploads/2019/02/Turkey-Judgeship-Advocacy-Analysis-brief-2018-ENG.pdf

122. See Venice Commission, Turkey Opinion on the Amendments to the Constitution adopted by the Grand National Assembly on 21 January 2017 and to be submitted to a national referendum on 16 April 2017, 110th Plenary Session, Venice, 10-11 March 2017, CDL-AD(2017)005, Opinion No. 875/2017, para. 19 (accessed on April 26, 2019), https://www.venice.coe.int/webforms/documents/default.aspx?pdffile=cdl-ad(2017)005-e

123. Ibid., para. 21.

124. This appeals system had practical consequences for the independent review of the first judicial decisions on detention and other pre-trial measures. For instance, in 2018 there were 40 Penal Courts of Peace and 60 criminal courts in Ankara. An arrest warrant produced by one of the 40 peace courts could be ap-

pealed at one of the 60 criminal courts, randomly selected. The randomness of the choice of an appeal body as well as the high number of judges that could be entrusted with such an appeal provided strong guarantees against possible influences by members of the executive or legislative branches. The closed-circuit system of appeal by criminal peace judges abolished this guarantee. For example, while in the old system around 100 judges in Ankara were involved in decisions on pretrial measures, now only 10 are empowered to decide on them. See "The Turkish Criminal Peace Judgeships and International Law," International Commission of Jurists (ICJ), February 2019, https://www.icj.org/wp-content/uploads/2019/02/Turkey-Judgeship-Advocacy-Analysis-brief-2018-ENG.pdf

125. "Turkey's descent into arbitrariness: The end of rule of law," *Stockholm Center for Freedom (SCF)*, April 2017, (accessed on April 26, 2019), https://stockholmcf.org/wp-content/uploads/2017/04/Turkey's-Descent-Into-Arbitrariness-The-End-Of-Rule-Of-Law.pdf

126. "The Turkish Criminal Peace Judgeships and International Law," *International Commission of Jurists (ICJ)*, February 2019, https://www.icj.org/wp-content/uploads/2019/02/Turkey-Judgeship-Advocacy-Analysis-brief-2018-ENG.pdf

127. See cases nos. E. 2014/164, K. 2015/12, 14.1.2015. Two of the dissenting voters, Alparslan Altan and Erdal Tercan, were dismissed and arrested after the coup attempt.

128. Venice Commission, Turkey Opinion on the Amendments to the Constitution adopted by the Grand National Assembly on 21 January 2017 and to be submitted to a national referendum on April 16, 2017, 110th Plenary Session, Venice, March 10-11, 2017, CDL-AD (2017)005, Opinion No. 875/2017, para. 50-52. https://www.venice.coe.int/webforms/documents/default.aspx?pdffile=cdl-ad(2017)005-e

129. Ibid., para. 22.

130. Yaman Akdeniz, "Analysis of the Draft Provision on the 'Presentation of media services via Internet' to the Turkish Law No. 6112 on the Establishment of Radio and Television Enterprises and Their Media Services," OSCE, February 28, 2018, (accessed on April 26, 2019), https://www.osce.org/representative-on-freedom-of-media/373846?download=true

131. Yaman Akdeniz and Kerem Altıparmak, *Turkey: Freedom of Expression in Jeopardy: Violations of the rights of authors, publishers and academics under the state of emergency*, (PEN, March 28, 2018), p.11, (accessed on April 26, 2019), https://www.englishpen.org/wp-content/uploads/2018/03/Turkey_Freedom_of_Expression_in_Jeopardy_ENG.pdf

132. "Report on the impact of the state of emergency on human rights in Turkey, including an update on the South-East (January-December 2017)," Office of the United Nations High Commissioner for Human Rights (OHCHR), March 2018, https://www.ohchr.org/Documents/Countries/TR/2018-03-19_Second_OHCHR_Turkey_Report.pdf

133. Ibid.

134. "Jailed head of lawyers association allowed to attend father's funeral in handcuffs," *Stockholm Center for Freedom (SCF)*, January 19, 2019, (accessed on April 26, 2019), https://stockholmcf.org/jailed-head-of-lawyers-association-allowed-to-attend-fathers-funeral-in-handcuffs/ ; "Our Statement on the Occasion of Day of the Endangered Lawyers," *The Arrested Lawyers' Initia-*

tive, January 24, 2019, (accessed on April 26, 2019), https://arrestedlawyers.org/2019/01/24/our-statement-on-the-occasion-of-day-of-the-endangered-lawyers/

135. "Threats to the independence of the legal profession in Turkey - systematic arrests and detention of lawyers / dismissals of judges and prosecutors," the Bar Human Rights Committee of England & Wales (BHRC), the International Bar Association's Human Rights Institute (IBAHRI) and the Law Society of England and Wales, September 18, 2018, (accessed on April 26, 2019), http://communities.lawsociety.org.uk/international/international-rule-of-law/lawyers-at-risk/un-submission-on-turkey-international-law-breaches-regarding-the-independence-of-the-legal-profession/5065977.fullarticle

136. "Cumhurbaşkanı Erdoğan: Bu karara uymuyorum, saygı da duymuyorum," *Hürriyet,* February 28, 2016, (accessed on April 26, 2019), http://www.hurriyet.com.tr/cumhurbaskani-erdogan-karara-uymuyorum-saygi-da-duymuyorum-40061344

137. As President Erdoğan has not observed any objective criterion in appointing members of the court, he has even appointed his personal advisors to the bench. Among the new members, appointed on August 25, 2016, were Recai Akyel, a senior presidential advisor, and Şevki Hakyemez, an academic who had made his support for the AKP public. The July 15, 2016 coup attempt has given Erdoğan the chance to dominate the high judicial bodies, along with other state organs. Since the failed coup, the Constitutional Court has abandoned its futile attempts at independence against Erdoğan. A blatant manifestation of this submission was the silence of the court when two of its members, Alpaslan Altan and Erdal Tercan, were dismissed and arrested the day after the coup attempt. In this way the law requiring that high court judges can only be investigated and tried by their own courts was violated. The court not only did not resist this lawlessness but actually was complicit in it. See "Anayasa Mahkemesi üyeleri tutuklandı," *Hürriyet,* July 20, 2016, (accessed on April 26, 2019), http://www.hurriyet.com.tr/anayasa-mahkemesi-uyeleri-tutuklandi-40156750

138. "On Emergency Decree Laws NO. 667-676 – Adopted Following the Failed Coup of 15 July 2016," Venice Commission, December 12, 2016, (accessed on April 26, 2019), http://www.venice.coe.int/webforms/documents/default.aspx?pdffile=CDL-AD(2016)037-e

139. "Turkey's Constitutional Court rejects CHP application to cancel 13 gov't decrees," *Stockholm Center for Freedom (SCF),* July 1, 2018, (accessed on April 26, 2019), https://stockholmcf.org/turkeys-constitutional-court-rejects-chp-application-to-cancel-13-govt-decrees/

140. "Altıparmak: AYM, artık bir anayasamız olmadığını ilan etti," *NTV,* November 5, 2016, (accessed on April 26, 2019), http://t24.com.tr/haber/aym-artik-bir-anayasamiz-olmadigini-ilan-etti,369214

141. "Int'l press bodies urge Turkish gov't to implement Constitutional Court decision to free journalists," *Stockholm Center for Freedom (SCF),* January 12, 2018, (accessed on April 26, 2019), https://stockholmcf.org/intl-press-bodies-urge-turkish-govt-to-implement-constitutional-court-decision-to-free-journalists/

142. 23 Temmuz 2016 tarihli Resmi Gazete, (accessed on April 26, 2019), http://www.resmigazete.gov.tr/eskiler/2016/07/20160723M2.pdf

143. "Danıştay ve Yargıtay'a yeni atamalar yapıldı," *Sabah,* July 25, 2016, (acces-

sed on April 26, 2019), http://www.sabah.com.tr/gundem/2016/07/25/dani-stay-ve-yargitaya-yeni-atamalar-yapildi

144. European Commisson's Progress Report on Turkey, EU Commission, November 11, 2016, (accessed on April 26, 2019), https://ec.europa.eu/neighbour-hood-enlargement/sites/near/files/pdf/key_documents/2016/20161109_report_turkey.pdf

145. "Turkish gov't asks 83 countries to extradite 452 people over alleged links to Gülen movement," *Stockholm Center for Freedom (SCF)*, November 14, 2018, (accessed on April 26, 2019), https://stockholmcf.org/turkish-govt-requests-83-countries-to-extradite-452-people-over-alleged-links-to-gulen-movement/

146. Anayasa değişikliği teklifine sert tepki," *Deutsche Welle-Türkçe*, December 11, 2016, (accessed on April 26, 2019), http://www.dw.com/tr/hukuk%C3%A7u-lardan-anayasa-de%C4%9Fi%C5%9Fiklik-teklifine-sert-tepki/a-36725812 ; See Kemal Gözler, *Elveda Anayasa:16 Nisan 2017'de Oylayacağımız Anayasa Değişikliği Hakkında Eleştiriler,* (Ekin Yayınları, Istanbul 2017).

147. "İçtüzük değişikliği teklifin detayları belli oldu," *NTV*, July 7, 2017, (accessed on April 26, 2019), http://www.ntv.com.tr/turkiye/ictuzuk-degisikligi-tbm-mde-ictuzuk-teklifinin-detaylari-belli-oldu,2Le9XEQGU06gpe36qZiiDw ; "İçtüzük değiyikliği TBMM'de kabul edildi," *CNN Türk*, 27 Temmuz 2017, (accessed on April 26, 2019), https://www.cnnturk.com/son-dakika-ictuzuk-degi-sikligi-tbmmde-kabul-edildi

148. "Mazlumder'e AKP operasyonu," *Artı Gerçek*, March 19, 2017, (accessed on April 26, 2019), https://www.artigercek.com/mazlumdere-akp-operasyonu

149. "Turkish gov't jails prominent social activist Osman Kavala after 2 weeks of detention," *Stockholm Center for Freedom (SCF)*, November 1, 2017, (accessed on April 26, 2019), https://stockholmcf.org/turkish-govt-jails-prominent-so-cial-activist-osman-kavala-after-2-weeks-of-detention/

150. "Af Örgütü'nün Türkiye yöneticisi tutuklandı," *Sözcü*, June 10, 2017, (accessed on April 26, 2019), http://www.sozcu.com.tr/2017/gundem/af-orgutunun-tur-kiye-yoneticisi-tutuklandi-1889185/

151. "Büyükada'da gözaltına alınan insan hakları savunucularına tutuklama," *Sözcü*, July 17, 2017, (accessed on April 26, 2019), http://www.sozcu.com.tr/2017/gundem/buyukadada-gozaltina-alinan-insan-haklari-savunucularina-tutukla-ma-talebi-1936361/ ; "Büyükada Tutuklamaları İktidar ve Medyasının Planlı Operasyonu," *Bianet*, July 19, 2017, (accessed on April 26, 2019), https://bianet.org/bianet/insan-haklari/188407-buyukada-tutuklamalari-iktidar-ve-me-dyasinin-planli-operasyonu

152. "250 bin üyeli İtalyan Barolar Konseyinden Bozdağ'a sert kınama," February 7, 2017, (accessed on June 21, 2017),https://washingtonhatti.com/2017/02/07/250-bin-avukat-uyeli-italyan-ulusal-barolar-konseyin-den-bozdaga-sert-kinama/

153. "Top police chief says 22,987 police officers dismissed over Gülen links," *Turkish Minute*, December 12, 2017, (accessed on April 26, 2019), https://www.turkishminute.com/2017/12/12/top-police-chief-says-22987-police-officers-dismissed-over-gulen-links/

154. "FETÖ Tutuklu Sayısı! Kaç Asker Kaç Sivil Var," *Milliyet*, May 6, 2017, (accessed on June 20, 2017), https://www.haber24.com/gundem/feto-tutuklu-sayisi-kac-asker-kac-sivil-var-h621178.html

155. "15,153 Turkish military personnel dismissed since failed coup: minister," *Turkish Minute*, October 29, 2018, (accessed on April 26, 2019), https://www.turkishminute.com/2018/10/29/15153-turkish-military-personnel-dismissed-since-failed-coup-minister/

156. "Polis koleji kapatılıyor," *Sabah*, February 27, 2015, (accessed on April 26, 2019), http://www.sabah.com.tr/gundem/2015/02/27/polis-koleji-kapatiliyor

157. "Askeri okullar kapatıldı, milli savunma üniversitesi kuruldu," *Hürriyet*, July 31, 2016, (accessed on April 26, 2019), http://www.hurriyet.com.tr/askeri-okullar-kapatildi-milli-savunma-universitesi-kuruldu-40176760

158. "Milli savunma Üniversitesi rektörlüğüne Erhan Afyoncu atandı," *Hürriyet*, October 4, 2016, (accessed on April 26, 2019), http://www.hurriyet.com.tr/erhan-afyoncu-milli-savunma-universitesi-rektorlugune-atandi-40239832

159. "Cezaevlerinden 38 bin kişi tahliye ediliyor," *Al Jazeera*, August 18, 2016, (accessed on April 26, 2019), http://www.aljazeera.com.tr/haber/cezaevlerinden-38-bin-kisi-tahliye-ediliyor

160. Semih İdiz, "Pressure Mounts on Turkey Over Radical Groups in Syria," *al-Monitor*, October 15, 2013, (accessed on April 26, 2019), http://www.al-monitor.com/pulse/originals/2013/10/turkey-must-control-jihadists-entering-syria.html

161. "HÜDA-PAR supports AKP member's 'new state' remarks," *Turkish Minute*, August 7, 2017, (accessed on April 26, 2019), https://www.turkishminute.com/2017/08/07/huda-par-supports-akp-members-new-state-remarks/

162. "CHP asks gov't whether SADAT trained ISIL," *Turkish Minute*, September 15, 2016, (accessed on April 26, 2019), https://www.turkishminute.com/2016/09/15/chp-asks-govt-whether-sadat-trained-isil/

163. "Kırmızı yelekler giyen Osmanlı Ocakları, Fatih Portakal'ı tehdit etti," *Gazete Duvar*, December 26, 2018, (accessed on April 26, 2019), https://www.gazeteduvar.com.tr/gundem/2018/12/26/kirmizi-yelekler-giyen-osmanli-ocaklari-fatih-portakali-tehdit-etti/ ; See also Abdullah Bozkurt, "Erdoğan, the godfather of the mafia syndicate in Turkey," *Turkish Minute*, August 1, 2017, (accessed on April 26, 2019), https://www.turkishminute.com/2017/08/01/opinion-erdogan-the-godfather-of-the-mafia-syndicate-in-turkey/

164. "Alleged paramilitary organization raising money to combat 'economic war' against Turkey," *Turkish Minute*, December 31, 2018, (accessed on April 26, 2019), https://www.turkishminute.com/2018/12/31/alleged-paramilitary-organization-raising-money-to-combat-economic-war-against-turkey/

165. "Adnan Tanrıverdi kimdir? SADAT nedir?" *Sözcü*, August 17, 2016, (accessed on April 26, 2019), http://www.sozcu.com.tr/2016/gundem/adnan-tanriverdi-kimdir-sadat-nedir-1355672/

166. Parliamentary question by CHP lawmaker Fikri Sağlar, August 22, 2016, (accessed on April 26, 2019), http://www2.tbmm.gov.tr/d26/7/7-7687s.pdf; Parliamentary question by CHP lawmaker Mahmut Tanal, August 19, 2016, (accessed on April 26, 2019), http://www2.tbmm.gov.tr/d26/7/7-7686s.pdf

167. "Erdoğan'ın özel olarak teşekkür ettiği HÜDA-PAR'dan referandum yorumu," *Türkiye*, April 17, 2017, (accessed on April 26, 2019), http://www.turkiyegazetesi.com.tr/politika/465627.aspx

168. "Anayasa Mahkemesi Hizbullah yargılamalarında ihlal kararı verdi," *Memurlar.net*, December 27, 2016, (accessed on April 26, 2019), http://www.memurlar.

net/haber/635059/

169. "Salih Mirzabeyoğlu tahliye edildi!" *CNN Türk*, July 22, 2014, (accessed on April 26, 2019), https://www.cnnturk.com/haber/turkiye/salih-mirzabeyoglu-tahliye-ediliyor-salih-mirzabeyoglu-kimdir

170. "Cumhurbaşkanı Erdoğan, Salih Mirzabeyoğlu ile görüştü," *CNN Türk*, December 1, 2014, (accessed on April 26, 2019), https://www.cnnturk.com/haber/turkiye/cumhurbaskani-erdogan-salih-mirzabeyoglu-ile-gorustu ; Abdullah Bozkurt, "Erdoğan saves jihadist network: The Vasat terror group in Turkey," *Stockholm Center for Freedom (SCF)*, February 20, 2018, (accessed on April 26, 2019), https://stockholmcf.org/commentary-erdogan-saves-jihadist-network-the-vasat-terror-group-in-turkey/

171. "DAİŞ Manisa'da aleni faaliyet yürütüyor," *Yeni Özgür Politika*, March 17, 2017, (accessed on April 26, 2019), http://yeniozgurpolitika.com/index.php?rupel=lezgin&id=2626

172. "İBDA-C'li cihatçı çeteci, darbe girişimine karşı polisin yanında çatıştı," *Sendika.org*, July 16, 2016, (accessed on April 26, 2019), https://www.youtube.com/watch?v=ZvPdVzpczvY

173. Sedat Peker said: "They should pray for our president [Erdoğan], who they call a dictator. God forbid, if his visit to this world ends even in natural ways, they will see what a dictator is. God willing, we will hang all those who are sympathetic to them [the Gülen movement] on the nearest flagpole. We will hang them on the nearest tree." He also said once he and his thugs were done in the streets, they would raid the prisons and hang those inmates linked to the Gülen movement as well. See "Sedat Peker: Cezaevlerini basacağız, ağaçlara asacağız", *Cumhuriyet*, July 16, 2017, (accessed on April 26, 2019), http://www.cumhuriyet.com.tr/video/video_haber/782673/Sedat_Peker__Cezaevlerini_basacagiz__agaclara_asacagiz.html

174. "Erdoğan'dan 15 Temmuz mesajı: Önce bu hainlerin kafasını kopartacağız," *BBC Turkish*, July 16, 2017, (accessed on April 26, 2019), http://www.bbc.com/turkce/haberler-turkiye-40622285

175. "Oluk oluk kan akacak," *Cumhuriyet*, October 9, 2015, (accessed on April 26, 2019), http://www.cumhuriyet.com.tr/haber/siyaset/384791/_Oluk_oluk_kan_akacak_.html

176. "Kim bu Osmanlı Ocakları?" *Hürriyet*, September 11, 2015, (accessed on April 26, 2019), http://www.hurriyet.com.tr/kim-bu-osmanli-ocaklari-30039635

177. "Eren Erdem, Kılıçdaroğlu'nun önüne mermi bırakanları açıkladı," *BirGün*, June 8, 2016, (accessed on June 21, 2017), http://www.birgun.net/haber-detay/eren-erdem-kilicdaroglu-nun-onune-mermi-birakanlari-acikladi-115275.html

178. "Fatih Tezcan: Fethullah Gülen öldürülmelidir," *Sol*, September 1, 2016, (accessed on April 26, 2019), http://haber.sol.org.tr/toplum/video-fatih-tezcan-fethullah-gulen-oldurulmelidir-167855

179. "Pro-gov't columnist suggests setting Silivri Prison ablaze due to Gülen movement inmates," *Turkish Minute*, 10 June 2017, (accessed on April 26, 2019), https://www.turkishminute.com/2017/06/10/video-pro-govt-columnist-suggests-setting-silivri-prison-ablaze-due-to-gulen-movement-inmates/

Chapter 3

1. Çağıl Kasapoğlu, "Bazı ülkeler Gülen okullarını kapatmaya neden direniyor?" *BBC Türkçe*, August 2 2016, (accessed on April 26, 2019), http://www.bbc.com/turkce/haberler-turkiye-36950705

2. See İlber Ortaylı, Toktamış Ateş, Eser Karakaş, *Barış Köprüleri - Dünyaya Açılan Türk Okulları*, (Ufuk Kitapları, Istanbul, 2005.)

3. See Ahmet Dönmez, *Yüzde On - Adil Düzenden Havuz Düzenine*, (Klas Kitap Yayınları, Istanbul, 2014.)

4. "Yolsuzluk operasyonunu yapan polislere gözaltı," *Evrensel*, July 22, 2014, (accessed on April 26, 2019), https://www.evrensel.net/haber/88717/yolsuzluk-operasyonunu-yapan-polislere-gozalti

5. "İslamofobi... İslamofaşizm...," Hasan Cemal, *T24*, October 25, 2016, (accessed on April 26, 2019), http://t24.com.tr/yazarlar/hasan-cemal/islamofobi-islamo-fasizm,15730

6. See "Erdoğan's Coup In Turkey -- A bizarre coup bid that was set to fail from the get-go," *Stockholm Center for Freedom (SCF)*, July 2017, (accessed on April 26, 2019), https://stockholmcf.org/wp-content/uploads/2017/07/15_July_Erdogans_Coup_13.07.2017.pdf

7. "Turkish minister: 48,000 jailed, 1,028 companies seized over Gülen links," *Turkish Minute*, November 16, 2017, (accessed on April 26, 2019), https://www.turkishminute.com/2017/11/16/turkish-minister-48000-jailed-1028-companies-seized-over-gulen-links/

8. See "Freedom of the press in Turkey: Far worse than you think," *Stockholm Center for Freedom (SCF)*, January 2017, (accessed on April 26, 2019), http://stockholmcf.org/wp-content/uploads/2017/02/Freedom_of_press_in_Turkey_26.01.2017.pdf

9. "Turkey Refuses To Recognize 29 Int'l Universities' Diplomas Over Alleged Coup Links," *Stockholm Center for Freedom (SCF)*, April 5, 2017, (accessed on April 26, 2019), https://stockholmcf.org/turkey-refuses-to-recognize-29-intl-universities-diplomas-over-alleged-coup-links/

10. "Erdoğan: 'FETÖ' için tavsiye kararı aldık," *Time Türk*, May 27, 2016, (accessed on April 26, 2019), http://www.timeturk.com/erdogan-feto-icin-tavsiye-karari-aldik/haber-157045

11. "İşte FETÖ kriterleri," *Kamu Haber Merkezi*, August 12, 2016, (accessed on April 26, 2019), http://www.kamuhabermerkezi.com/iste-feto-kriterleri-20013h.htm

12. "Turkey orders detention of 222 people over Gülen links in one day," *Turkish Minute*, January 15, 2019, (accessed on April 26, 2019), https://www.turkishminute.com/2019/01/15/turkey-orders-detention-of-222-people-over-gulen-links-in-one-day/

13. See Ergil 2012. Also see Jon Pahl, *Fethullah Gülen: A Life of Hizmet* (Blue Dome Press, Clifton NJ, 2019). According to Gülen's birth certificate he was born in 1941. However, his birth registration was made a few years later than his real date of birth. For more information, see https://www.fgulen.com/tr/hayati-tr/hayat-kronolojisi/fgulen-com-1941-1959-Hayat-Kronolojisi

14. "1941-1959 Hayat Kronolojisi," *fgulen.com*, June 10, 2006, (accessed on April 26, 2019), https://www.fgulen.com/tr/hayati-tr/hayat-kronolojisi/fgu-

len-com-1941-1959-Hayat-Kronolojisi

15. See Ergene 2005, p. 40.

16. See Can 2000.

17. See Gülen 2000.

18. Ibid.

19. Ergene 2005, p. 42.

20. Mercan 2016.

21. Ibid.

22. "Fethullah Hoca Papa'yla görüştü," *Hürriyet*, February 10, 1998, (accessed on April 26, 2019), http://www.hurriyet.com.tr/fethullah-hoca-papayla-gorustu-39005791

23. "Efsanevi Reha Muhtar - Fethullah Gülen Konuşması," *YouTube*, July 16, 2013, (accessed on April 26, 2019), https://www.youtube.com/watch?v=cHM-2fOhv1Y&t=363s

24. "Fethullah Gülen ve Terör," *fgulen.com*, February 1, 2015, (accessed on April 26, 2019), http://fgulen.com/tr/turk-basininda-fethullah-gulen/fethullah-gulen-hakkinda-dizi-yazilar-dosyalar/fethullah-gulen-web-sitesi-ozel-dosyalar/47549-fethullah-gulen-ve-teror

25. Fethullah Gülen, "İntihar," *Herkül*, (accessed on April 26, 2019), http://www.herkul.org/bamteli/intihar-2/

26. See AKP's Party Program, (accessed on June 22, 2017) http://www.akparti.org.tr/site/akparti/parti-programi

27. Bülent Keneş, "İslamî olana karşı siyasal İslamcılık," *Zaman*, January 26, 2014, (accessed on April 26, 2019), http://bulentkenes.blogspot.se/2014/01/islami-olana-kars-siyasal-islamclk.html

28. Ibid.

29. "TMK'da tuzağı Zaman deşifre etmişti," *fgulen.com*, December 1, 2013, (accessed on April 26, 2019), http://fgulen.com/tr/turk-basininda-fethullah-gulen/fethullah-gulen-hakkinda-haberler/fethullah-gulen-hakkinda-2013-haberleri/37464-tmkda-tuzagi-zaman-desifre-etmisti

30. Joe Lauria, "Reclusive Turkish Imam Criticizes Gaza Flotilla," *The Wall Street Journal*, June 4, 2010, (accessed on April 26, 2019), https://www.wsj.com/articles/SB10001424052748704025304575284721280274694

31. See the official results of June 12, 2011 general elections, YSK, http://www.ysk.gov.tr/ysk/docs/Kararlar/2011Pdf/2011-1070.pdf

32. Bülent Keneş, "Islamist vs. Islamic: Erdogan's deep-rooted hatred of the Gülen movement," *Politurco*, April 28, 2018, (accessed on April 26, 2019), http://www.politurco.com/islamist-vs-islamic-erdogans-deep-rooted-hatred-of-the-gulen-movement.html

33. "On February 7, "specially authorized" prosecutor Sadrettin Sarıkaya in Istanbul summoned the head of the Turkish National Intelligence Organisation (MIT), Hakan Fidan, his predecessor Emre Taner, the former deputy undersecretary of MIT Afet Gunes and two other MIT officials to testify – as suspects – as part of the ongoing investigation of the Kurdistan Committees Union (KCK), which the prosecutors claim is controlled by the outlawed Kurdistan Workers' Party (PKK) and as such engaged in terrorist activities. Hundreds

of Kurdish politicians, dozens of journalists and prominent intellectuals have been arrested since the KCK investigation was launched in 2009. However, the prosecutor's latest move is unprecedented, and has revealed the existence of deep fissures within the Turkish state, over which the ruling Justice and Development Party (AKP) was supposed to have established full control after having vanquished the military and redesigned the composition of the judiciary." See Halil M. Karaveli, "The Coalition Crumbles: Erdogan, the Gülenists, and Turkish Democracy," *The Turkey Analyst*, February 20, 2012, (accessed on April 26, 2019), https://www.turkeyanalyst.org/publications/turkey-analyst-articles/item/395-the-coalition-crumbles-erdogan-the-gülenists-and-turkish-democracy.html ; "'7 Şubat'ta Gül, Hakan Fidan'a 'ifade ver' dedi; Erdoğan 'gitme' dedi," *T24*, February 21, 2014, (accessed on April 26, 2019), http://t24.com.tr/haber/7-subatta-gul-hakan-fidana-ifade-ver-dedi-erdogan-gitme-dedi,251631

34. "Those who have somehow been our partners during our 10 years in power will not be our partners in the next 10 years. Throughout the last 10 years we had partners in what we accomplished in civilian-military relations, liberties, law and justice. Even if they were liberals, they were somehow our partners, although they did not like us during this process. However, the period of re-building [the state] lies ahead. This period will not be as they had hoped. Those who walked together with us in the past will be partners of the forces against us tomorrow because the new Turkey and the future will not be a future and an era they will accept. So, we will have a tougher job." See "Babuşcu: Gelecek 10 yıl, liberaller gibi eski paydaşlarımızın arzuladığı gibi olmayacak," *T24*, April 1, 2013, (accessed on April 26, 2019), http://t24.com.tr/haber/babuscu-onumuzdeki-10-yil-liberaller-gibi-eski-paydaslarimizin-kabullenecegi-gibi-olmayacak,226892

35. "Gülen Cemaati'ne dava 'uzak ihtimal değil'," *BBC Türkçe*, December 20, 2013, (accessed on April 26, 2019), http://www.bbc.com/turkce/haberler/2013/12/131220_rengin_analiz

36. "Zaman: Dershane yasası taslağı doğruysa, eğitime büyük darbe vurulur!" *T24*, November 14, 2013, (accessed on April 26, 2019), http://t24.com.tr/haber/zaman-dershane-yasasi-taslagi-dogruysa-egitime-buyuk-darbe-vurulur,243948 ; "Erdoğan: Dershanelerde geri adım yok, cemaat bize saldırıyı durdursun!" *T24*, November 20. 2103, (accessed on April 26, 2019), http://t24.com.tr/haber/erdogan-diyarbakir-sonrasi-gazetecilerin-sorularini-yanitliyor,244443

37. "Dumanlı: Gülen cemaati, dershane kapatmayı desteklediği AKP'ye yakıştıramıyor," *T24*, October 14, 2013, (accessed on April 26, 2019), http://t24.com.tr/haber/dumanli-gulen-cemaati-dershane-kapatmayi-destekledigi-akpye-yakistiramiyor,241872

38. "Berat Albayrak: Ben de FETÖ okulunda okudum!" *Demokrat Samsun*, July 29, 2016, (accessed on April 26, 2019), http://www.demokratsamsun.com/siyaset/berat-albayrak-bende-feto-okulunda-okudum-h13842.html

39. Selahattin Günday, "17 Aralık: Darbe mi yolsuzluk mu?" *Al Jazeera*, December 17, 2014, (accessed on April 26, 2019), http://www.aljazeera.com.tr/al-jazeera-ozel/17-aralik-darbe-mi-yolsuzluk-mu

40. "Erdoğan: Cadı avıysa, biz bu cadı avını yapacağız, bunu da bilin!" *T24*, May 11, 2014, (accessed on April 26, 2019), http://t24.com.tr/haber/erdogan-cadi-aviysa-biz-bu-cadi-avini-yapacagiz-bunu-da-bilin,258112

41. Bülent Keneş, "Viva la muerte: Şeyhim Edebali, sen yoluna ben yoluma!"

TR7/24, October 18, 2016, (accessed on April 26, 2019), http://www.tr724.com/viva-la-muerte-seyhim-edebali-sen-yoluna-ben-yoluma-akif-umut-avaz/

42. "Erdoğan: Bir adam gibi ölmek var bir de madam gibi," *BirGün*, October 15, 2016, (accessed on April 26, 2019), http://www.birgun.net/haber-detay/erdogan-bir-adam-gibi-olmek-var-bir-de-madam-gibi-131496.html

43. Keneş, "Viva la muerte…"

44. See "Melih Gökçek'in 'Alevi-Sünni çatışması' sözlerine tepki!" *Halkın Habercisi*, October 10, 2016, (accessed on April 26, 2019), http://www.halkinhabercisi.com/melih-gokcekin-alevi-sunni-catismasi-sozlerine-tepki

45. "Turkey's Ankara Mayor Gökçek hints 'genocide' for followers of Gülen movement," *Stockholm Center for Freedom (SCF)*, June 3, 2017, (accessed on April 26, 2019), https://stockholmcf.org/turkeys-ankara-mayor-gokcek-hints-genocide-for-followers-of-gulen-movement/

46. "Turkish court acquits Erdoğanist gang leader who threatened Gülen-linked people with hanging," *Stockholm Center for Freedom (SCF)*, June 21, 2018, (accessed on April 26, 2019), https://stockholmcf.org/turkish-court-acquits-erdoganist-gang-leader-who-threatened-gulen-linked-people-with-hanging/

47. "Pro-Erdoğan mafia leader tells prosecutor he stands behind call to take up arms," *Turkish Minute*, February 8, 2019, (accessed on April 26, 2019), https://www.turkishminute.com/2019/02/08/pro-erdogan-mafia-leader-tells-prosecutor-he-stands-behind-call-to-take-up-arms/

48. "Erdoğan'dan İnanılmaz Sözler," *Gazeteport*, September 13, 2016, (accessed on April 26, 2019), http://gazeteport.com/2016/erdogandan-inanilmaz-sozler-69733/

49. "Başbakan Erdoğan'a kefenli karşılama," *CNN Türk*, December 22, 2013, (accessed on April 26, 2019), https://www.cnnturk.com/turkiye/basbakan-erdogana-kefenli-karsilama ; "Erdoğan'a kefenli karşılama," *Anadolu Ajansı*, December 22, 2013, (accessed on April 26, 2019), http://aa.com.tr/tr/turkiye/erdogana-kefenli-karsilama/195814

50. "Başbakan'a yine kefenli karşılama," December 27, 2013, *nediyor.com*, (accessed on April 26, 2019), https://nediyor.com/basbakana-yine-kefenli-karsilama/

51. "Urfa'da Erdoğan'ı kefenle karşıladılar," *Balıklıgöl.com*, March 10, 2014, (accessed on April 26, 2019), http://www.balikligol.com/haber/urfada-erdogani-kefenle-karsiladilar-25759.html

52. "Başbakan'a Hatay'da kefenli karşılama," *Haber7*, March 22, 2014, (accessed on April 26, 2019), http://www.haber7.com/foto-galeri/29153-basbakana-hatayda-kefenli-karsilama/p1

53. Fikret Aydemir, "Kefenli karşılama," *Akşam*, January 19, 2014, (accessed on April 26, 2019), http://www.aksam.com.tr/yazarlar/fikret-aydemir-bruksel/kefenli-karsilama/haber-277645

54. "Ahmet Davutoğlu'na kefenli karşılama," *Haber Vitrini*, March 19, 2014, (accessed on April 26, 2019), http://habervitrini.com/gundem/ahmet-davutogluna-kefenli-karsilama-300978

55. "Niğde Ak Parti Gençlik Kollarından Darbe Girişimine Kefenli Protesto," *Hedef Halk*, July 21, 2016, (accessed on April 26, 2019), http://www.hedefhalk.com/nigde-ak-parti-genclik-kollarindan-darbe-girisimine-kefenli-protesto-809775h.htm

56. "Ömer Halisdemir davasında Fethullah Gülen'i idam ettiler," *Posta*, March 20, 2017, (accessed on April 26, 2019), http://www.posta.com.tr/omer-halisde-mir-davasinda-fethullah-gulen-i-idam-ettiler-haberi-1278711

57. "Fetullah Gülen idam edildi," https://www.youtube.com/watch?v=yK3PML-ws3Q0

58. "Pazar'da F. Gülen maketi idam edildi!" *Pazar53*, July 28, 2016, (accessed on April 26, 2019), http://www.pazar53.com/pazarda-f-gulen-maketi-idam-edil-di-25g.htm

59. "Bursa'da FETÖ'ye temsili idam," *Olay*, July 20, 2016, (accessed on April 26, 2019), https://www.olay.com.tr/bursada-fetoye-temsili-idam-78826h.htm

60. "'Adalet Yürüyüşü'ne yeni tehdit: Şehadet için rabbimize yalvarıyoruz," *Gazete Manifesto*, June 28, 2017, (accessed on April 26, 2019), http://gazetemanifesto.com/2017/06/28/adalet-yuruyusune-yeni-tehdit-sehadet-icin-rabbimize-yal-variyoruz/

61. "AKP'li yönetici Kılıçdaroğlu'nu ölümle tehdit etti: Reis'in tek bir kelimesi-yle koşar öldürürüz!" *TR7/24*, June 23, 2017, (accessed on April 26, 2019), http://www.tr724.com/akpli-yoneticisi-kilicdaroglunu-olumle-tehdit-etti-rei-sin-tek-bir-kelimesiyle-kosar-oldururuz/

62. "Bakan Zeybekçi: Gebertin bizi diye yalvaracaklar," *BirGün*, September 1, 2016, (accessed on April 26, 2019), http://www.birgun.net/haber-detay/bakan-zey-bekci-gebertin-bizi-diye-yalvaracaklar-122392.html

63. "Yeni Söz ve Milat yazarı Hüseyin Adalan: FETÖ'cülerin bebeklerine kadar kat-li vacibtir," *Haberdar*, May 7, 2017, (accessed on April 26, 2019), http://www.haberdar.com/gundem/yeni-soz-ve-milat-yazari-huseyin-adalan-feto-culer-in-bebeklerine-kadar-katli-vacibtir-h51024.html

64. "Pro-Erdogan troll says 'the best Gülenist is a dead Gülenist," *Turkish Minute*, September 10, 2018, (accessed on April 26, 2019), https://www.turkishminute.com/2018/09/10/pro-erdogan-troll-says-the-best-gulenist-is-a-dead-gulenist/

65. "Pro-Erdoğan troll calls on gov't to assassinate Gülenists," *Turkey Purge*, May 13, 2017, (accessed on April 26, 2019), https://turkeypurge.com/pro-erdogan-troll-calls-on-govt-to-assassinate-gulen-followers

66. "Pro-Erdoğan journalists call for assassination of Gülen followers abroad," *Turkish Minute*, June 15, 2017, (accessed on April 26, 2019), https://www.turkishminute.com/2017/06/15/pro-erdogan-journalists-call-for-assassina-tion-of-gulen-followers-abroad/

67. "Erdoğan: Cezalarını tamamlayıp dışarı çıkanlar olursa, milletimiz sokakta gördüğünde gereken cezayı verecektir," *GriHat*, June 7, 2017, (accessed on April 26, 2019), http://grihat.com/erdogan-cezalarini-tamamlayip-disa-ri-cikanlar-olursa-milletimiz-sokakta-gordugunde-gereken-cezayi-verecektir/

68. "Turkey's energy minister: I would strangle Gülenists wherever I see them," *Turkey Purge*, September 11, 2017, (accessed on April 26, 2019), https://turkey-purge.com/video-turkeys-energy-minister-i-would-strangle-gulenists-wher-ever-i-see-them

69. "Erdoganist gang leader says will hang all people linked with Gülen move-ment," *Stockholm Center for Freedom (SCF)*, July 16, 2017, (accessed on April 26, 2019), https://stockholmcf.org/erdoganist-gang-leader-says-will-hang-all-people-linked-with-gulen-movement/ ; "Sedat Peker planını açıkladı: Cezaev-lerini basacağız ve...," *ABC Gazetesi*, July 16, 2017, (accessed on April 26, 2019),

http://www.abcgazetesi.com/sedat-peker-planini-acikladi-cezaevlerini-basa-cagiz-ve-58874h.htm

70. "FETÖ'cü hainler cezaevinde kalkışma peşinde!" *Türkiye*, September 8, 2016, (accessed on April 26, 2019), http://www.turkiyegazetesi.com.tr/gundem/400711.aspx ; "Hainler cezaevinde kalkışma peşinde," *Akşam*, 8 Eylül 2016, (accessed on April 26, 2019), http://www.aksam.com.tr/guncel/hainler-cezaevinde-kalkisma-pesinde/haber-547851 ; "Silivri'de firar hazırlığı," *Odatv*, 26 Ekim 2016, (accessed on April 26, 2019), http://odatv.com/silivride-firar-hazirligi-2610161200.html ; "FETÖ'den cezaevinde kalkışma hazırlığı," *Medya Gündemi*, October 26, 2016, (accessed on April 26, 2019),http://www.medyagundem.com/fetoden-cezaevinde-kalkisma-hazirligi/; "FETÖ'den cezaevinde kalkışma hazırlığı," *Star*, 2 Nisan 2017, (accessed on April 26, 2019), http://www.star.com.tr/guncel/fetoden-cezaevinde-kalkisma-hazirligi-haber-1203081/ ; Cezaevinde kalkışma hazırlığı," *Yeni Şafak*, April 2, 2017, (accessed on April 26, 2019), http://www.yenisafak.com/gundem/cezaevinde-kalkisma-hazirligi-2637218

71. See "Erdoğan's Coup", *Stockholm Center for Freedom (SCF)*, https://stockholmcf.org/wp-content/uploads/2017/07/15_July_Erdogans_Coup_13.07.2017.pdf

72. Haluk Kalafat, "İdam Hakkında AKP Dün Ne Diyordu? Bugün Ne Diyor?" *Bianet*, November 2, 2016, (accessed on April 26, 2019), http://bianet.org/bianet/siyaset/180283-idam-hakkinda-akp-dun-ne-diyordu-bugun-ne-diyor

73. "Erdoğan: Bir referandum da idam için yaparız," *BBC Türkçe*, April 11, 2017, (accessed on April 26, 2019), http://www.bbc.com/turkce/haberler-turkiye-39565796

74. Özge Artunç, "Türkiye idam defterini tekrar açacak mı?" *Deutsche Welle* Türkçe, April 26, 2017, (accessed on April 26, 2019), http://www.dw.com/tr/t%C3%B-Crkiye-idam-defterini-tekrar-a%C3%A7acak-m%C4%B1/a-38591543

75. "ORC'nin anketine göre, halkın yüzde 91'i idam istiyor!" *T24*, July 27, 2016, (accessed on April 26, 2019), http://t24.com.tr/haber/orcnin-anketine-gore-halkin-yuzde-91i-idam-istiyor,352073

76. "Türkiye'de vatandaşların yüzde 82'si ordunun yönetime el koymasını istemiyor," *Sanal Basın*, July 19, 2017, (accessed on April 26, 2019), http://www.sanalbasin.com/turkiyede-vatandaslarin-yuzde-82si-ordunun-yonetime-el-koymasini-istemiyor-14742729/

77. "İşte Erdoğan'ın okuduğu şiir!" *Haber7*, May 21 2017, (accessed on April 26, 2019), http://www.haber7.com/siyaset/haber/2336436-iste-erdoganin-okudugu-siir

78. "Oğlunun şehadet haberini alan baba: Ayıp olmasa güler oynarım," *Aydın Post*, June 26, 2017, (accessed on April 26, 2019), http://www.aydinpost.com/oglunun-sehadet-haberini-alan-baba-ayip-olmasa-guler-oynarim-277184h.htm

79. "Mursi gibi bir akıbete uğrarsam..." *Milliyet*, May 17, 2015, (accessed on April 26, 2019), http://www.milliyet.com.tr/erdogan-dan-kayseri-mesajlari/siyaset/detay/2060470/default.htm

80. "Vatan için Azrail'e aleykümselam deriz," *Milliyet*, May 18, 2015, (accessed on April 26, 2019), http://www.milliyet.com.tr/vatan-icin-azrail-e-aleykumselam/siyaset/detay/2060564/default.htm

81. Osman Ulagay, "CHP yaşama, AKP ölüme odaklı," *T24*, May 22, 2015, (ac-

cessed on April 26, 2019), http://t24.com.tr/yazarlar/osman-ulagay/chp-yasama-akp-olume-odakli,11941

82. This is a list of just some of the 240 insults and hate speech against the Gulen movement uttered by President Erdogan that the Stockholm Center for Freedom (SCF) compiled in a report titled "Erdoğan's vile campaign of hate speech - A case study: Targeting of the Gülen Movement," May 2017, http://stockholmcf.org/wp-content/uploads/2017/06/Erdogans-Vile-Campaign-Of-Hate-Speech-Case-Study-Targeting-Of-The-Gulen-Movement_2017.pdf

83. See Smith 2011; Sherrer 2008; Bain et al 2014.

84. Erdoğan's vile campaign of hate speech - A case study: Targeting of the Gülen Movement," *Stockholm Center for Freedom (SCF)*, May 2017.

85. https://www.google.se/search?q=FETO&oq=FETO&aqs=-chrome.0.69i59j0l5.1884j1j7&sourceid=chrome&ie=UTF-8

86. "Erdoğan'a dava açan 21 kişiden 7'si tutuklandı," *BirGün*, January 17, 2017, (accessed on June 23, 2017), http://www.birgun.net/haber-detay/erdogan-a-dava-acan-21-kisiden-7-si-tutuklandi-143520.html ; "Erdoğan'a 'hakaret' davası açan 21 kişiye 'FETÖ' operasyonu: 17 gözaltı," *ABC Gazetesi*, January 10, 2017, (accessed on June 23, 2017), http://www.abcgazetesi.com/erdogana-hakaret-davasi-acan-21-kisiye-feto-operasyonu-17-gozalti-39816h.htm

87. "Turkey sees record hike in investigations, prosecutions for allegedly insulting president," *Turkish Minute*, December 9, 2018, (accessed on April 26, 2019), https://www.turkishminute.com/2018/12/09/turkey-sees-record-hike-in-investigations-prosecutions-for-allegedly-insulting-president/

88. "Adalet Bakanlığından 'Cumhurbaşkanı Erdoğan'a hakaret' açıklaması," *Anadolu Ajansı*, June 29, 2017, (accessed on April 26, 2019), http://aa.com.tr/tr/turkiye/adalet-bakanligindan-cumhurbaskani-erdogana-hakaret-aciklamasi/850764

89. "2016'da Erdoğan'ı eleştirmenin bilançosu: 46 bin işlem, 5 bin kamu davası, 1080 mahkumiyet!" *TR7/24*, June 28, 2017, (accessed on April 26, 2019), http://www.tr724.com/2016da-erdoganin-elestirmenin-bilancosu-46-bin-islem-5-bin-kamu-davasi-1080-mahkumiyet/

90. "Hakim Murat Aydın Trabzon'a atanmasını 'sürgün' olarak niteledi," *CNN Türk*, June 13, 2016, (accessed on April 26, 2019), https://www.cnnturk.com/turkiye/hakim-murat-aydin-trabzona-atanmasini-surgun-olarak-niteledi

91. "Cumhurbaşkanına Hakarete Beraat" Haberi, Erdoğan'ın Şikayetiyle Engellendi," *Bianet*, April 13, 2017, (accessed on April 26, 2019), https://m.bianet.org/bianet/medya/185430-bianet-in-cumhurbaskanina-hakarete-beraat-haberi-erdogan-in-sikayetiyle-engellendi

92. "Erdoğan: Köklerini kurutacağız," *memleket.com*, October 19, 2016, (accessed on April 26, 2019), http://www.memleket.com.tr/erdogan-koklerini-kurutacagiz-970160h.htm

93. "Erdoğan'dan 'Paralel Yapı' açıklaması: Bana ihanet ettiler, bazı özel adımlar var," *Habertürk*, October 18, 2015, (accessed on April 26, 2019), http://www.haberturk.com/gundem/haber/1155174-cumhurbaskani-erdogan-aciklama-yapiyor

94. "Ve Paralel Yapı Kırmızı Kitapta," *Sabah*, January 2, 2015, (accessed on April 26, 2019), http://www.sabah.com.tr/gundem/2015/01/02/ve-paralel-yapi-kirmizi-kitapta

95. "Cumhurbaşkanı Erdoğan, aTV-aHaber Ortak Yayınına Katıldı," *Türkiye Cumhurbaşkanlığı Sitesi*, October 30, 2015, (accessed on April 26, 2019), https://www.tccb.gov.tr/haberler/410/35814/cumhurbaskani-erdogan-atv-a-haber-ortak-yayinina-katildi.html

96. "Erdoğan ilk kez açıkladı; FETÖ'nün adı artık illegal terör örgütü," *Medya Gündemi*, April 30, 2016, (accessed on April 26, 2019), http://www.medyagundem.com/erdogan-ilk-kez-acikladi-fetonun-adi-artik-illegal-teror-orgutu/

97. "No progress toward media freedom in Turkey, IPI report finds," *IPI*, February 11, 2019, (accessed on April 26, 2019), https://freeturkeyjournalists.ipi.media/no-progress-toward-media-freedom-in-turkey-ipi-report-finds/

98. "Erdoğan açıkladı: MGK Fethullah Gülen için karar aldı," *Hürriyet*, May 27, 2016, (accessed on April 26, 2019), http://www.hurriyet.com.tr/erdogan-dan-chpye-cok-sert-hakaret-tepkisi-40109914

99. "Hükümetten önemli FETÖ kararı," *Takvim*, May 30, 2016, (accessed on April 26, 2019), http://www.takvim.com.tr/guncel/2016/05/30/hukumetten-onemli-feto-karari

100. https://www.google.se/search?q=FET%C3%96&source=lnms&sa=X&ved=0ahUKEwirldXqha3VAhWEJJoKHc-jD8gQ_AUICSgA&biw=1366&bih=662&dpr=1

101. Published in early 2016, the peace declaration accuses the Turkish government of carrying out heavy-handed operations in Turkey's southeastern region, where outlawed PKK militants and the military have been engaged in clashes since the breakdown of a cease-fire between the two in July 2015. It was signed by more than 1,000 intellectuals from both inside and outside Turkey, including U.S. philosopher Noam Chomsky. The peace declaration frustrated President Erdoğan and the AKP government, leading to retribution against the academics. Some of the insults Erdoğan used against them included "so-called intellectuals," "a flock called intellectuals," "traitors" and "rough copies of intellectuals." See "YÖK Says Boğaziçi Academic Fired For Signing Peace Declaration," *Stockholm Centre for Freedom (SCF)*, May 9, 2017, (accessed on April 26, 2019), https://stockholmcf.org/yok-says-bogazici-academic-fired-for-signing-peace-declaration/

102. Twenty-one people including artisans, teachers and village headmen had launched legal action against Erdoğan at the Antalya Court of First Instance on February 11, 2014, arguing that Erdoğan insulted them when he said, referring to the Gülen movement, "We will enter their lairs." These people had claimed damages. However, police officers from the counterterrorism department simultaneously raided their houses. Nine of them were arrested on charges of membership in a terrorist organization, while detention warrants were issued for 12 of them and seven of them were arrested and imprisoned. In such a setting, it is nearly impossible for any victim to launch any kind of action against Erdoğan for his insults and hate speech. See "Erdoğan'ın 'inlerine gireceğiz' sözüne dava açan yedi kişi tutuklandı," *Diken*, January 17, 2017, (accessed on April 26, 2019), http://www.diken.com.tr/erdoganin-inlerine-girecegiz-sozlerine-dava-acan-yedi-kisi-tutuklandi/

103. "Erdoğan: Cadı avıysa, biz bu cadı avını yapacağız, bunu da bilin!" *T24*, May 11, 2014, (accessed on April 26, 2019), http://t24.com.tr/haber/erdogan-cadi-aviysa-biz-bu-cadi-avini-yapacagiz-bunu-da-bilin,258112

104. "FETÖcü'lerin Giremediği Kuaför," *Aksu TV*, October 27, 2016, (accessed on

April 26, 2019), https://www.youtube.com/watch?v=sGmgFu5Ez4Q

105. "Bahabey'e 'FETÖ'cüler giremez' pankartı," Çorum Haber, (accessed on April 26, 2019), http://www.Çorumhaber.net/haber/amp/57457

106. "Çalışma Bakanlığı'ndan fişleme: KHK mağdurlarının başka işe girmesi engellenecek," *Yarın*, September 25, 2017, (accessed on April 26, 2019), http://yarinhaber.net/emek/59943/calisma-bakanligindan-fisleme-khk-magdurlari-nin-baska-ise-girmesi-engellenecek

107. Erdoğan's vile campaign of hate speech - A case study: Targeting of the Gülen Movement," *Stockholm Center for Freedom (SCF)*, May 2017, http://stock-holmcf.org/wp-content/uploads/2017/06/Erdogans-Vile-Campaign-Of-Hate-Speech-Case-Study-Targeting-Of-The-Gulen-Movement_2017.pdf

108. "Mağdur edebiyatı yapanlar ihanet içinde," *Hürriyet*, October 26, 2016, (accessed on April 26, 2019), http://www.hurriyet.com.tr/magdur-edebiyati-yapan-lar-ihanet-icinde-40259964

109. Erdoğan's vile campaign of hate speech - A case study: Targeting of the Gülen Movement," *Stockholm Center for Freedom (SCF)*, May 2017, http://stock-holmcf.org/wp-content/uploads/2017/06/Erdogans-Vile-Campaign-Of-Hate-Speech-Case-Study-Targeting-Of-The-Gulen-Movement_2017.pdf

110. "Mass Torture and Ill-Treatment In Turkey," *Stockholm Center for Freedom (SCF)*, June 2007, http://stockholmcf.org/wp-content/uploads/2017/06/Mass-Torture-And-Ill-Treatment-In-Turkey_06.06.2017.pdf

111. Ibid.

112. Hayrettin Karaman, "Zaman dostların çekişme zamanı değildir," *Yeni Şa-fak*, February 2, 2017, (accessed on April 26, 2019), http://www.yenisafak.com/yazarlar/hayrettinkaraman/zaman-dostlarin-cekisme-zamani-de-gildir-2035923 ; "AKP'nin Fetvacısı Hayrettin Karaman'dan İç Savaş ve Ölüm Fetvası," *Zaman Avustralya*, February 2, 2017, (accessed on April 26, 2019), http://www.zamanaustralia.com/2017/02/akpnin-fetvacisi-hayrettin-kara-mandan-ic-savas-ve-olum-fetvasi

113. "Erdoğan: 'Bunu Ancak Kafir Yapar,'" *haberler.com*, July 30, 2016, (accessed on April 26, 2019), https://www.haberler.com/erdogan-bunu-ancak-kafir-yapar-8659679-haberi/

114. "FETÖ'ye merhamet vatana ihanettir," *Kırküç*, August 11, 2016, (accessed on June 21, 2017) http://gazetekirkuc.com/fetoye-merhamet-vatana-ihanettir/

115. "Erdoğan'dan FETÖ açıklaması: Kim ki mağduriyet edebiyatı yapıyor, ihanet içindedir," *Sputnik*, October 26, 2016, (accessed on April 26, 2019), https://tr.sputniknews.com/politika/201610261025488880-erdogan-feto-magdur/

Chapter 4

1. See *Convention on the Prevention and Punishment of the Crime of Genocide* https://treaties.un.org/doc/publication/unts/volume%2078/volume-78-i-1021-english.pdf

2. "Erdoğan: FETÖ'nün kökünü kazıyacağız!" *aHaber*, August 11, 2016, (accessed on April 26, 2019), http://www.ahaber.com.tr/webtv/gundem/cumhurbas-kani-erdogan-fetonun-kokunu-kaziyacagiz ; "Cumhurbaşkanı Erdoğan, FETÖ ile mücadelede net mesajlar verdi," *Star*, May 21, 2017, (accessed on April

26, 2019), http://www.star.com.tr/politika/cumhurbaskani-erdogandan-by-lock-ve-bank-asya-vurgusu-haber-1219703/

3. "Cumhurbaşkanı Erdoğan: FETÖ'cüler ya imha olacaklar ya da defolup gidecekler," *Haber1461*, October 19, 2016, (accessed on April 26, 2019), http://www.haber1461.com/cumhurbaskani-erdogan-fetoculer-ya-imha-olacak-lar-ya-da-defolup-gidecekler.html

4. "Genocides, Politicides, and Other Mass Murder Since 1945," *Genocide Prevention Advisory Network*, (accessed on April 26, 2019), http://www.gpanet.org/content/genocides-politicides-and-other-mass-murder-1945-stages-2008

5. Alpkaya 2002, p.126.

6. Gregory H. Stanton, "What Is Genocide?" *Genocide Watch*, (accessed on April 26, 2019), http://www.genocidewatch.org/genocide/whatisit.html

7. "Statements by Hitler and Senior Nazis Concerning Jews and Judaism," *phdn. org*, (accessed on April 26, 2019), https://www.phdn.org/archives/www.ess. uwe.ac.uk/genocide/statements.htm

8. See "Erdoğan's vile campaign of hate speech - A case study: Targeting of the Gülen Movement," *Stockholm Center for Freedom (SCF)*, May 2017, (accessed on April 26, 2019), http://stockholmcf.org/wp-content/uploads/2017/06/Erdo-gans-Vile-Campaign-Of-Hate-Speech-Case-Study-Targeting-Of-The-Gulen-Movement_2017.pdf

9. "Başbakan Erdoğan'ın 14 Ocak 2014 tarihli TBMM Grup Toplantısı konuşmasının tam metni," January 14, 2014, (accessed on June 21, 2017), ht-tps://www.akparti.org.tr/tbmm/haberler/basbakan-erdoganin-14-ocak-tarih-li-tbmm-grup-toplantisi-konusmasinin/57705 and also https://www.youtube. com/watch?v=UEgRtK2C_EU

10. "Erdoğan, CFR'da konuştu," *Sputnik*, September 23, 2017, (accessed on June 22, 2017), https://tr.sputniknews.com/rsfmradio.com/2014_09_23/erdogan-cfr-konusmasi/

11. "Erdoğan: Cadı avıysa, biz bu cadı avını yapacağız, bunu da bilin!" *T24*, May 11, 2014, (accessed on April 26, 2019), http://t24.com.tr/haber/erdogan-ca-di-aviysa-biz-bu-cadi-avini-yapacagiz-bunu-da-bilin,258112

12. "Erdoğan: Pensilvanya'daki şarlatanın sesine kulak veren..." *Milliyet*, August 3, 2016, (accessed on April 26, 2019), http://www.milliyet.com.tr/erdogan-pen-silvanya-daki-sarlatani-siyaset-2288810/

13. "Erdoğan: FETÖ'nün kökünü kazımak boynumuzun borcu," *BBC Türkçe*, August 14, 2016, (accessed on April 26, 2019), http://www.bbc.com/turkce/haber-ler-turkiye-37078024

14. "Cumhurbaşkanı Erdoğan: Hala bu ihanet çetesinin içinde yer alanlar vatan hainidir," *Habertürk*, August 30, 2016, (accessed on April 26, 2019), http://www.haberturk.com/gundem/haber/1289890-cumhurbaskani-erdogan-bu--ihanet-cetesinin-icinde-yer-alanlar-vatan-hainidir

15. "Erdoğan: FETÖ'cüleri vatandaşlıktan atacağız," *Haber7*, October 15, 2016, (accessed on April 26, 2019), http://www.haber7.com/siyaset/haber/2172170-er-dogan-fetoculeri-vatandasliktan-atacagiz

16. "Erdoğan'dan Fethullah Gülen'e: Gelsene," *Sputnik*, October 29, 2016, (accessed on April 26, 2019), https://tr.sputniknews.com/politi-ka/201610291025537854-erdogan-fethullah-gulen-gelsene/

17. "Özür ve Tazminat Gerçekleşti, Ablukanın Kalkması Konusunda da İlerleme Var," November 21, 2016, (accessed on April 26, 2019), https://www.tccb.gov. tr/haberler/410/61089/ozur-ve-tazminat-gerceklesti-ablukanin-kalkmasi-ko-nusunda-da-ilerleme-var.html

18. Elihu D Richter, Yael Stein, Alex Barnea and Marc Sherman, "Can we prevent Genocide by preventing Incitement?" *Genocide Watch*, November 2009, (accessed on April 26, 2019), http://www.genocidewatch.org/images/Articles_Can_we_prevent_genocide_by_preventing_incitement.pdf

19. Ibid.

20. Thomas E. Davies, *How the Rome Statute Weakens the International Prohibition on Incitement to Genocide*, September 28, 2009, (accessed on April 26, 2019), https://harvardhrj.com/2009/09/how-the-rome-statute-weakens-the-interna-tional-prohibition-on-incitement-to-genocide/

21. "Suspicious Deaths And Suicides In Turkey," *Stockholm Center for Freedom (SCF)*, March 22, 2017, (accessed on April 26, 2019), http://stockholmcf. org/wp-content/uploads/2017/03/Suspicious-Deaths-And-Suicides-In-Tur-key_22.03.2017.pdf

22. "Mass Torture And Ill-Treatment In Turkey," *Stockholm Center for Freedom (SCF)*, June 2017, (accessed on April 26, 2019), http://stockholmcf.org/ wp-content/uploads/2017/06/Mass-Torture-And-Ill-Treatment-In-Tur-key_06.06.2017.pdf

23. "Doctor Jailed Due To Alleged Gülen Links Dies Of Heart Attack In Prison," *Stockholm Center for Freedom (SCF)*, March 24, 2017, (accessed on April 26, 2019), https://stockholmcf.org/doctor-jailed-due-to-alleged-gulen-links-dies-of-heart-attack-in-prison/

24. "Woman Miscarried Twins In Turkish Prison, Dead Babies Not Returned To Family," *Stockholm Center for Freedom* (SCF), June 23, 2017, (accessed on April 26, 2019), https://stockholmcf.org/woman-miscarried-twins-in-turkish-pris-on-dead-babies-not-returned-to-family/

25. "Jailed For Months Over Alleged Gülen Links, 62-Year-Old Teacher Dies Of Cancer In Turkish Prison," *Stockholm Center for Freedom (SCF)*, June 8, 2017, (accessed on April 26, 2019), https://stockholmcf.org/jailed-for-months-over-alleged-gulen-links-62-year-old-teacher-dies-of-cancer-in-turkish-prison/

26. "61-Year-Old Businessman Dies From Poor Conditions In Turkey's Elbistan Prison," *Stockholm Center for Freedom (SCF)*, June 6, 2017, (accessed on April 26, 2019), https://stockholmcf.org/61-year-old-businessman-dies-from-poor-conditions-in-turkeys-elbistan-prison/

27. "Suspicious Deaths And Suicides In Turkey," *Stockholm Center for Freedom (SCF)*, March 22, 2017, (accessed on April 26, 2019), http://stockholmcf. org/wp-content/uploads/2017/03/Suspicious-Deaths-And-Suicides-In-Tur-key_22.03.2017.pdf

28. "Turkish gov't asks 83 countries to extradite 452 people over alleged links to Gülen movement," *Stockholm Center for Freedom (SCF)*, November 14, 2018, (accessed on April 26, 2019), https://stockholmcf.org/turkish-govt-requests-83-countries-to-extradite-452-people-over-alleged-links-to-gulen-movement/

29. "A Blank Check: Turkey's Post-Coup Suspension of Safeguards Against Tor-ture," *Human Rights Watch*, October 25, 2016, (accessed on April 26, 2019), https://www.hrw.org/report/2016/10/25/blank-check/turkeys-post-coup-sus-

pension-safeguards-against-torture

30. "Suspicious Deaths And Suicides In Turkey," *Stockholm Center for Freedom (SCF)*, March 22, 2017, (accessed on April 26, 2019), http://stockholmcf. org/wp-content/uploads/2017/03/Suspicious-Deaths-And-Suicides-In-Turkey_22.03.2017.pdf

31. Ibid.

32. Ibid.

33. "Başbakan hedef gösterdi, uyuşturucu bağımlısı öldürdü," *Shaber*, August 9, 2014, (accessed on April 26, 2019), http://www.shaber3.com/gundem/Basbakan-hedef-gosterdi-uyusturucu-bagimlisi-oldurdu/1058345/

34. "Atalay Filiz de 'FETÖ'ye sığındı: Halk idam istiyor, ben halkın talebini yerine getirdim," *Diken*, March 9, 2017, (accessed on April 26, 2019), http://www.diken.com.tr/atalay-filiz-de-fetoye-sigindi-halk-idam-istiyor-ben-halkin-talebini-yerine-getirdim/

35. "Sedat Peker planını açıkladı: Cezaevlerini basacağız ve...," *ABC Gazetesi*, July 16, 2017, (accessed on September 11, 2017), http://www.abcgazetesi.com/sedat-peker-planini-acikladi-cezaevlerini-basacagiz-ve-58874h.htm

36. "Erdoğan: Cezalarını tamamlayıp dışarı çıkanlar olursa, milletimiz sokakta gördüğünde gereken cezayı verecektir," *GriHat*, June 7, 2017, (accessed on April 26, 2019), http://grihat.com/erdogan-cezalarini-tamamlayip-disari-cikanlar-olursa-milletimiz-sokakta-gordugunde-gereken-cezayi-verecektir/

37. Özbek 2008, p. 81.

38. Çolak 2005, p. 208.

39. "Convention against Torture and Other Cruel, Inhuman or Degrading Treatment or Punishment," (accessed on April 26, 2019), http://www.ohchr.org/EN/ProfessionalInterest/Pages/CAT.aspx

40. Lemkin, *Axis Rule...*, p.79.

41. Jorgensen 2001, p. 290; Obote-Odora 2002, p. 397; Önok 2003, p. 151.

42. Rosenbaum 1993, p. 16.

43. Türk Ceza Kanunu (TCK) Madde 94, (accessed on April 26, 2019), http://www.turkhukuksitesi.com/mevzuat.php?mid=3925

44. *Convention for the Protection of Human Rights and Fundamental Freedoms*, (accessed on April 26, 2019), http://www.echr.coe.int/Documents/Collection_Convention_1950_ENG.pdf

45. *European Convention for the Prevention of Torture and Inhuman or Degrading Treatment or Punishment*, (accessed on April 26, 2019), https://rm.coe.int/16806dbaa3

46. *Türkiye Cumhuriyeti Anayasası*, (accessed on April 26, 2019), https://www.tbmm.gov.tr/anayasa/anayasa82.htm

47. "Türk Ceza Kanunu, 94. Madde'nin gerekçesi," (accessed on April 26, 2019), http://www.turkhukuksitesi.com/serh.php?did=1168

48. "Mass Torture and Ill-Treatment In Turkey," *Stockholm Center for Freedom (SCF)*, June 2007, (accessed on April 26, 2019), http://stockholmcf.org/wp-content/uploads/2017/06/Mass-Torture-And-Ill-Treatment-In-Turkey_06.06.2017.pdf

49. Rengin Arslan, "OHAL ve Avrupa İnsan Hakları Sözleşmesi: Hukukçular ne diyor?" *BBC Türkçe*, July 22, 2016, (accessed on April 26, 2019), http://www.bbc.com/turkce/36860670

50. July 23, 2016 tarihli Kanun Hükmünde Kararname (accessed on April 26, 2019), http://www2.tbmm.gov.tr/d26/1/1-0746.pdf

51. "A Blank Check - Turkey's Post-Coup Suspension of Safeguards Against Torture," Human Rights Watch, October 25, 2016, (accessed on April 26, 2019), https://www.hrw.org/report/2016/10/25/blank-check/turkeys-post-coup-suspension-safeguards-against-torture

52. "Istanbul Protocol: The Manual on Effective Investigation and Documentation of Torture and Other Cruel, Inhuman or Degrading Treatment or Punishment," United Nations High Commissioner for Human Rights, (accessed on April 26, 2019), https://s3.amazonaws.com/PHR_Reports/istanbul-protocol_opt.pdf

53. Selin Girit, "Gözaltında işkence iddiaları: Yüreğimin en pis yerine yazdım," *BBC Türkçe*, November 28, 2016, (accessed on April 26, 2019), http://www.bbc.com/turkce/haberler-turkiye-38126711

54. Kemal Göktaş, "Avukattan acı itirafı: Korktum işkenceye sessiz kaldım," *Cumhuriyet*, October 24, 2016, (accessed on April 26, 2019), http://www.cumhuriyet.com.tr/haber/turkiye/620855/Avukattan_aci_itiraf__Korktum__iskence-ye_sessiz_kaldim.html

55. "Darbeci Askerlere İşkence Görüntüleri" July 20, 2016, (accessed on April 26, 2019) https://www.youtube.com/watch?v=Racum9mZZx8

56. "Gözlatında akli dengesini yitiren öğretmen tekrar cezaevine kondu," *TR7/24*, February 27, 2017, (accessed on April 26, 2019), http://www.tr724.com/gozaltinda-akli-dengesini-yitiren-tugba-ogretmen-tekrar-cezaevine-kondu/

57. "AKP'li Metiner'den vahim sözler: İşkence'ye inceleme yok," *Cumhuriyet*, October 2, 2016, (accessed on April 26, 2019), http://www.cumhuriyet.com.tr/haber/turkiye/608880/AKP_li_Metiner_den_vahim_sozler__iskenceye_ince-leme_yok.html

58. "Ekonomi Bakanı: Bu darbecilere öyle bir ceza vereceğiz ki 'gebertin bizi' diye yalvaracaklar!", *T24*, August 10, 2016, (accessed on April 26, 2019), http://t24.com.tr/haber/ekonomi-bakani-bu-darbecilere-oyle-bir-ceza-verecegiz-ki-ge-bertin-bizi-diye-yalvaracaklar,352845

59. "Cezaevlerinden 38 bin kişi tahliye ediliyor," *Al Jazeera*, August 18, 2016, (accessed on April 26, 2019), http://www.aljazeera.com.tr/haber/cezaevlerin-den-38-bin-kisi-tahliye-ediliyor

60. "Adalet Bakanı Bozdağ'dan 2017 vaadi: 175 yeni cezaevi," *Sol*, December 22, 2016, (accessed on April 26, 2019), http://haber.sol.org.tr/toplum/adalet-bakani-bozdagdan-2017-vaadi-175-yeni-cezaevi-179975

61. "Cezaevlerinde Yer Kalmadı: Mayıs 2017 itibarıyla 221 bin 607 tutuklu," *Dokuz8 Haber*, May 19, 2017, (accessed on April 26, 2019), https://medium.com/@dokuz8HABER/cezaevlerinde-yer-kalmad%C4%B1-may%C4%B1s-2017-iti-bar%C4%B1yla-221-bin-607-tutuklu-18e4dc97e3e6

62. "Occupancy rate in Turkish prisons more than 40,000 above capacity," *Turkish Minute*, November 14, 2018, (accessed on April 26, 2019), https://www.turkishminute.com/2018/11/14/occupancy-rate-in-turkish-prisons-mo-re-than-40000-above-capacity/

63. "Emniyet'ten 'gizli' talimat iddiası: Gözaltı birimlerini uygun hale getirin," *Agos*, September 9, 2016, (accessed on April 26, 2019), http://www.agos.com.tr/tr/yazi/16504/emniyet-ten-gizli-talimat-iddiasi-gozalti-birimlerini-uygun-hale-getirin

64. "Af Örgütü: Darbe Girişiminde Gözaltına Alınanlara İşkence ve Tecavüz," Bianet, July 25, 2016, (accessed on April 26, 2019), https://m.bianet.org/bianet/insan-haklari/177141-af-orgutu-darbe-girisiminde-gozaltina-alinanlara-iskence-ve-tecavuz

65. "Ankara Adliyesi'ne 100 metre mesafede gördüğü işkenceyi anlattı," *TR7/24*, August 6, 2017, (accessed on April 26, 2019), http://www.tr724.com/ankara-adliyesine-100-metre-mesafede-gordugu-iskenceyi-anlatti/

66. "Mass Torture and Ill-Treatment In Turkey," *Stockholm Center for Freedom (SCF)*, June 2007, http://stockholmcf.org/wp-content/uploads/2017/06/Mass-Torture-And-Ill-Treatment-In-Turkey_06.06.2017.pdf

67. Erdoğan Öztürk, "Dokuma gözaltı merkezi oldu," *Sabah*, August 13, 2016, (accessed on April 26, 2019), http://www.sabah.com.tr/akdeniz/2016/08/13/dokuma-gozalti-merkezi-oldu

68. "15 Temmuz Gecesi Fidan'ı uğurlayan Yavuz: Genelkurmay'daki ifademi ölüm tehditleri altında verdim," *Sputnik*, March 7, 2017, (accessed on April 26, 2019), https://tr.sputniknews.com/turkiye/201703071027523444-darbe-gecesi-mit-mustesari-fidani-ugurlayan-kubra-yavuz-genelkurmaydaki-ifademi-olum-tehdidi-altinda-verdim/

69. "Askerlere camide işkence," *Sol*, July 16, 2016, (accessed on April 26, 2019), http://haber.sol.org.tr/toplum/askerlere-camide-iskence-162145

70. "Sorguda kaburgamı kıran asker bir ay sonra FETÖ'den tutuklandı," *Odatv*, March 2, 2017, (accessed on April 26, 2019), http://odatv.com/genelkurmayin-listeyi-yeniden-kontrol-etmesini-istiyorum-0203171200.html

71. "Domuz bağı, suyla boğma, elektrik, kafanın klozete sokulması," *Shaber*, April 24, 2017, (accessed on April 26, 2019), http://www.shaber3.com/domuz-bagi-suyla-bogma-elektrik-kafanin-klozete-sokulmasi-haberi/1284758/

72. "ÖKK'daki darbe girişimi davası," *Habertürk*, February 28, 2017, (accessed on June 23, 2017), http://www.haberturk.com/yerel-haberler/haber/11094976-okkdaki-darbe-girisimi-davasi

73. "SCF Reveals Mass Torture And Abuse In An Unofficial Detention Facility In Turkey's Capital," *Stockholm Center for Freedom (SCF)*, May 7, 2017, (accessed on April 26, 2019), http://stockholmcf.org/scf-reveals-mass-torture-and-abuse-in-an-unofficial-detention-facility-in-turkeys-capital/

74. "Savcı işkence suç duyurusunu KHK'ye dayanarak reddetti," *Evrensel*, January 16, 2017, (accessed on April 26, 2019), https://www.evrensel.net/haber/304217/savci-iskence-suc-duyurusunu-khkye-dayanarak-reddetti

75. "Muşta ile dayak, copla tecavüz girişimi, eşe tecavüz tehdidi!.." *Shaber*, February 16, 2017, (accessed on April 26, 2019), http://www.shaber3.com/musta-ile-dayak-copla-tecavuz-girisimi-ese-tecavuz-tehdidi-haberi/1280700/

76. "Turkey Prosecutor Drops Probe Into Torture-Led Death Under Police Custody," *Stockholm Center for Freedom (SCF)*, August 5, 2017, (accessed on April 26, 2019), https://stockholmcf.org/turkey-prosecutor-drops-probe-into-torture-led-death-under-police-custody/

77. "Gözaltında ölen öğretmenin babası gözyaşları içinde anlattı," *Cumhuriyet*, August 5, 2016, (accessed on April 26, 2019), http://www.cumhuriyet.com.tr/haber/turkiye/580062/Gozaltinda_olen_ogretmenin_babasi_gozyaslari_icinde_anlatti.html

78. "Suspicious Deaths of Turkey's Purge (July 2016 – October 2018), *Turkey Purge*, October 18, 2018, (accessed on April 26, 2019), https://turkeypurge.com/wp-content/uploads/2018/10/dosya-2.pdf

79. "Avukatlar darbecileri savunmak istemiyor," *Sabah*, July 24, 2016, (accessed on April 26, 2019), http://www.sabah.com.tr/gundem/2016/07/24/avukatlar-darbecileri-savunmak-istemiyor

80. Çiğdem Özcan, "Aradığınız insana şu an ulaşılamıyor," *Evrensel*, August 9, 2016, (accessed on April 26, 2019), https://www.evrensel.net/haber/287253/aradiginiz-insana-su-an-ulasilamiyor

81. "Istanbul Protocol: The Manual on Effective Investigation and Documentation of Torture and Other Cruel, Inhuman or Degrading Treatment or Punishment," (accessed on April 26, 2019), https://s3.amazonaws.com/PHR_Reports/istanbul-protocol_opt.pdf

82. "Turkey arrests ÇHD head Selçuk Kozağaçlı on terrorism charges," *Stockholm Center for Freedom (SCF)*, November 13, 2017, (accessed on April 26, 2019), https://stockholmcf.org/turkey-arrests-chd-head-selcuk-kozagacli-on-terrorism-charges/

83. "ÇHD: FETÖ zanlıları arasında tecavüze uğrayıp bağırsak ameliyatı olanlar var!" *You Tube*, October 16, 2016, (accessed on April 26, 2019), https://www.youtube.com/watch?v=o9S3u8mQ4LM

84. "Kozağaçlı: Tecavüze uğrayıp bağırsak ameliyatı olanlar var," *T24*, October 16, 2016, (accessed on April 26, 2019), https://t24.com.tr/video/chd-genel-baskaninin-iddiasi-feto-zanlilari-arasinda-tecavuze-ugrayip-bagirsak-ameliyati-olanlar-var,3445

85. Hilal Köse, "Eski işkence aletleri geri döndü," *Cumhuriyet*, September 13, 2016, (accessed on April 26, 2019), http://www.cumhuriyet.com.tr/haber/turkiye/599848/Eski_iskence_aletleri_geri_dondu.html

86. Emin Çölaşan, "Cezaevine düşmeye gör," *Sözcü*, July 25, 2017, (accessed on April 26, 2019), http://www.sozcu.com.tr/2017/yazarlar/emin-colasan/cezaevine-dusmeye-gor-1944893/

87. "Eski tip işkence geri geldi; askı, elektrik!.." *T24*, September 14, 2016, (accessed on April 26, 2019), http://t24.com.tr/haber/eski-tip-iskence-geri-geldi-aski-elektrik,359800

88. "Suspicious Deaths And Suicides In Turkey -- Updated List (As of January 25, 2019)," *Stockholm Center for Freedom (SCF)*, (accessed on April 26, 2019), http://stockholmcf.org/suspicious-deaths-and-suicides-in-turkey-updated-list/

89. Nil Soysal, "FETÖ sendromu toplumu tıpkı bir virüs gibi sardı!" *Sözcü*, June 23, 2017, (accessed on April 26, 2019), http://www.sozcu.com.tr/2017/gundem/feto-sendromu-toplumu-tipki-bir-virus-gibi-sardi-1905898/; "Psychotherapist Tries To Get Recognition For 'FETÖ Syndrome' For Widespread Gülenophobia In Turkey," Stockholm Center for Freedom (SCF), June 25, 2017, (accessed on April 26, 2019), https://stockholmcf.org/psychotherapist-tries-to-get-recognition-for-feto-syndrome-for-gulenophobia-in-turkey/

90. "More Turks Report Anxiety, Stress and depression Under Erdogan's Rule," *Stockholm Center for Freedom (SCF)*, August 13, 2017, (accessed on April 26, 2019), https://stockholmcf.org/wp-content/uploads/2017/08/More-Turks-Report-Anxiety-Stress-and-depression-Under-Erdogan's-Rule_aug.132017.pdf

91. "10 kişiden 1'i ilaç kullanıyor," *Milliyet*, March 24, 2017, (accessed on April 26, 2019), http://www.milliyet.com.tr/10-kisiden-1-i-ilac-kullaniyor-gundem-2419359/

92. "Turkey's Health Ministry Response to opposition lawmaker's question," Turkish Parliament, July 12, 2013, (accessed on April 26, 2019), http://www2.tbmm.gov.tr/d24/7/7-29113sgc.pdf

93. Haluk Çolak, *Güncel Ceza Hukuku*, (Bilge Yayınevi, Ankara, 2005), p. 208.

94. "Thousands of Turks Seek Asylum in Germany," *The American Interest*, May 9, 2017, (accessed on April 26, 2019), https://www.the-american-interest.com/2017/05/09/thousands-of-turks-seek-asylum-in-germany/

95. "Report on the human rights situation in South-East Turkey (July 2015 to December 2016)" Office of the United Nations High Commissioner for Human Rights , March 10, 2017, (accessed on April 26, 2019), http://www.ohchr.org/Documents/Countries/TR/OHCHR_South-East_TurkeyReport_10March2017.pdf

96. Kürşat Akyol, "Turkey could find itself facing hefty legal bill for mass purges," *al-Monitor*, September 19, 2016, (accessed on April 26, 2019), http://www.al-monitor.com/pulse/originals/2016/09/turkey-risks-thousands-of-civil-death-lawsuits.html#ixzz4oRaQAneR

97. "Enforced disappearances in Turkey -- Updated List As of January 9, 2019," *Stockholm Center for Freedom (SCF)*, January 9, 2019, (accessed on April 26, 2019), https://stockholmcf.org/enforced-disappearences-in-turkey-2/ ; "2 more men abducted by armed group in Ankara: report," *Turkish Minute*, February 15, 2019, (accessed on April 26, 2019), https://www.turkishminute.com/2019/02/15/2-more-men-abducted-by-armed-group-in-ankara-report/

98. Cem Küçük, "Medeni ölüme mahkum yazarlar listesi," *Yeni Şafak*, February 10, 2015, (accessed on April 26, 2019), http://www.yenisafak.com/yazarlar/cemkucuk/medeni-olume-mahkum-yazarlar-listesi-2007775 ; Cem Küçük, "Medeni Ölüm' mekanizmaları!" *Star*, January 16, 2016, (accessed on April 26, 2019), http://www.star.com.tr/yazar/medeni-olum-mekanizmalari-yazi-1082729/

99. In a 2006 judgment, the ECtHR defined as "civil death" the sanctions imposed, on grounds of civil disobedience, on Osman Murat Ülke, who refused to do his mandatory military service, in addition to the prison sentence he faced. See "Avrupa İnsan Hakları Mahkemesi Ülke-Türkiye Davası, Kararın Özet Çevirisi," January 24, 2006, (accessed on April 26, 2019), http://www.aihmiz.org.tr/?q=tr/content/ulke-karari

100. "Cemaat operasyonunda 12 Eylül'deki gibi 500 bin kişiyi alırız," *T24*, August 5, 2014, (accessed on April 26, 2019), http://t24.com.tr/haber/cemaat-operasyonunda-12-eyluldeki-gibi-500-bin-kisiyi-aliriz,266563

101. "Interior minister says more than 500,000 detained, 30,000 arrested over Gülen links," *Turkish Minute*, February 14, 2019, (accessed on April 26, 2019), https://www.turkishminute.com/2019/02/14/interior-minister-says-more-than-500000-detained-30000-arrested-over-gulen-links/

102. "Turkey: Almost 130,000 purged public sector workers still awaiting justice,"

Amnesty International, October 25, 2018, (accessed on April 26, 2019), https://www.amnesty.org/en/latest/news/2018/10/almost-130000-purged-sector-workers-still-awaiting-justice-in-turkey/

103. "15 Temmuz hukuksuzluğunun bilançosu: Asker, polis, hakim, savcı, vali, kaymakam 50 bin tutuklu, 155 bin gözaltı," *TR7/24*, May 28, 2017, (accessed on April 26, 2019), http://www.tr724.com/15-temmuz-hukuksuzlugunun-bilancosu-50-bin-tutuklu-155-bin-gozalti/

104. Ibid.

105. "Purged beyond return? No remedy for Turkey's dismissed public sector workers," *Amnesty Internationals*, October 2018, (accessed on April 26, 2019), https://www.amnesty.org/download/Documents/EUR4492102018ENGLISH.PDF

106. "Turkish gov't jailed 77,081 people since controversial coup attempt in 2016 over alleged links to Gülen movement," *Stockholm Center for Freedom (SCF)*, April 18, 2018, (accessed on April 26, 2019), https://stockholmcf.org/turkish-govt-jailed-77081-people-since-controversial-coup-attempt-in-2016-over-alleged-links-to-gulen-movement/

107. "Turkish Defence Minister Akar: 15,153 military officers including 150 generals and admirals dismissed over Gülen links," *Stockholm Center for Freedom (SCF)*, October 27, 2018, (accessed on April 26, 2019), https://stockholmcf.org/turkish-defence-minister-akar-15153-military-officers-including-150-generals-and-admirals-dismissed-over-gulen-links/

108. "15 Temmuz hukuksuzluğunun bilançosu: Asker, polis, hakim, savcı, vali, kaymakam 50 bin tutuklu, 155 bin gözaltı," *TR7/24*, May 28, 2017, http://www.tr724.com/15-temmuz-hukuksuzlugunun-bilancosu-50-bin-tutuklu-155-bin-gozalti/

109. "Turkish Defence Minister Akar: 15,153 military officers including 150 generals and admirals dismissed over Gülen links," Stockholm Center for Freedom (SCF), October 27, 2018, https://stockholmcf.org/turkish-defence-minister-akar-15153-military-officers-including-150-generals-and-admirals-dismissed-over-gulen-links/

110. "CoE's Muižnieks Expresses Concern About Turkey's New Supreme Board Of Judges And Prosecutors," Stockholm Center for Freedom (SCF), June 8, 2017, (accessed on April 26, 2019), https://stockholmcf.org/coes-muiznieks-expresses-concern-about-turkeys-new-supreme-board-of-judges-and-prosecutors/

111. "15 Temmuz hukuksuzluğunun bilançosu: Asker, polis, hakim, savcı, vali, kaymakam 50 bin tutuklu, 155 bin gözaltı," TR7/24, May 28, 2017, http://www.tr724.com/15-temmuz-hukuksuzlugunun-bilancosu-50-bin-tutuklu-155-bin-gozalti/

112. "Jailed head of lawyers association allowed to attend father's funeral in handcuffs," *Stockholm Center for Freedom (SCF)*, January 19, 2019, (accessed on April 26, 2019), https://stockholmcf.org/jailed-head-of-lawyers-association-allowed-to-attend-fathers-funeral-in-handcuffs/ ; "Our Statement on the Occasion of Day of the Endangered Lawyers," The Arrested Lawyers' Initiative, January 24, 2019, (accessed on April 26, 2019), https://arrestedlawyers.org/2019/01/24/our-statement-on-the-occasion-of-day-of-the-endangered-lawyers/

113. "Free thought under siege in Turkey: The crackdown on education," *Stockholm*

Center for Freedom (SCF), July 2018, (accessed on April 26, 2019), https://stockholmcf.org/wp-content/uploads/2018/07/The-Crackdown-On-Education-in-Turkey_june_2018.pdf

114. "How the state of emergency affected universites: Distribution of academics dismissed by decree-laws by university," *Cumhuriyet*, July 11, 2017, (accessed on April 26, 2019), http://www.cumhuriyet.com.tr/haber/egitim/778904/OHAL_universiteleri_nasil_etkiledi__KHK_larla_ihrac_edilen_akademisyenlerin_universitelere_gore_dagilimi.html

115. "Free thought under siege in Turkey: The crackdown on education," *Stockholm Center for Freedom (SCF)*, July 2018, (accessed on April 26, 2019), https://stockholmcf.org/wp-content/uploads/2018/07/The-Crackdown-On-Education-in-Turkey_june_2018.pdf

116. "Turkish vice president says gov't took over 1,004 companies across 42 provinces," *Stockholm Center for Freedom (SCF)*, November 1, 2018, (accessed on April 26, 2019), https://stockholmcf.org/turkish-vice-president-says-govt-took-over-1004-companies-across-42-provinces/

117. "15 Temmuz hukuksuzluğunun bilançosu: Asker, polis, hakim, savcı, vali, kaymakam 50 bin tutuklu, 155 bin gözaltı," TR7/24, May 28, 2017, http://www.tr724.com/15-temmuz-hukuksuzlugunun-bilancosu-50-bin-tutuklu-155-bin-gozalti/

118. "TMSF Kayyım Olunan Şirketler," January 21, 2019, https://www.tmsf.org.tr/tr/Sirket/Kayyim?Page=10&Rows=100

119. "Turkish vice president says gov't took over 1,004 companies across 42 provinces," *Stockholm Center for Freedom (SCF)*, November 1, 2018, https://stockholmcf.org/turkish-vice-president-says-govt-took-over-1004-companies-across-42-provinces/

120. "ÇGD Head Says Over 900 Press Cards Canceled, 151 Journalists Jailed In Post-Coup Turkey," *Stockholm Center for Freedom* (SCF), August 5, 2017, (accessed on April 26, 2019), https://stockholmcf.org/cgd-head-says-over-900-press-cards-canceled-151-journalists-jailed-in-post-coup-turkey/

121. "Jailed and wanted journalists in Turkey -- Updated List," *Stockholm Center for Freedom* (SCF), February 15, 2019, (accessed on April 26, 2019), http://stockholmcf.org/updated-list/

122. Kerem Altıparmak, "OHAL KHK'leri "Sivil Ölüm" mü Demek?" *Bianet*, September 6, 2016, (accessed on April 26, 2019), https://bianet.org/bianet/bianet/178496-ohal-khk-leri-sivil-olum-mu-demek

123. AYM, 25.2.2010 gün ve E. 2008/17, K. 2010/44 sayılı kararı.

124. "Meslekten ihraç edilenler özelde çalışabilir mi, özel sektörde iş imkanı," Öğretmenler İçin, July 15, 2017, (accessed on April 26, 2019), http://www.ogretmenlericin.com/meb/kamudan-haber/meslekten-ihrac-edilenler-ozelde-calisabilir-mi-ozel-sektorde-is-imkani-18888.html

125. "SGK '36 kod' ile fişleme yapıyor," *Sol*, September 25, 2017, (accessed on April 26, 2019), http://haber.sol.org.tr/toplum/sgk-36-kod-ile-fisleme-yapiyor-210992

126. Rengin Arslan, "KHK'larla ihraç edilen memurlar: Mağduruz, bizi soruşturun," *BBC Türkçe*, November 8, 2016, (accessed on April 26, 2019), http://www.bbc.com/turkce/haberler-turkiye-37904717

127. "Lisansı iptal edilen öğretmenlere bir daha çalışma izni verilmeyecek," *Mymemur.com*, October 3, 2016, (accessed on April 26, 2019), http://www.mymemur.com.tr/lisansi-iptal-edilen-ogretmenlere-bir-daha-calisma-izni-verilmeyecek-81635h.htm

128. "FETÖ mağduru anne: '8 aylık hasta bebeğin suçu ne?'" *Yurt Gazetesi*, March 21, 2017, (accessed on April 26, 2019), http://www.mynet.com/haber/yasam/feto-magduru-anne-8-aylik-hasta-bebegin-sucu-ne-2944654-1

129. Kürşat Akyol, "Turkey could find itself facing hefty legal bill for mass purges," *al-Monitor*, September 19, 2016, (accessed on April 26, 2019), http://www.al-monitor.com/pulse/originals/2016/09/turkey-risks-thousands-of-civil-death-lawsuits.html#ixzz4oRaQAneR

130. Kerem Altıparmak, "OHAL KHK'leri "Sivil Ölüm" mü Demek?" *Bianet*, September 6, 2016, (accessed on April 26, 2019), https://bianet.org/bianet/bianet/178496-ohal-khk-leri-sivil-olum-mu-demek

131. Niemietz/Almanya, 16.12. 1992, Series A no. 251-B, para. 29.

132. "Avrupa İnsan Hakları Mahkemesi Ülke-Türkiye Davası, Kararın Özet Çevirisi," January 24, 2006 http://www.aihmiz.org.tr/?q=tr/content/ulke-karari

133. ARTICLE 2- The Republic of Turkey is a democratic, secular and social state governed by rule of law, within the notions of public peace, national solidarity and justice, respecting human rights, loyal to the nationalism of Atatürk, and based on the fundamental tenets set forth in the preamble.

134. Kerem Altıparmak, "OHAL KHK'leri "Sivil Ölüm" mü Demek?" *Bianet*, September 6, 2016, (accessed on April 26, 2019), https://bianet.org/bianet/bianet/178496-ohal-khk-leri-sivil-olum-mu-demek

135. ARTICLE 15- (As amended on April 16, 2017; Act No. 6771) In times of war, mobilization, a state of emergency, the exercise of fundamental rights and freedoms may be partially or entirely suspended, or measures derogating the guarantees embodied in the Constitution may be taken to the extent required by the exigencies of the situation, as long as obligations under international law are not violated. (As amended on May 7, 2004; Act No. 5170) Even under the circumstances indicated in the first paragraph, the individual's right to life, the integrity of his/her corporeal and spiritual existence shall be inviolable except where death occurs through acts in conformity with law of war; no one shall be compelled to reveal his/her religion, conscience, thought or opinion, nor be accused on account of them; offences and penalties shall not be made retroactive; nor shall anyone be held guilty until so proven by a court ruling.

136. Bkz. Sidabras ve Džiautas, para. 59.

137. See Naidin/Romania, no. 38162/07, 21.10.2104, para. 54.

138. Kerem Altıparmak, "Bu Bir Olağanüstü Hal KHK'si Değildir," *Bianet*, July 25, 2016, (accessed on April 26, 2019), https://bianet.org/bianet/hukuk/177136-bu-bir-olaganustu-hal-khk-si-degildir

139. See CDL-AD(2012)028-e, Amicus Curiae Brief on the Law on determining a criterion for limiting the exercise of public office, access to documents and publishing, the co-operation with the bodies of the state security ("Lustration Law") of "the former Yugoslav Republic of Macedonia" adopted by the Venice Commission At its 93rd Plenary Session (Venice, 14-15 December 2012), (accessed on April 26, 2019), https://www.venice.coe.int/webforms/documents/?pdf=CDL-AD(2012)028-e

140. Oxford English Dictionary "Genocide" citing Raphael Lemkin's "Axis Rule in Occupied Europe", ix. 79.

141. "Son dakika: FETÖ üyelerine baskın! Toplantı halindeyken yakalandılar..." *Milliyet*, March 2, 2017, (accessed on April 26, 2019), http://www.milliyet.com.tr/son-dakika-feto-uyeleri-toplanti-gundem-2405970/ ; Bülent Keneş, "İnsanlığımızı kurtaran 12 dev adam," *TR7/24*, March 7, 2017, (accessed on April 26, 2019), http://www.tr724.com/insanligimizi-kurtaran-12-dev-adam-haber-analiz-akif-umut-avaz/

142. "Turkey: Almost 130,000 purged public sector workers still awaiting justice," *Amnesty International*, October 25, 2018, https://www.amnesty.org/en/latest/news/2018/10/almost-130000-purged-sector-workers-still-awaiting-justice-in-turkey/

143. "Turkey Arrests Newly Married Kutlu Couple Over Alleged Gülen Links," *Stockholm Center for Freedom* (SCF), July 10, 2017, (accessed on April 26, 2019), https://stockholmcf.org/turkey-arrests-bridegroom-kutlu-as-bride-kutlu-still-under-interrogation-over-alleged-gulen-links/

144. "Doktora götürülmeyen kadın nezarette tek başına doğum yaptı," *Gazete Karınca*, March 28, 2017, (accessed on April 26, 2019), http://gazetekarinca.com/2017/03/doktora-goturulmeyen-kadin-nezarette-tek-basina-dogum-yapti/

145. "Nurhayat Yıldız, zindanda karnındaki ikizlerini kaybetti!" *Mağduriyetler*, June 23, 2017, (accessed on April 26, 2019), http://magduriyetler.com/2017/06/23/nurhayat-yildiz-zindanda-karnindaki-ikizlerini-kaybetti/

146. "Report on the impact of the state of emergency on human rights in Turkey, including an update on the South-East (January-December 2017)," *Office of the United Nations High Commissioner for Human Rights (OHCHR)*, March 2018, (accessed on April 26, 2019), https://www.ohchr.org/Documents/Countries/TR/2018-03-19_Second_OHCHR_Turkey_Report.pdf , "Opposition deputy: Police detain another woman shortly after delivery," *Turkey Purge*, August 1, 2017, (accessed on April 26, 2019), https://turkeypurge.com/opposition-deputy-police-detain-another-woman-shortly-after-delivery

147. Faruk Turhan, "Yeni Türk Ceza Kanunu'na Göre Uluslararası Suçların Cezalandırılması," *Hukuki Perspektifler Dergisi*, Sayı 3, Nisan 2005, p. 14.

148. Duygu Ayber, "Tutuklu kadın sayısı üçe katlandı: Çıplak arama artık rutin," *Journo*, February 23, 2017, (accessed on April 26, 2019), https://journo.com.tr/tutuklu-kadin-sayisi-ciplak-arama

149. "Jailing women in Turkey: Systematic campaign of persecution and fear," *Stockholm Center for Freedom (SCF)*, April 2017, (accessed on April 26, 2019), http://stockholmcf.org/wp-content/uploads/2017/04/Jailing-women-in-Turkey.pdf

150. "743 children jailed with their mothers in Turkey, rights group reveals," *Turkish Minute*, November 23, 2018, (accessed on April 26, 2019), https://www.turkishminute.com/2018/11/23/743-children-jailed-with-their-mothers-in-turkey-rights-group-reveals/

151. 10th General Report on the CPT's activities (1999) including a section on Women deprived of their liberty, paragraph 27, www.cpt.coe.int/en/docsannual.htm

152. Türkiye Büyük Millet Meclisi Genel Kurul Tutanağı 26. Dönem 2. Yasama Yılı 68. Birleşim (2017, February 9), https://www.tbmm.gov.tr/devel-

op/owa/tutanak_sd.birlesim_baslangic?P4=22844&P5=H&web_user_
id=15455253&PAGE1=1&PAGE2=74

153. "Report on the impact of the state of emergency on human rights in Turkey,
including an update on the South-East (January-December 2017)," Office of
the United Nations High Commissioner for Human Rights (OHCHR), March
2018, https://www.ohchr.org/Documents/Countries/TR/2018-03-19_Second_
OHCHR_Turkey_Report.pdf

154. Emin Çölaşan, "Hukukçular yazıyor," *Sözcü*, October 2, 2016, (accessed on April 26, 2019), http://www.sozcu.com.tr/2016/yazarlar/emin-colasan/hukukcu-
lar-yaziyor-1423418/

155. "Yeni Söz ve Milat yazarı Hüseyin Adalan: FETÖ'cülerin bebeklerine kadar kat-
li vacibtir," *Haberdar,* May 7 2017, (accessed on April 26, 2019), http://www.
haberdar.com/gundem/yeni-soz-ve-milat-yazari-huseyin-adalan-feto-culer-
in-bebeklerine-kadar-katli-vacibtir-h51024.html

156. "Cezaevine eşini ziyarete giden anne tutuklandı, 5 çocuk ortada kaldı," *Kronos*,
23 Ocak 2017, (accessed on April 26, 2019), http://www.kronos.news/tr/cezae-
vi-ziyaretinde-anne-de-gozaltinda-alindi-5-cocuk-ortada-kaldi/

157. Emin Çölaşan, "Hukukçular yazıyor," *Sözcü*, October 2, 2016, (accessed on April 26, 2019), http://www.sozcu.com.tr/2016/yazarlar/emin-colasan/hukukcu-
lar-yaziyor-1423418/

Chapter 5

1. Gregory H. Stanton, "The Ten Stages of Genocide," *Genocide Watch*, (accessed
on April 26, 2019), http://genocidewatch.net/genocide-2/8-stages-of-geno-
cide/

2. "Nefret Suçlarıyla Mücadele Konferansları Konuşma Metinleri," (accessed on
April 26, 2019), http://rightsagenda.org/nefret-suclariyla-mucadele-konfer-
anslari-konusma-metinleri/

3. Nuri Elibol, "Gizlenen FETÖ'cüler nasıl tespit ediliyor?" *Türkiye*, August 15,
2016, (accessed on April 26, 2019), http://www.turkiyegazetesi.com.tr/yazarlar/
nuri-elibol/592812.aspx ; Saygı Öztürk, "Savcılar, FETÖ'cüleri 8 kriterle belir-
leyecek," Sözcü, 29 Mayıs 2017, (accessed on April 26, 2019), http://www.soz-
cu.com.tr/2017/gundem/savcilar-fetoculeri-8-kriterle-belirleyecek-1873005/ ;
Ebru Karatosun, "13 adımda FETÖ'den tutuklanma kriterleri," *Türkiye*, January
31, 2017, (accessed on April 26, 2019), http://www.turkiyegazetesi.com.tr/gun-
dem/442810.aspx ; "FETÖ'cü memurları belirlemede 11 kriter!" *memurhaber.
com*, August 2, 2017, (accessed on April 26, 2019), http://www.memurhaber.
com/fetocu-memurlari-belirlemede-11-kriter-foto-galerisi-1705450.htm

4. "Opinion On Emergency Decree Laws Nos. 667-676 Adopted Following The
Failed Coup On 15 July 2016," Venice Commission, December 9-10, 2016, (accessed on April 26, 2019), http://www.venice.coe.int/webforms/documents/
default.aspx?pdffile=CDL-AD(2016)037-e

5. "Turkish navy algorithm detects 4,500 allegedly Gülen-linked officers among
800,000 profiled," *Turkish Minute*, September 11, 2018, (accessed on April
26, 2019), https://www.turkishminute.com/2018/09/11/turkish-navy-algo-
rithm-detects-allegedly-4500-gulen-linked-officers-among-800000-profiled/

6. "15 July: Erdoğan's Coup," Stockholm Center for Freedom (SCF), July 2017, https://stockholmcf.org/wp-content/uploads/2017/07/15_July_Erdogans_Coup_13.07.2017.pdf

7. "Medyatava tiraj raporu," 5 Ocak 2015, http://www.medyatava.com/tiraj/2015-01-05

8. MADDE 30 – Kanuna uygun şekilde basın işletmesi olarak kurulan basımevi ve eklentileri ile basın araçları, suç aleti olduğu gerekçesiyle zapt ve müsadere edilemez veya işletilmekten alıkonulamaz. Bkz. Türkiye Cumhuriyeti Anayasası, https://www.tbmm.gov.tr/anayasa/anayasa82.htm

9. July 27, 2016 tarihli Resmi Gazetede yayımlanan 668 Sayılı KHK, http://www.resmigazete.gov.tr/eskiler/2016/07/20160727M2-1.pdf

10. "Zaman Gazetesinin eski ekibine operasyon," Cumhuriyet, July 27, 2016, http://www.cumhuriyet.com.tr/haber/turkiye/574815/Zaman_gazetesinin_eski_ekibine_operasyon.html

11. "FETÖ'cüleri tespit etmek için 12 soru," Milli Gazete, August 15, 2016, http://milligazete.com.tr/haber/886434/iste-fetoculeri-tespit-etmek-icin-sorulan--12-soru

12. "Bank Asya," Wikipedia, https://tr.wikipedia.org/wiki/Bank_Asya

13. "TFF Birinci ligin adı Bank Asya ligi oldu," tff.org, January 16, 2008, (accessed on April 26, 2019), http://www.tff.org/default.aspx?pageID=287&ftxtID=3027

14. Neşe Karanfil, "700 bin kişi sorgulanıyor," Hürriyet, September 21, 2016, (accessed on April 26, 2019), http://www.hurriyet.com.tr/700-bin-kisis-orgulaniyor-40228664

15. "FETÖ sanığının Bank Asya savunması itibar görmedi," Anadolu Ajansı, May 10, 2017, (accessed on April 26, 2019), http://aa.com.tr/tr/turkiye/feto-saniginin-bank-asya-savunmasi-itibar-gormedi/815213

16. "Bank Asya'da 1.2 milyon kişiye ödeme yapılacak," Sabah, December 16, 2016, (accessed on April 26, 2019), http://www.sabah.com.tr/ekonomi/2016/12/16/bank-asyada-12-milyon-kisiye-odeme-yapilacak-bank-asya-odemelerini-nasil-alacagim

17. "Aksiyon İşçi Sendikaları Konfederasyonu," Wikipedia, (accessed on April 26, 2019), https://tr.wikipedia.org/wiki/Aksiyon_İşçi_Sendikaları_Konfederasyonu

18. "Aktif Eğitimciler Sendikası kuruldu," egitimciyiz.com, May 18, 2012, (accessed on April 26, 2019), http://www.egitimciyiz.com/aktif-egitimciler-sendikasi-kuruldu.html/

19. Koray Çalışkan, "Cemaatten mühim bir siyasi adım," Radikal, January 10, 2013, (accessed on April 26, 2019), http://www.radikal.com.tr/yazarlar/koray-caliskan/cemaatten-muhim-bir-siyasi-adim-1165373/

20. "667 sayılı Kanun Hükmünde Kararname," Resmi Gazete, July 23, 2016, (accessed on April 26, 2019), http://www.resmigazete.gov.tr/eskiler/2016/07/20160723.pdf

21. "Bursa'da 19 FETÖ'cü Aktif-Sen üyesi adliyele sevkedildi," Milliyet, September 28, 2016, (accessed on April 26, 2019), http://www.milliyet.com.tr/aktif-sen-uyesi-19-feto-cu-adliyeye-bursa-yerelhaber-1570438/ ; "Antalya'da Aktif-Sen üyesi 30 tutuklu sanığın yargılanmasına başlandı," memurlar.net, February 7, 2017, (accessed on April 26, 2019), http://www.memur-

lar.net/haber/644648/aktif-sen-uyesi-30-tutuklu-sanigin-yargilanmasi-na-baslandi.html ; "Adana'da Aktif-Sencilere FETÖ Davası açıldı," *Sabah*, November 26, 2016, (accessed on April 26, 2019), http://www.sabah.com.tr/guney/2016/11/26/aktif-sencilere-feto-davasi-acildi

22. "Aktif-Sen üyesine 6 yıl üç ay ceza verildi," *ogretmenlersitesi.com*, March 17, 2017, (accessed on April 26, 2019), http://www.ogretmenlersitesi.com/haber/aktif-sen-uyesine-6-yil-3-ay-ceza-verildi-h38068.html

23. "Çalışma ve Sosyal Güvenlik Bakanlığından: 4688 sayılı kamu görevlileri sendikaları ve toplu sözleşme kanunu gereğince kamu görevlileri sendikaları ile konfederasyonların üye sayılarına ilişkin 2016 Temmuz istatistikleri," *Resmi Gazete*, http://www.resmigazete.gov.tr/main.aspx?home=http://www.resmigazete.gov.tr/eskiler/2016/07/20160704.htm&main=http://www.resmigazete.gov.tr/eskiler/2016/07/20160704.htm

24. "Jailed head of lawyers association allowed to attend father's funeral in handcuffs," *Stockholm Center for Freedom (SCF)*, January 19, 2019, (accessed on April 26, 2019), https://stockholmcf.org/jailed-head-of-lawyers-association-allowed-to-attend-fathers-funeral-in-handcuffs/ ; "Our Statement on the Occasion of Day of the Endangered Lawyers," *The Arrested Lawyers' Initiative*, January 24, 2019, (accessed on April 26, 2019), https://arrestedlawyers.org/2019/01/24/our-statement-on-the-occasion-of-day-of-the-endangered-lawyers/

25. Tülay Canbolat, "FETÖ'cülerin sağlık dernekleri durmuyor," *Sabah*, August 19, 2016, (accessed on April 26, 2019), http://www.sabah.com.tr/ankara-baskent/2016/08/19/fetoculerin-saglik-dernekleri-durmuyor ; "FETÖ'nün sağlık yapılanmasına operasyon: 24 gözaltı," *CNN Türk*, 15 Mayıs 2016, https://www.cnnturk.com/turkiye/fetonun-saglik-yapilanmasina-operasyon-24-gozalti ; "Denizli'de FETÖ'nün sağlık yapılanması davası," *Milliyet*, June 12, 2017, (accessed on April 26, 2019), http://www.milliyet.com.tr/denizli-de-feto-nun-saglik-yapilanmasi-denizli-yerelhaber-2103966/

26. "Denizli'de FETÖ'nün sağlık ayağı hakim karşısında," *Denizli Gazetesi*, June 9, 2017, (accessed on April 26, 2019), http://www.denizligazetesi.com/haberler/guncel/denizlide-fetonun-saglik-ayagi-hakim-karsisinda/64182/

27. "Adana'da FETÖ sanığı işadamlarına dava," *Milliyet*, May 5,,2017, (accessed on April 26, 2019), http://www.milliyet.com.tr/adana-da-feto-sanigi-is-adamlari-hakkindaki-adana-yerelhaber-2019181/ ; "Denizli'de işadamlarına yönelik ikinci FETÖ Davası," *Hürriyet*, May 2, 2017, (accessed on April 26, 2019), http://www.hurriyet.com.tr/denizlide-isadamlarina-yonelik-2nci-feto-dava-40444879 ; "Bartın'da ,FETÖ davasında işadamları hakim karşısında," *haberler.com*, April 28, 2017, (accessed on April 26, 2019), https://www.haberler.com/bartin-da-feto-davasinda-isadamlari-hakim-9555015-haberi/

28. "Ticaret Köprüsünden 300 milyon dolarlık ihracat gelecek," *Dünya*, October 27, 2011, (accessed on April 26, 2019), https://www.dunya.com/gundem/ticaret-koprusunden-300-milyon-dolarlik-ihracat-gececek-haberi-157528 ; "Türkiye'nin Afrika açılımında Gülen okulları ve TUSKON'un rolü büyük," *T24*, January 7, 2013, (accessed on April 26, 2019), http://t24.com.tr/haber/ft-turkiyenin-afrika-aciliminda-gulen-okullari-ve-tuskonun-rolu-buyuk,221159

29. "Erdoğan Hukukta otoban istedi, zenginliği demokrasiye bağladı," *Hürriyet*, March 7, 2010, (accessed on April 26, 2019), http://www.hurriyet.com.tr/erdogan-hukukta-otoban-istedi-zenginligi-demokrasiye-bagladi-14030784

30. "668 numaralı KHK," *Resmi Gazete*, July 27, 2016, (accessed on April 26, 2019), http://www.resmigazete.gov.tr/eskiler/2016/07/20160727M2-1..pdf

31. "Yeşilsırt'ta FETÖ operasyonu: İki tutuklama. Yüzlerce kitaba el konuldu," *Muratlı Hizmet*, (accessed on April 26, 2019), http://muratlihizmetgazetesi.com/yesilsirt-ta-feto-operasyonu-2-tutuklama

32. "Kadirli'de FETÖ kitaplarını çöpe atan imam yakalandı," (accessed on July 1, 2017), https://www.osmaniye.net/osmaniye-haber/kadirli-de-feto-nun-kitaplarini-cope-atan-imam-yakalandi

33. "FETÖ kitaplarını gömen avukat yakalandı," *Beyaz Gazete*, July 30, 2016, (accessed on April 26, 2019), http://beyazgazete.com/haber/2016/7/30/feto-kitaplarini-gomen-avukat-yakalandi-3402665.html

34. "Düzce'de FETÖ kitaplarını yakarken yakalanan şahıs tutuklandı," *haberler.com*, July 25, 2016, (accessed on April 26, 2019), https://www.haberler.com/duzce-de-feto-nun-kitaplarini-yakarken-yakalanan-8645759-haberi/

35. "FETÖ'cü darbeciler Kur'anı atmış," *memurlar.net*, July 28, 2016, (accessed on April 26, 2019), http://www.memurlar.net/album/11052/11.resim

36. "Kitap üzerindeki parmak izinden FETÖ sorumlusu yakalandı," *memurlar.net*, December 7, 2016, (accessed on April 26, 2019), http://www.memurlar.net/haber/630415/

37. "MEB yasaklı yayınlar listesi," *Karar*, 17 Ekim 2016, (accessed on April 27, 2019), http://www.karar.com/guncel-haberler/meb-yasakli-yayinlar-listesi-257583#

38. "FETÖ'cülerin yazdığı ders kitapları imha edilecek," *Ulke TV*, September 8, 2016, (accessed on July 3, 2017), http://www.ulke.com.tr/guncel/haber/698902-fetoculerin-yazdigi-ders-kitaplari-imha-edilecek

39. "Digitürk tarihçesi," Digitürk, (accessed on April 26, 2019), https://www.digiturk.com.tr/kurumsal/tarihce/

40. "TMSF, Akşam Gazetesi ve Digitürk'e el koydu," *Radikal*, May 24, 2013, (accessed on April 27, 2019), http://www.radikal.com.tr/ekonomi/tmsf-aksam-gazetesi-ve-digiturke-el-koydu-1134857/

41. "Ethem Sancak, AKP yönetiminde," *T24*, May 21, 2017, (accessed on April 27, 2019), http://t24.com.tr/haber/ethem-sancak-akp-yonetimine-girdi,405236

42. "CHP'li Tanrıkulu: Digitürk'ün ihalesiz olarak Katarlılara satıldığı iddiası doğru mu?" *Haber46*, July 16, 2015, (accessed on April 26, 2019), https://www.haber46.com.tr/politika/tanrikulu-digiturkun-ihalesiz-olarak-katarlilara-satildigi-iddiasi-dogru-mu-h103931.html

43. "Digitürk 7 kanalı yayından kaldırdı," *Hürriyet*, October 8, 2015, (accessed on April 27, 2019), http://www.hurriyet.com.tr/digiturk-7-kanali-yayindan-kaldirdi-samanyolundan-aciklama-geldi-30261195

44. "Digitürk'e tepkiler çığ gibi: Kumandalı protesto. CHP bütün teşkilatlarından çıkarıyor," *Hukuki Haber*, October 10, 2015, (accessed on July 3, 2017) http://www.hukukihaber.net/gundem/digiturk-depremi-tepkiler-cig-gibi-kumandali-protesto-h64715.html

45. Erdem Gül, "Kılıçdaroğlu'ndan Digitürk'e boykot çağrısı," *Cumhuriyet*, October 9, 2015, (accessed on April 27, 2019) http://www.cumhuriyet.com.tr/haber/siyaset/384097/Kilicdaroglu_ndan_Digiturk_u_boykot_cagrisi.html

46. Sami Menteş, "Digitürk iptali FETÖ üyeliği delili oldu," *Odatv*, April 24, 2017,

(accessed on April 27, 2019), http://odatv.com/digiturk-iptali-feto-uyeligi-ne-delil-oldu-2404171200.html

47. "Cumhurbaşkanı Erdoğan, aTV-aHaber Ortak Yayınına Katıldı," *Türkiye Cumhurbaşkanlığı Sitesi*, October 30, 2015, (accessed on April 27, 2019), https://www.tccb.gov.tr/haberler/410/35814/cumhurbaskani-erdogan-atv-a-haber-ortak-yayinina-katildi.html

48. "Erdoğan ilk kez açıkladı; FETÖ'nün adı artık illegal terör örgütü," *Medya Gündemi*, April 30, 2016, (accessed on April 27, 2019), http://www.medyagundem.com/erdogan-ilk-kez-acikladi-fetonun-adi-artik-illegal-teror-orgutu/

49. "Hükümetten önemli FETÖ kararı," *Takvim*, May 30, 2016, (accessed on April 27, 2019), http://www.takvim.com.tr/guncel/2016/05/30/hukumetten-onemli-feto-karari

50. https://www.google.se/search?q=FETO&oq=FETO&aqs=-chrome.0.69i59j0l5.1884j1j7&sourceid=chrome&ie=UTF-8

51. "Adalet Bakanı Bekir Bozdağ'dan 'tek tip kıyafet' açıklaması," *T24*, July 18, 2017, (accessed on April 27, 2019), http://t24.com.tr/haber/adalet-bakani-bekir-bozdagdan-tek-tip-kiyafet-aciklamasi,414964

52. "Coup suspects to wear identical brown uniforms in court, Turkish ministry says," *Turkish Minute*, August 5, 2017, (accessed on April 27, 2019), https://www.turkishminute.com/2017/08/05/coup-suspects-to-wear-identical-brown-uniforms-in-court-turkish-ministry-says/

53. "No progress toward media freedom in Turkey, IPI report finds," *IPI*, February 11, 2019, (accessed on April 27, 2019), https://freeturkeyjournalists.ipi.media/no-progress-toward-media-freedom-in-turkey-ipi-report-finds/

54. "Nefret Suçlarıyla Mücadele Konferansları Konuşma Metinleri," *Human Rights Agenda Foundation*, (accessed on April 27, 2019), http://rightsagenda.org/nefret-suclariyla-mucadele-konferanslari-konusma-metinleri/

55. UN Human Rights Committee, *General Comment 18: Non-Discrimination*, Parag. 7, November 10, 1989, (accessed on April 27, 2019), https://www.refworld.org/docid/453883fa8.html

56. Türkiye'de Ayrımcılık, Irkçılık ve Nefret Suçları, *Human Rights Agenda Foundation*, June 14, 2005, (accessed on July 12, 2017), http://www.rightsagenda.org/index.php?option=com_content&view=article&id=198:takmatuerkiye-de-ayrmclk-irkclk-ve-nefret-suclar&catid=52:takmaraporlar&Itemid=91

57. Amnesty International, *Take A Step To Stamp Out Torture*, (Amnesty International Publications, London, 2000.) p. 37.

58. Bernard E. Whitley Jr. and Mary E. Kite, *The Psychology of Prejudice and Discrimination*, (Thomson Wadsworth Wadsworth Publishing, Canada, 2006), p.10.

59. Ibid., p. 3-4.

60. OSCE, *Ministerial Council Decision No. 4/03 on tolerance and non-discrimination*, Maastricht Ministerial Council Meeting, December 2, 2003, (accessed on April 27, 2019), https://www.osce.org/mc/19382

61. OSCE, *Ministerial Council Decision No. 12/04 on tolerance and non-discrimination*, Sofia Ministerial Council Meeting, December 7, 2004, (accessed on April 27, 2019), https://www.osce.org/mc/23133?download=true ; OSCE, *Permanent Council Decision No. 621: Tolerance and the fight against racism, xenophobia*

and discrimination, July 29, 2004, (accessed on April 27, 2019), https://www.osce.org/pc/35610

62. Ibid.

63. "Everyone is entitled to all the rights and freedoms set forth in this Declaration, without distinction of any kind, such as race, colour, sex, language, religion, political or other opinion, national or social origin, property, birth or other status. Furthermore, no distinction shall be made on the basis of the political, jurisdictional or international status of the country or territory to which a person belongs, whether it be independent, trust, non-self-governing or under any other limitation of sovereignty." See *Universal Declaration of Human Rights*, (accessed on April 27, 2019), http://www.un.org/en/universal-declaration-human-rights/

64. "Each State Party to the present Covenant undertakes to respect and to ensure to all individuals within its territory and subject to its jurisdiction the rights recognized in the present Covenant, without distinction of any kind, such as race, colour, sex, language, religion, political or other opinion, national or social origin, property, birth or other status." See *International Covenant on Civil and Political Rights,* Adopted and opened for signature, ratification and accession by General Assembly resolution 2200A (XXI) of 16 December 1966, entry into force March 23, 1976, in accordance with Article 49, (accessed on April 27, 2019), https://www.ohchr.org/en/professionalinterest/pages/ccpr.aspx

65. "The enjoyment of the rights and freedoms set forth in this Convention shall be secured without discrimination on any ground such as sex, race, colour, language, religion, political or other opinion, national or social origin, association with a national minority, property, birth or other status." See *European Convention on Human Rights as amended by Protocols Nos. 11 and 14,* European Court of Human Rights, Council of Europe, (accessed on April 27, 2019), https://www.echr.coe.int/Documents/Convention_ENG.pdf

66. "The member States of the Council of Europe signatory hereto,

    Having regard to the fundamental principle according to which all persons are equal before the law and are entitled to the equal protection of the law;

    Being resolved to take further steps to promote the equality of all persons through the collective enforcement of a general prohibition of discrimination by means of the Convention for the Protection of Human Rights and Fundamental Freedoms signed at Rome on 4 November 1950 (hereinafter referred to as "the Convention");

    Reaffirming that the principle of non-discrimination does not prevent States Parties from taking measures in order to promote full and effective equality, provided that there is an objective and reasonable justification for those measures,

    Have agreed as follows:

    Article 1 – General prohibition of discrimination

    1 - The enjoyment of any right set forth by law shall be secured without discrimination on any ground such as sex, race, colour, language, religion, political or other opinion, national or social origin, association with a national minority, property, birth or other status.

    2 - No one shall be discriminated against by any public authority on any ground such as those mentioned in paragraph 1." See CoE, *Protocol No. 12 to the Con-*

vention for the Protection of Human Rights and Fundamental Freedoms, Rome, 4.XI.2000, (accessed on April 27, 2019), https://rm.coe.int/CoERMPublicCommonSearchServices/DisplayDCTMContent?documentId=0900001680080622

67. "The enjoyment of the rights set forth in this Charter shall be secured without discrimination on any ground such as race, colour, sex, language, religion, political or other opinion, national extraction or social origin, health, association with a national minority, birth or other status." See the *Art. E of the Part V of the amended European Social Charter*, Strasbourg, 3.V.1996, (accessed on April 27, 2019), https://rm.coe.int/168007cf93

68. "1. Any discrimination based on any ground such as sex, race, colour, ethnic or social origin, genetic features, language, religion or belief, political or any other opinion, membership of a national minority, property, birth, disability, age or sexual orientation shall be prohibited."

"2. Within the scope of application of the Treaty establishing the European Community and of the Treaty on European Union, and without prejudice to the special provisions of those Treaties, any discrimination on grounds of nationality shall be prohibited." See Article 21 of the Chapter III (titled "Equality") of "the European Union Declaration of Fundamental Rights (2000/C 364/01)," Official Journal of the European Communities, 18.12.2000, (accessed on April 27, 2019), http://www.europarl.europa.eu/charter/pdf/text_en.pdf

69. "Jailed and wanted journalists in Turkey -- Updated List," *Stockholm Center for Freedom (SCF)*, April 26, 2019, (accessed on April 27, 2019), http://stockholmcf.org/updated-list/

70. "2 more men abducted by armed group in Ankara: report," *Turkish Minute*, February 15, 2019, (accessed on April 27, 2019), https://www.turkishminute.com/2019/02/15/2-more-men-abducted-by-armed-group-in-ankara-report/ ; "Black Sites Turkey," *Correctiv*, December 11, 2018, (accessed on April 27, 2019), https://correctiv.org/en/top-stories-en/2018/12/06/black-sites/ ; "Enforced disappearences in Turkey: Updated List As of January 09, 2019," *Stockholm Center for Freedom (SCF)*, (accessed on April 27, 2019), https://stockholmcf.org/enforced-disappearances-in-turkey-2/ ; "Enforced disappearences in Turkey," *Stockholm Center for Freedom (SCF)*, June 2017, (accessed on April 27, 2019), https://stockholmcf.org/wp-content/uploads/2017/06/Enforced-Dissappearences-in-Turkey_22_June_2017.pdf

71. "Erdoğan's vile campaign of hate speech - A case study: Targeting of the Gülen Movement," *Stockholm Center for Freedom (SCF)*, May 2017, (accessed on April 27, 2019), http://stockholmcf.org/wp-content/uploads/2017/06/Erdogans-Vile-Campaign-Of-Hate-Speech-Case-Study-Targeting-Of-The-Gulen-Movement_2017.pdf

72. Augustine Brannigan, "Criminology and the Holocaust: Xenophobia, Evolution and Genocide," *Crime & Delinquency*, Vol. 44, No. 2, 1998, p. 262.

73. "Dünyaca tanınan İslam Alimi Ali Cuma'dan Diyanet'e 'Firak-ı Dalle' reddiyesi," *TR7/24*, October 24, 2016, (accessed on April 27, 2019), http://www.tr724.com/dunyaca-taninan-islam-alimi-ali-cumadan-diyanete-kendi-kusurlarini-baskalarinda-goruyorlar/

74. "Diyanet FETÖ raporu açıklandı!" *Sabah*, July 26 2017, (accessed on April 27, 2019), http://www.sabah.com.tr/gundem/2017/07/26/son-dakika-diyanet-feto-raporu-aciklandi

75. "Fethullah Hoca Papa'yla görüştü," *Hürriyet*, February 10, 1998, (accessed on April 27, 2019), http://www.hurriyet.com.tr/fethullah-hoca-papayla-gorustu-39005791

76. "Bartholomeos: Liberalleşme için Gülen'le çalışıyoruz," *Dünya Bülteni*, April 12, 2012, (accessed on July 18, 2017), http://www.dunyabulteni.net/haber/205739/bartholomeos-liberallesme-icin-gulenle-calisiyoruz

77. "Erdoğan gördüğümüz kadarı ile FETÖ Pakistan'da..." *DHA*, November 17 2016, (accessed on July 18, 2017), http://www.dha.com.tr/erdogan-gordugumuz-kadari-ile-feto-pakistanda_1383943.html

78. Tamer Korkmaz, "Hoca kılıklı haçlı artığı," *Yeni Şafak*, February 22, 2017, (accessed on April 27, 2019), http://www.yenisafak.com/yazarlar/tamerkorkmaz/hoca-kilikli-hacli-artigi-2036347

79. "Devlet Bahçeli ilk 'evet' mitingini yaptı," *Vatan*, March 18, 2017, (accessed on April 27, 2019), http://www.gazetevatan.com/devlet-bahceli-ilk-evet-mitingini-yapti-1049396-siyaset/

80. Ali Karahasanoğlu, "Gülen, belam gibi baş aşağı gitmekten korkuyormuş," *Yeni Akit*, April 4, 2017, (accessed on April 27, 2019), http://www.yeniakit.com.tr/yazarlar/ali-karahasanoglu/gulen-belam-gibi-basasagi-gitmekten-korkuyormus-18915.html

81. Aytunç Altındal, "Vatikan'ın gizli kardinali Gülen," *Sabah*, April 2, 2017, (accessed on April 27, 2019), http://www.sabah.com.tr/webtv/turkiye/vatikanin-gizli-kardinali-gulen

82. "Hate Speech Against Christians in Erdoğan's Turkey," *Stockholm Center for Freedom (SCF)*, August 21, 2017, (accessed on April 27, 2019), https://stockholmcf.org/wp-content/uploads/2017/08/Hate-Speech-Against-Christians-in-Erdoğan's-Turkey_21.08.2017.pdf

83. "Çocuk bakanların öğretmenleri açığa alındı," *Haberdar*, April 26, 2017, (accessed on April 27, 2019), http://www.haberdar.com/gundem/cocuk-bakan-in-ogretmenleri-aciga-alindi-h50056.html

84. "Skandal, 23 Nisan çocuğu Başbakan'a Fetö'nün projesini savundu," *Haber Vitrini*, April 24, 2017, (accessed on April 27, 2019), http://www.habervitrini.com/gundem/skandal-23-nisan-cocugu-basbakan-a-feto-nun-projesini-ovdu-886557

85. "Emniyet Genel Müdürlüğünde İhraç Edilen Toplam Personel Sayısı ve Unvanı," *Kamu Biz*, February 14, 2017, (accessed on April 27, 2019), http://www.kamubiz.com/emniyet/emniyet-genel-mudurlugunde-ihrac-edilen-toplam-personel-sayisi-h322.html

86. "'FETÖ' operasyonlarında kaç kişi tutuklandı?"; *T24*, April 2, 2017, (accessed on April 27, 2019), http://t24.com.tr/haber/feto-operasyonlarinda-kac-kisi-tutuklandi,397075

87. "Emniyet'in göz bebeği polis kolejleri neden kapatıldı?" *Shaber*, October 17, 2015, (accessed on April 27, 2019), http://www.shaber3.com/emniyetin-goz-bebegi-polis-kolejleri-neden-kapatildi-haberi/1179222/

88. "Türkiye'de 9 bin 213 polis yemin etti," *Milliyet*, March 19, 2017, (accessed on April 27, 2019), http://www.milliyet.com.tr/turkiye-de-9-bin-213-polis-yemin-gundem-2416553/

89. "Bakanlık bilançoyu açıkladı: 169 general, 7 bin 98 albay ve alt rütbeler, 8 bin

815 emniyet mensubu…," *GriHat*, July 13, 2017, (accessed on April 27, 2019), https://grihat.com/cemaat-sorusturmalari-kapsaminda-169-bin-13-kisi-hakkinda-islem-yapildi/

90. "Komuta kademesi üniformalarıyla sabah namazında," *Sol*, July 28, 2017, (accessed on April 27, 2019), http://haber.sol.org.tr/toplum/komuta-kademesi-uniformalariyla-sabah-namazinda-204459 ; "El Bab'da minbere çıkan Zekai Paşa'dan net mesaj!" *Haber7*, July 27, 2017, (accessed on April 27, 2019), http://www.haber7.com/guncel/haber/2364997-el-babda-minbere-cikan-zekai-pasadan-net-mesaj

91. "Erdoğan ve İBDA-C lideri Mirzabeyoğlu'nun sürpriz görüşmesi," *BirGün*, November 30, 2014, (accessed on July 16, 2017), http://www.birgun.net/haber-detay/erdogan-ve-ibda-c-lideri-mirzabeyoglu-nun-surpriz-gorusmesi-71897.html

92. "Sedat Peker o görüşmeyi anlattı," *Milliyet*, June 17, 2015, (accessed on April 27, 2019), http://www.milliyet.com.tr/sedat-peker-o-gorusmeyi-anlatti-gundem-2075245/

93. Ipek Yezdani, "Türkiye'den cihada 10 bin kişi gitti," *Hürriyet*, June 27, 2915, (accessed on April 27, 2019), http://www.hurriyet.com.tr/turkiye-den-cihada-10-bin-kisi-gitti-29383934

94. Human Rights Watch (HRW), *Entrenching Impunity Government Responsibility for International Crimes in Darfur*, 2008, (accessed on April 27, 2019), https://www.hrw.org/legacy/features/darfur/fiveyearson/report4.html

95. "Gözaltındayken Serbest Bırakılan Işid Militanları TBMM Gündeminde," *Haberler*, December 13, 2015, (accessed on April 27, 2019), https://www.haberler.com/gozaltindayken-serbest-birakilan-isid-militanlari-7964792-haberi/

96. Mahmut Akpınar, "AKP, tarikatları siyasallaştırıp radikalleştiriyor," *TR7/24*, May 3, 2017, (accessed on April 27, 2019), http://www.tr724.com/akp-tarikatlari-siyasallastirip-radikallestiriyor-mahmut-akpinar-yazdi/

97. Ümit Çetin, "Başbakan: Yüzde 50'yi evinde zor tutuyorum," *Hürriyet*, June 4, 2013, (accessed on April 27, 2019), http://www.hurriyet.com.tr/basbakan-yuzde-50-yi-evinde-zor-tutuyorum-23429709

98. "Erdoğan halkı meydanlara çağırdı," *Gerçek Gündem*, July 16 , 2016, (accessed on April 27, 2019), http://www.gercekgundem.com/erdogan-halki-meydanlara-cagirdi-220301h.htm

99. "Fetö'nün Kitapçısı Yağmalandı," *Haberler*, July 16, 2016, (accessed on April 27, 2019), https://www.haberler.com/feto-nun-kitapcisi-yagmalandi-8615240-haberi/

100. "6-7 Ekim'in acı bilançosu 50 ölü," *Hürriyet*, November 6, 2014, (accessed on April 27, 2019), http://www.hurriyet.com.tr/6-7-ekim-in-aci-bilancosu-50-olu-27525777

101. "The next sultan?," *The Economist*, August 16, 2014, (accessed on April 27, 2019), https://www.economist.com/news/europe/21612237-recep-tayyip-erdogans-plans-presidency-next-sultan

102. Alper Görmüş, "Savaşa dönüşmüş siyaset, medya, sosyal medya," *Al Jazeera Turk*, October 2, 2015, (accessed on April 27, 2019), http://www.aljazeera.com.tr/gorus/savasa-donusmus-siyaset-medya-sosyal-medya ; Ömer Taşpınar, "İktidar, medya ve kutuplaşma," *T24*, 18 Ağustos 2014, (accessed on April 27, 2019) http://t24.com.tr/yazarlar/omer-taspinar/iktidar-medya-ve-kutuplasma,9977

103. Murat Belge, "Demokratik Muhalefet," *Birikim*, June 19, 2017, (accessed on April 27, 2019), http://www.birikimdergisi.com/haftalik/8376/demokratik-muhalefet#.WYSg2YiGPIU

104. See "Freedom of the press in Turkey: Far worse than you think," *Stockholm Center for Freedom (SCF)*, January 2017, (accessed on April 27, 2019), http://stockholmcf.org/wp-content/uploads/2017/02/Freedom_of_press_in_Turkey_26.01.2017.pdf

105. "Yenikapı'daki mitinge kaç milyon kişi katıldı?," *Hürriyet*, August 7, 2016, (accessed on April 27, 2019), http://www.hurriyet.com.tr/buyuk-bulusma-haydi--yenikapi-mitingine-40183980

106. "Havuz medyası Gül'e savaş açtı," *Politika Kulvarı*, June 16, 2015, (accessed on April 27, 2019), http://www.politikakulvari.com/haber/guncel_1/havuz-medyasi-gule-savas-acti/3371.html

107. "Bülent Arınç'ın damadı Ekrem Yeter 'FETÖ'den tutuklandı," *BirGün*, June 5, 2017, (accessed on July 19, 2017), http://www.birgun.net/haber-detay/bulent-arinc-in-damadi-ekrem-yeter-feto-den-tutuklandi-162980.html

108. Human Rights Watch (HRW), *Silencing Turkey's Media: The Government's Deepening Assault on Critical Journalism*, December 15, 2016, (accessed on April 27, 2019), https://www.hrw.org/report/2016/12/15/silencing-turkeys-media/governments-deepening-assault-critical-journalism ; "Ahmet Altan tutuklandı," *Cumhuriyet*, 23 Eylül 2016, (accessed on April 27, 2019), http://www.cumhuriyet.com.tr/haber/turkiye/604139/Ahmet_Altan_tutuklandi.html

109. "FETÖ'nün ev sahipliğinde CHP, HDP ve PKK'lı terör platformu!" *Medya Gündem*, January 30, 2016, (accessed on April 27, 2019), http://www.medyagundem.com/fetonun-ev-sahipliginde-chp-hdp-ve-pkkli-teror-platformu/

110. See "Turkey's descent into arbitrariness: The end of rule of law," *Stockholm Center for Fredoom (SCF)*, April 2017, (accessed on April 27, 2019), https://stockholmcf.org/wp-content/uploads/2017/04/Turkey's-Descent-Into-Arbitrariness-The-End-Of-Rule-Of-Law.pdf

111. Cengiz Çandar, "Will state of emergency become the new normal for Turkey?" *al-Monitor*, October 3, 2016, (accessed on April 27, 2019), http://www.al-monitor.com/pulse/originals/2016/10/turkey-state-of-emergency-becomes-new-normal.html

112. Alon Ben-Meir, "Erdogan: Sultan of an Illusionary Ottoman Empire," *The Globalist*, March 9, 2017, (accessed on April 27, 2019), https://www.theglobalist.com/erdogan-sultan-of-an-illusionary-ottoman-empire-turkey/

113. Steven M. Collins, "Is Erdogan leading Turkey into isolation?" April 25, 2017, (accessed on April 27, 2019), http://stevenmcollins.com/WordPress/is-erdogan-leading-turkey-into-isolation/

114. "Fed up with EU, Erdogan says Turkey could join Shanghai bloc," *Reuters*, November 20, 2016, (accessed on April 27, 2019), http://www.reuters.com/article/us-turkey-europe-erdogan-idUSKBN13F0CY

115. Fox-IT, *Expert Witness Report on ByLock Investigation*, September 13, 2017, (accessed on April 27, 2019), https://foxitsecurity.files.wordpress.com/2017/09/bylock-fox-it-expert-witness-report-english.pdf ; "Pro-Erdoğan Daily: MIT Prepares A New List Of 130,000 ByLock Users," *Stockholm Center for Freedom (SCF)*, May 30, 2017, (accessed on April 27, 2019), https://stockholmcf.org/pro-erdogan-daily-mit-prepares-a-new-list-of-130000-bylock-users/

116. Güven Gürkan Öztan, "Son dönemeç: Namlu, sokak ve savaş," *BirGün,* October 24, 2016, (accessed on April 27, 2019), http://www.birgun.net/haber-detay/son-donemec-namlu-sokak-ve-savas-132664.html ; "Sinan Oğan: AKP esnafa kamplarda silah eğitimi veriyor," *Demokrat Haber,* 15 Şubat 2017, (accessed on April 27, 2019), http://www.demokrathaber.org/siyaset/sinan-ogan-akp-esnafa-kamplarda-silah-egitimi-veriyor-h79797.html

117. "Erdoğan: Türkiye yeni bir kurtuluş savaşı veriyor," *Yeniçağ,* 26 Kasım 2016, (accessed on April 27, 2019), http://www.yenicaggazetesi.com.tr/erdogan-turkiye-yeni-bir-kurtulus-savasi-veriyor-151526h.htm

118. "Pro-Erdoğan Turkish Journalists Call For Assassination Of Gülen Followers Abroad," *Stockholm Center for Freedom (SCF),* June 15, 2017, (accessed on April 27, 2019), https://stockholmcf.org/pro-erdogan-turkish-journalists-call-for-assassination-of-gulen-followers-abroad/ ; "Canlı yayında Hizmet Hareketi gönüllülerine suikast çağrısı," *TR7/24,* 15 Haziran 2017, (accessed on April 27, 2019), http://www.tr724.com/canli-yayinda-hizmet-hareketi-gonullulerine-suikast-cagrisi/

119. In a public speech delivered on March 8, 2017, Interior Minister Süleyman Soylu revealed that the government was plotting to do something abroad to critics from the Gülen movement: "They think they can go and flee to Germany. ... One day, these FETO terrorists may be shocked to see where they are located, you know. I'm telling you from here, it is not that easy. ... Both the security and strategy of this country [Turkey] have now changed. We won't leave those who betrayed Turkey alone wherever they may be around the world." "Bir de başımıza Almanya çıktı," *Hürriyet,* March 8, 2017, (accessed on April 27, 2019), http://www.hurriyet.com.tr/gundem/bir-de-basimiza-almanya-cikti-40388917

120. "MİT'te 'insan kaçırma ve infaz bürosu kuruldu," *TR7/24,* June 16 , 2017, (accessed on April 27, 2019), http://www.tr724.com/mitte-insan-kacirma-ve-infaz-burosu-kuruldu/ ; "Former intel chief calls for use of ASALA, MOSSAD tactics to kill Gulen followers," *Turkish Minute,* January 15, 2018, (accessed on April 27, 2019), https://www.turkishminute.com/2018/01/15/former-intel-chief-calls-for-use-of-asala-mossad-tactics-to-kill-gulen-followers/

121. Journalists Cem Küçük and Fuat Uğur, staunch supporters of Turkish President Recep Tayyip Erdoğan, name former *Zaman* daily Editor-in-Chief Ekrem Dumanlı, former *Today's Zaman* columnist Emre Uslu, former *Today's Zaman* Ankara Bureau Chief Abdullah Bozkurt and former *Today's Zaman* columnist professor İhsan Yılmaz as the first who should be assassinated. "Blow the brains out of 3 to 5 of them. Look how frightened they'll be. Kill that Ekrem Dumanli, Emre Uslu now... Abdullah Bozkurt lives in Stockholm. His home address is known by the [Turkish] state. [Turkish intelligence] knows where Emre Uslu lives. All those dastards. The dog known as Ihsan Yilmaz travels around Australia and New Zealand," Kucuk said. See "Pro-Erdoğan journalists call for assassination of colleagues in exile," *Turkish Minute,* December 22, 2017, (accessed on April 27, 2019), https://www.turkishminute.com/2017/12/22/video-pro-kurdish-mp-says-he-received-intel-on-plans-to-kill-turkish-dissidents-in-europe/ ; Also see "Pro-Erdoğan Turkish journalists call for assassination of Gülen followers abroad," *Stockholm Center for Freedom (SCF),* June 15, 2017, (accessed on April 27, 2019), https://stockholmcf.org/pro-erdogan-turkish-journalists-call-for-assassination-of-gulen-followers-abroad/

122. Former speechwriter of Turkish President Erdoğan and current ruling AKP

deputy Aydın Ünal threatened Turkish journalists in exile with extrajudicial killings, in his column published in the pro-Erdoğan *Yeni Safak* daily. Strongly criticizing journalists in exile for covering the case of Reza Zarrab, a Turkish-Iranian gold trader who was arrested in Miami in March 2016 on charges of evading US sanctions on Iran, Ünal said: "Better to get ready for intra-organization extrajudicial killings instead of carrying out operations over judicial theater [the Zarrab case]." The AKP deputy listed the names of journalists to be targeted: Ekrem Dumanlı, Adem Yavuz Arslan, Celil Sağır, Bülent Keneş, Abdulhamit Bilici, Erhan Başyurt, Emre Uslu, Akın İpek and Can Dündar. See "Erdogan's deputy threatens journalists with extrajudicial killings," *Turkish Minute*, December 4, 2017, (accessed on April 27, 2019), https://www.turkishminute.com/2017/12/04/erdogans-deputy-threatens-journalists-with-extrajudicial-killings/

123. "Pro-Erdoğan journalist suggests killing family members of jailed Gülen followers in Turkey," *Stockholm Center for Freedom (SCF)*, December 12, 2017, (accessed on April 27, 2019), https://stockholmcf.org/pro-erdogan-journalist-suggests-killing-family-members-of-jailed-gulen-followers-in-turkey/

124. "Erdoğan vows to pursue Gülen movement followers who 'escaped the sword,'" *Turkish Minute*, February 25, 2018, (accessed on April 27, 2019), https://www.turkishminute.com/2018/02/25/erdogan-vows-to-pursue-gulen-movement-followers-who-escaped-the-sword/

125. Emin Çölaşan, "Cezaevine düşmeye gör," *Sözcü*, July 25, 2017, (accessed on April 27, 2019), http://www.sozcu.com.tr/2017/yazarlar/emin-colasan/cezaevine-dusmeye-gor-1944893/ ; "Doluluk yüzde 100'ü aştı, cezaevleri salgın hastalık alarmı veriyor," *TR7/24*, December 17, 2016, (accessed on April 27, 2019), http://www.tr724.com/doluluk-yuzde-110-asti-cezaevleri-salgin-hastalik-alarmi-veriyor/

126. As of December 18, 2018, a total of 1,934 people has been given life sentences by Turkish courts in sham trials related to a 2016 coup attempt. Of these convicts, 978 were jailed for life while 956 were sentenced to aggravated life imprisonment. See "Turkish courts hands down 1,934 life sentences in coup-related trials: report," *Turkish Minute*, December 18, 2018, (accessed on April 27, 2019), https://www.turkishminute.com/2018/12/18/turkish-courts-hands-down-1934-life-sentences-in-coup-related-trials-report/

127. "MİT, 122 bin kişilik ByLock listesini savcılığa teslim etti," *Cumhuriyet*, March 1, 2017, (accessed on April 27, 2019), http://www.cumhuriyet.com.tr/haber/turkiye/687857/MiT__122_bin_kisilik_ByLock_listesini_savciliga_teslim_etti.html

128. "15 Temmuz hukuksuzluğunun bilançosu: Asker, polis, hakim, savcı, vali, kaymakam 50 bin tutuklu, 155 bin gözaltı," *TR7/24*, 28 Mayıs 2017, (accessed on April 27, 2019), http://www.tr724.com/15-temmuz-hukuksuzlugunun-bilancosu-50-bin-tutuklu-155-bin-gozalti/

129. "Suspicious Deaths And Suicides In Turkey," *Stockholm Center for Freedom (SCF)*, March 22, 2017 (accessed on April 27, 2019), http://stockholmcf.org/wp-content/uploads/2017/03/Suspicious-Deaths-And-Suicides-In-Turkey_22.03.2017.pdf ; "Suspicious Deaths And Suicides In Turkey – Updated List As of January 25, 2019," *Stockholm Center for Freedom (SCF)*, (accessed on April 27, 2019), http://stockholmcf.org/suspicious-deaths-and-suicides-in-turkey-updated-list/

130. Gregory H. Stanton, "The 10 Stages of Genocide," *Genocide Watch*, (accessed on April 27, 2019), http://genocidewatch.org/genocide/tenstagesofgenocide.html

131. "Report on the impact of the state of emergency on human rights in Turkey, including an update on the South-East (January-December 2017)," *Office of the United Nations High Commissioner for Human Rights (OHCHR)*, March 2018, (accessed on April 27, 2019), https://www.ohchr.org/Documents/Countries/TR/2018-03-19_Second_OHCHR_Turkey_Report.pdf ; "Opposition deputy: Police detain another woman shortly after delivery," *Turkey Purge*, August 1, 2017, (accessed on April 27, 2019), https://turkeypurge.com/opposition-deputy-police-detain-another-woman-shortly-after-delivery ; "Turkish Police Waiting At Mother's Hospital Room To Detain Her Just After Delivery," *Stockholm Center for Freedom (SCF)*, October 14, 2017, (accessed on April 27, 2019), https://stockholmcf.org/turkish-police-waiting-at-mothers-hospital-room-to-detain-her-just-after-delivery/

132. "Mass torture and ill-treatment in Turkey," *Stockholm Center for Freedom (SCF)*, June 6, 2017, (accessed on April 27, 2019), https://stockholmcf.org/wp-content/uploads/2017/06/Mass-Torture-And-Ill-Treatment-In-Turkey_06.06.2017.pdf

133. "Şişeyle komalık edilen öğretmen [YAZI DİZİSİ-1]," *TR7/24*, September 23, 2016, (accessed on April 27, 2019), https://medium.com/tr724/%C5%9Fi%C5%9Feyle-komal%C4%B1k-edilen-%C3%B6%C4%9Fretmen-yazi-di%CC%87zi%CC%87si%CC%87-1-a00edc63fc80

134. Levent Kenez, "Sippenhaft nedir bilir misin?" *TR7/24*, October 17, 2016, (accessed on April 27, 2019), http://www.tr724.com/sippenhaft-nedir-bilir-misin/

135. "Eşi evde bulunamayınca gözaltına alınan 3 çocuk annesi tutuklandı," *TR7/24*, March 15, 2017, (accessed on April 27, 2019), http://www.tr724.com/esi-evde-bulunamayinca-gozaltina-alinan-3-cocuk-annesi-elif-yildirim-nerede/

136. "Ali Fuat Yılmazer'in iki kızı da tutuklandı," *Aktif Haber*, March 2, 2017, (accessed on April 27, 2019), http://aktifhaber.com/gundem/ali-fuat-yilmazer-in-iki-kizi-da-tutuklandi-h93513.html

137. "Detained Mother Of Five Children Released By Court With 50.000 TL Bail," *Stockholm Center for Freedom (SCF)*, January 30, 2017, (accessed on April 27, 2019), https://stockholmcf.org/detained-mother-of-five-children-released-by-court-with-50-000-tl-bail/ ; "Cezaevine eşini ziyarete giden anne tutuklandı, 5 çocuk ortada kaldı," *Kronos*, January 23, 2017, (accessed on April 27, 2019), https://kronoshaber1.com/tr/cezaevi-ziyaretinde-anne-de-gozaltinda-alindi-5-cocuk-ortada-kaldi/

138. "Adalet Bakanı Bekir Bozdağ'dan 'tek tip kıyafet' açıklaması," *T24*, July 18, 2017, (accessed on April 27, 2019), http://t24.com.tr/haber/adalet-bakani-bekir-bozdagdan-tek-tip-kiyafet-aciklamasi,414964

139. "15 Temmuz hukuksuzluğunun bilançosu: Asker, polis, hakim, savcı, vali, kaymakam 50 bin tutuklu, 155 bin gözaltı," *TR7/24*, May 28, 2017, (accessed on April 27, 2019), http://www.tr724.com/15-temmuz-hukuksuzlugunun-bilancosu-50-bin-tutuklu-155-bin-gozalti/

140. Darren Boyle, "Erdogan cancels 50,000 passports in latest post-coup crackdown in Turkey as he tells Western leaders who criticise him: 'Mind your own business!'" *Daily Mail*, July 30, 2016, (accessed on April 27, 2019), http://www.

dailymail.co.uk/news/article-3715856/Erdogan-cancels-50-000-passports-lat-est-post-coup-crackdown-Turkey-tells-Western-leaders-criticise-Mind-busi-ness.html ; "4,806 Passports Owned By Alleged Gülen Followers Seized At Is-tanbul Airport In One Year," *Stockholm Center for Freedom (SCF)*, July 10, 2017, (accessed on April 27, 2019), https://stockholmcf.org/4806-passports-owned-by-alleged-gulen-followers-seized-at-istanbul-airport-in-one-year/

141. "Arbitrary deprivation of nationality and denial of consular services to Turkish citizens," *ISI*, July 2017, (accessed on April 27, 2019), http://www.institutesi. org/policy-brief-Turkey-arbitrary-deprivation-of-nationality_2017.pdf

142. "Suspicious Deaths And Suicides In Turkey – Updated List," *Stockholm Center for Freedom (SCF)*, January 25, 2019, (accessed on April 27, 2019), http:// stockholmcf.org/suspicious-deaths-and-suicides-in-turkey-updated-list/

143. Richter, Stein, Barnea, Sherman, "Can we prevent Genocide by preventing Incitement?" Genocide Watch, November 2009, (accessed on April 27, 2019), http://www.genocidewatch.org/images/Articles_Can_we_prevent_genocide_by_preventing_incitement.pdf

144. Bahadır Bumin Özarslan, "Soykırım Suçunun Önlenmesi ve Cezalandırılması Sözleşmesi Açısından Hocalı Katliamı," *Türksam*, July 13, 2016, (accessed on July 15, 2017), http://www.turksam.org/tr/makale-detay/1286-soykirim-su-cunun-onlenmesi-ve-cezalandirilmasi-sozlesmesi-acisindan-hocali-katliami

145. Brannigan 1998, p. 262.

146. Day & Vandiver 2000, pp. 45-46.

147. "The Responsibility to Protect," *ICISS*, December 2001, (accessed on April 27, 2019), http://www.globalr2p.org/media/files/iciss_report.pdf

148. Gregory H. Stanton, "The 12 Ways to Deny a Genocide," *Genocide Watch*, June 15, 2005, (accessed on April 27, 2019), http://www.genocidewatch.org/geno-cide/12waystodenygenocide.html

149. "Bozdağ'a göre cezaevlerinde işkence yok: İftira, yalan, propaganda," *Diken*, October 15, 2016, (accessed on April 27, 2019), http://www.diken.com.tr/ bozdaga-gore-cezaevlerinde-iskence-yok-iftira-yalan-propaganda/

150. "AKP deputy chairman claims no violation of human rights in Turkey," *Turkish Minute*, January 13, 2019, (accessed on April 27, 2019), https://www.turkish-minute.com/2019/01/13/akp-deputy-chairman-claims-no-violation-of-hu-man-rights-in-turkey/

151. "OHAL mağdurlarından haberi yok mu?," *Yeni Asya*, June 5, 2017, (accessed on April 27, 2019), http://www.yeniasya.com.tr/gundem/ohal-magdurlarin-dan-haberi-yok-mu_434309

152. "Erdoğan'a göre 'tutuklu gazeteci yok': 'Hepsi yalan, kendilerinin gazete-ci olduğunu iddia ediyorlar'," *Gazete Karınca*, July 12, 2017, (accessed on April 27, 2019), http://gazetekarinca.com/2017/07/erdogana-gore-tutuk-lu-gazeteci-yok-hepsi-yalan-kendilerinin-gazeteci-oldugunu-iddia-ediyor-lar/ ; "Erdoğan calls Turkey's jailed journalists 'thieves, child abusers, terror-ists'," *Turkish Minute*, March 22, 2017, (accessed on April 27, 2019), https:// www.turkishminute.com/2017/03/22/erdogan-calls-turkeys-jailed-journal-ists-thieves-child-abusers-terrorists/ ; "Erdoğan's senior advisor says there are no journalists in jail in Turkey," *Turkish Minute*, December 19, 2018, (accessed on April 27, 2019), https://www.turkishminute.com/2018/12/19/erdogans-senior-advisor-says-there-are-no-journalists-in-jail-in-turkey/ ; "Erdoğan

claims reforms under his rule made Turkey's media more democratic and free,"
Turkish Minute, January 9, 2019, (accessed on April 27, 2019), https://www.
turkishminute.com/2019/01/09/erdogan-claims-reforms-under-his-rule-
made-turkeys-media-more-democratic-and-free/

153. "Erdoğan claims Turkey is one of only a few countries with a full-fledged democracy," *Turkish Minute,* December 27, 2018, (accessed on April 27, 2019),
https://www.turkishminute.com/2018/12/27/erdogan-claims-turkey-is-one-
only-a-few-countries-with-a-full-fledged-democracy/

154. World Justice Project, *Rule of Law Index 2017–2018,* February 2019, (accessed
on April 27, 2019), https://worldjusticeproject.org/sites/default/files/docu-
ments/WJP_ROLI_2017-18_Online-Edition.pdf; "World Justice Project shows
Turkey among world's worst for rule of law," *Stockholm Center for Freedom
(SCF),* February 1, 2019, (accessed on April 27, 2019), https://stockholmcf.org/
world-justice-project-shows-turkey-among-worlds-worst-for-rule-of-law/   ;
"OHAL mağdurlarından haberi yok mu?" *Yeni Asya,* June 5, 2017, (accessed
on April 27, 2019), http://www.yeniasya.com.tr/gundem/ohal-magdurlarin-
dan-haberi-yok-mu_434309

155. "Türkiye, Demokrasi ve Özgürlüklerin Batı Ülkelerinin Bile Ötesinde Yaşandığı
Bir Ülke," *TCCB,* March 17, 2017, accessed on April 27, 2019), https://www.
tccb.gov.tr/haberler/410/73358/turkiye-demokrasi-ve-ozgurluklerin-ba-
ti-ulkelerinin-bile-otesinde-yasandigi-bir-ulke.html

156. "Democracy Index 2018," *The Economist Intelligence Unit's Democracy Index,*
January 8, 2019, (accessed on April 27, 2019), https://www.eiu.com/topic/
democracy-index ; "Turkey ranks 110th among 160 countries in The Economist's democracy index," *Turkish Minute,* January 9, 2019, accessed on April
27, 2019), https://www.turkishminute.com/2019/01/09/turkey-ranks-110th-
among-160-countries-in-the-economists-democracy-index/

Conclusion

1   https://www.turkishminute.com/2020/05/10/pro-erdogan-writer-sparks-
outrage-with-plans-to-massacre-neighbors-in-event-of-coup-attempt/

BIBLIOGRAPHY

A Blank Check: Turkey's Post-Coup Suspension of Safeguards Against Torture, Human Rights Watch, October 2016.

Aktan, Gündüz; "Devletlerarası Hukuka Göre Ermeni Meselesi," *Türkiye Günlüğü*, Sayı 64, 2001.

Aktar, Ayhan; *Varlık Vergisi ve Türkleştirme Politikaları*, İletişim Yayınları, Istanbul, 2014

Akün, Neslihan Verda; "Uluslararası Hukukta ve Türk Hukuku'nda Soykırım (Jenosid) Suçu," *Milletlerarası Hukuk ve Milletlerarası Özel Hukuk Bülteni*, Yıl. 24, Sayı. 1-2, 2004.

Akün, Neslihan Verda, "Soykırım Suçunun Önlenmesi ve Cezalandırılmasına Dair Sözleşme'nin Uygulanmasına İlişkin Dava (26 Şubat 2007 Tarihli Karar)," *Milletlerarası Adalet Divanı Kararları (1990-2007)*, Beta Basım Yayım Dağıtım, Istanbul, 2008, s. 24-37.

Alpkaya, Gökçen; "Eski Yugoslavya İçin Uluslararası Ceza Mahkemesi," Turhan Kitabevi, Ankara, 2002

Akdeniz, Yaman and Altıparmak, Kerem; *Turkey: Freedom of Expression in Jeopardy Violations of the rights of authors, publishers and academics under the State of Emergency*, PEN, March 28, 2018.

Arıcan, Mehmet; "Türk Ceza Hukukunda Soykırım Suçu," *Kriminoloji Dergisi*, Cilt 1, Sayı 2, Temmuz 2009.

Aygün, Hüseyin; *Dersim 1938 ve Zorlu İskan (Dersim 1938 and the Forced Resettlement)*, Dipnot Publishing, 2009.

Bain, Paul G.; Vaes, Jeroen; and Leyens, Jacques-Philippe; *Humanness and Dehumanization*, Taylor & Francis, 2014.

Barutçu, Faik Ahmet; *Siyasi Anılar 1939-1954*, (Milliyet Yayınları, Istanbul, 1977), p. 263.

Başak, Cengiz, *Uluslararası Ceza Mahkemeleri ve Uluslararası Suçlar*, Turhan Kitabevi, Ankara, 2003.

Brannigan, Augustine; "Criminology and the Holocaust: Xenophobia, Evolution and Genocide," *Crime & Delinquency*, Vol. 44, No. 2, 1998

Can, Eyüp; *Ufuk Turu*, Doğan Kitap, Istanbul, 2000.

Chalk, Frank and Jonassohn, Kurt; *The History and Sociology of Genocide*, Yale University Press London, 1990.

Chigas, George; The Politics of Defining Justice after the Cambodian Genocide," *Journal of Genocide Research*, Vol. 2, 2000, pp. 245-265.

Çolak, Haluk; *Güncel Ceza Hukuku*, Bilge Yayınevi, Ankara, 2005.

Dadrian, Vahakn N.; Structural-Functional Components of Genocide: A Victimological Approach," (ed) Israel Drapkin, Victimology, Vol. III, Lexington MA, 1974, pp.123-136.

Day, Edward & Vandiver M.; "Criminology and Genocide Studies," *Crime, Law & Social Change*, No. 34, 2000.

Değirmenci, Olgun; "Uluslararası Ceza Mahkemelerinin Kararları Işığında Mukayeseli Hukukta ve Türk Hukukunda Soykırım Suçu (TCK md. 76)," *Türkiye Barolar Birliği Dergisi*, Sayı 70, 2007.

De Zayas, Alfred; "The Istanbul Pogrom of 6–7 September 1955 in the Light of International Law," *Genocide Studies and Prevention*, Vol. 2, Iss. 2, 2007, pp. 137-

154.

Doğru, Osman; İnsan *Hakları Uluslararası Mevzuatı*, (Beta Yayınları, Istanbul, 1998), p. 250.

Dönmez, Ahmet; *Yüzde On - Adil Düzenden Havuz Düzenine*, Klas Kitap Yayınları, Istanbul, 2014.

Erdoğan's Coup in Turkey, Stockholm Center for Freedom, Stockholm, July 2017.

Erdoğan's vile campaign of hate speech - A case study: Targeting of the Gülen Movement, Stockholm Center for Freedom (SCF), Stockholm, May 2017.

Ergene, Enes; *Geleneğin Modern Çağa Tanıklığı*, Yeni Akademi Yayınları, Istanbul, 2005.

Ergil, Doğu, *Fethullah Gülen and the Gülen Movement in 100 Questions*, Blue Dome Press, Clifton, NJ, 2012.

European Commisson's Progress Report on Turkey, EU Commission, November 2016.

Expert Witness Report on ByLock Investigation, Fox-IT, September 2017.

Free thought under siege in Turkey: The crackdown on education, Stockholm Center for Freedom (SCF), Stockholm, July 2018.

Fluckiger, Jay D.; *Surviving the Taliban: The Incredible, True Story of a Convert*, Cedar Fort Inc, 2011.

Freedom of the press in Turkey: Far worse than you think, Stockholm Center for Freedom, Stockholm, January 2017.

Göktepeoğlu, Ercan, "Uluslararası Hukukta ve Türk Hukukunda Soykırım Suçu (The Crime of Genocide in International and Turkish Law)," *TAAD*, Yıl: 5, Sayı: 19, Ekim 2014, s. 797-838.

Gülen, Fethullah, *Küçük Dünyam*, Nil Yayınları, Istanbul, 2000.

Horowitz, Irving L.; *Genocide; State Power and Mass Murder*, Routledge, New Brunswich NJ, 1977.

Jorgensen, Nina H. B.; "The Definition of Genocide: Joining the Dots in the Light of Recent Practice," *International Criminal Law*, Volume 1, Issue 3/4, July 2001.

Kakar, M. Hassan, *Afghanistan: The Soviet Invasion and the Afghan Response, 1979–1982*," University of California Press, 1995.

Koca, Mahmut; "The Crime of Genocide in the New Turkish Penal Code," *Annales*, 2010a, XLII, N. 59, p. 255-283.

——, "Türk Ceza Kanununda Soykırım Suçu," *Türkiye Adalet Akademisi Dergisi*, No 1, April 2010b, p. 22.

Kocaoğlu, Serhat Sinan; "Suçların Suçu: Soykırım," Türkiye Barolar Birliği Dergisi, Sayı 90, 2010.

Koçoğlu, Yahya; *Azınlık Gençleri Anlatıyor*, Metis Yayınları, Istanbul, 2001.

Kuper, Leo; "Theoretical Issues Relating to Genocide: Uses and Abuses," ed. George J. Andreopoulos, *Genocide; Conceptual and Historical Dimensions*, University of Pennsylvania Press, Philadelphia, 1994, s. 31-46.

Lemkin, Raphael, *Axis Rule in Occupied Europe: Laws of Occupation, Analysis of Goverment Proposals for Redress,* Carnegie Endowment for International Peace, Division of International Law, *1944.*

Levin, Nora; *The Holocaust: The Destruction of European Jewry 1933-1945*, Knopf Publishing Group, New York, 1968.

——; *The Holocaust: The Destruction of European Jewry 1933-1945*, (Schocken, New York, 1973), p. 20.

Mass Torture and Ill-Treatment in Turkey, Stockholm Center for Freedom (SCF), Stockholm, June 2017.

Mercan, Faruk; *Demokrasiden Geriye Dönüş Yok - Dünden Bugüne Fethullah Gülen'in Düşünce* İstikameti, Blue Dome Press, NJ, 2016.

Monroe, Kristen Renwick; *Ethics in an Age of Terror and Genocide: Identity and Moral Choice*, Princeton, NJ: Princeton University Press, 2012.

Morsink, Johannes; "Cultural Genocide, the Universal Declaration, and Minority Rights," *Human Rights Quarterly*, 1999, vol. 211, pp.1009-60.

Obote-Odora, Alex; "Complicity in Genocide as Understood Through the ICTR Experience," *International Criminal Law Review, Volume 2, Issue 4, November 2002.*

Ortaylı, İlber; Ateş, Toktamış, Karakaş, Eser, *Barış Köprüleri - Dünyaya Açılan Türk Okulları*, Ufuk Kitapları, Istanbul, 2005.

Ökte, Faik; *Varlık Vergisi Faciası*, Nebioğlu Yayınevi, Istanbul, 1951.

Önok, Rifat Murat; *Tarihî Perspektifiyle Uluslararası Ceza Divanı*, Turhan Kitabevi, Ankara, 2003.

Örmeci, Ozan; "Narsisist liderlik ve Recep Tayyip Erdoğan örneği," *Uluslararası Politika Akademisi*, 27 Temmuz 2014, (accessed on April 26, 2019), http://politikaakademisi.org/2014/07/27/narsisist-liderlik-ve-recep-tayyip-erdogan-analizi/

Özbek, Veli Özer; *TCK İzmir Şerhi, Yeni Türk Ceza Kanunu'nun Anlamı*, (Seçkin Yayınevi, Ankara, 2008), p. 81.

Pahl, Jon; *Fethullah Gülen: A Life of Hizmet* (Blue Dome Press, Clifton NJ, 2019)

Post, Jerrold M. "Saddam Hussein of Iraq: A Political Psychology Profile," *Political Psychology*, vol. 12(2), June 1991, (accessed on April 26, 2019), https://www.researchgate.net/publication/268044923_Saddam_Hussein_of_Iraq_A_Political_Psychology_Profile

Read, Peter; *The Stolen Generations: The Removal of Aboriginal Children in New South Wales 1883 to 1969*, NSW Department of Aboriginal Affairs, Sydney, 2006.

Report on the human rights situation in South-East Turkey (July 2015 to December 2016), Office of the United Nations High Commissioner for Human Rights (OHCHR), March 2017.

Report on the impact of the state of emergency on human rights in Turkey, including an update on the South-East (January-December 2017), Office of the United Nations High Commissioner for Human Rights (OHCHR), March 2018.

Rosenbaum, Alan S.; *Prosecuting Nazi War Criminals*, Boulder, 1993.

Rummel, Rudolph J.; *Statistics of Democide: Genocide and Mass Murder since 1900*, Center for National Security Law, School of Law, University of Virginia, 1997.

Sherrer, Hans; *Dehumanization Is Not an Option: An Inquiry into the Exercise of Authority Against Perceived Wrongdoers*, Createspace Independent Publishing Platform, 2008.

Silencing Turkey's Media: The Government's Deepening Assault on Critical Journalism, Human Rights Watch, December 2016.

Smith, David Livingstone; *Less Than Human: Why We Demean, Enslave and Exterminate Others*, St. Martin's Press, 2011.

Suspicious Deaths and Suicides in Turkey, Stockholm Center for Freedom (SCF), Stockholm, March 2017.

Tezcan, Durmuş; Erdem, Mustafa Ruhan, Önok, Murat; *5237 Sayılı Türk Ceza Kanunu'na Göre Teorik ve Pratik Ceza Özel Hukuku*, Seçkin Yayınevi, Ankara, 2006.

Thornton, Russell; "Aboriginal North American Population and Rates of Decline, ca.

A.D. 1500-1900," *Current Anthropology*, April 1997, no. 38, vol. 2, pp. 310-315.

Turhan, Faruk "Yeni Türk Ceza Kanununda Uluslararası Suçlar," Süleyman Demirel Üniversitesi, (a paper presented on November 20-21, 2004). Accessed April 26, 2019, http://www.ceza-bb.adalet.gov.tr/makale/101.doc

Turhan, Faruk; "Yeni Türk Ceza Kanunu'na Göre Uluslararası Suçların Cezalandırılması," *Hukuki Perspektifler Dergisi*, Sayı 3, Nisan 2005.

Turkey's descent into arbitrariness: The end of rule of law, Stockholm Center for Fredoom (SCF), Stockholm, April 2017.

Walker, Christopher J.; *Armenia: The Survival of a Nation*, Palgrave Macmillan, 1990.

Warrick, Joby; *Black Flags: The Rise of ISIS*, Doubleday, 2015.

Whitley Jr, Bernard E. and Kite, Mary E.; *The Psychology of Prejudice and Discrimination*, Routledge, 2006.

Yaşlı, Fatih; *Türkçü Faşizmden Türk-İslam Ülküsüne*, Yordam Kitap, Istanbul, 2017.

Yonan, Gabriele; *Asur soykırımı: Unutulan bir holocaust*, çev. Erol Sever, Pencere Yay., Istanbul, 1999.

INDEX